PRAISE FOR

STEPHEN DANDO-COLLINS AND

CAESAR VERSUS POMPEY

"A triumph! At first blush, it might be easy to think this story has been told. But the story that's told is incomplete. Too often, Pompey the Great stands in the shadow of Julius Caesar. In *Caesar Versus Pompey*, Stephen Dando-Collins invites Pompey to step out of the shadows and stand in the light, shoulder to shoulder with Caesar.

"The story of these two titans is dramatic, full of twists and turns, partnerships and betrayals. Without one, there is no other.

"By telling the story of Pompey and Caesar in the way that only he can, Dando-Collins fills in an important gap in the dramatic events that culminated in the collapse of the Roman Republic. Pompey and Caesar needed each other, and any student or fan of Roman history needs this important book."
> — PHILLIP BARLAG, AUTHOR OF *EVIL ROMAN EMPERORS*
> AND HOST OF *THE GREATS OF HISTORY* PODCAST

"Stephen Dando-Collins never fails to provide a thrilling and educational read."
> — CAMERON REILLY, CO-HOST, *THE LIFE OF CAESAR* PODCAST

"Stephen Dando-Collins is the modern-age's foremost dramatizer of ancient Greek and Roman history."
> — ROBIN HAWDON, BRITISH PLAYWRIGHT AND AUTHOR
> OF *ALMOST FAMOUS; THE LAND, THE LAND;* AND
> *DINNER WITH CHURCHILL*

"(Dando-Collins is) the legions' foremost living authority."
> — *ARTS AND LETTERS MONTHLY*

CAESAR
VERSUS POMPEY

ALSO BY STEPHEN DANDO-COLLINS

Seven Against Thebes: The Quest of the Original Magnificent Seven

Rebels Against Rome: 400 Years of Rebellions Against the Rule of Rome

Constantine at the Bridge: How the Battle of the Milvian Bridge Created Christian Rome

Conquering Jerusalem: The AD 66–73 Roman Campaign to Crush the Jewish Revolt

Cyrus the Great: Conqueror, Liberator, Anointed One

Caligula: The Mad Emperor of Rome

Rise of an Empire: How One Man United Greece to Defeat Xerxes's Persians

The Ides: Caesar's Murder and the War for Rome

Blood of the Caesars: How the Murder of Germanicus Led to the Fall of Rome

Mark Antony's Heroes: How the Third Gallica Legion Saved an Apostle and Created an Emperor

Cleopatra's Kidnappers: How Caesar's Sixth Legion Gave Egypt to Rome and Rome to Caesar

Nero's Killing Machine: The True Story of Rome's Remarkable Fourteenth Legion

Caesar's Legion: The Epic Saga of Julius Caesar's Elite Tenth Legion and the Armies of Rome

CAESAR
VERSUS POMPEY

DETERMINING ROME'S GREATEST GENERAL, STATESMAN & NATION-BUILDER

STEPHEN DANDO-COLLINS

TURNER
PUBLISHING COMPANY

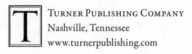

TURNER PUBLISHING COMPANY
Nashville, Tennessee
www.turnerpublishing.com

Cover and Book Design by William Ruoto
Maps ©2001 by D. L. McElhannon

Library of Congress Cataloging-in-Publication Data
Names: Dando-Collins, Stephen, author.
Title: Caesar versus Pompey : determining Rome's greatest general,
   statesman & nation-builder / Stephen Dando-Collins.
Description: Nashville, Tennessee : Turner Publishing Company, [2024] |
   Includes bibliographical references and index.
Identifiers: LCCN 2023032887 (print) | LCCN 2023032888 (ebook) | ISBN
   9781684428953 (paperback) | ISBN 9781684428960 (hardcover) | ISBN
   9781684428977 (epub)
Subjects: LCSH: Caesar, Julius. | Pompey, the Great, 106 B.C.-48 B.C. |
   Generals—Rome—Biography. | Statesmen—Rome—Biography. |
   Rome—History—Republic, 265-30 B.C. | Rome—Politics and
   government—265-30 B.C.
Classification: LCC DG265 .D36 2024 (print) | LCC DG265 (ebook) | DDC
   937/.050922—dc23/eng/20231228
LC record available at https://lccn.loc.gov/2023032887
LC ebook record available at https://lccn.loc.gov/2023032888

Printed in the United States of America

1 2 3 4 5 6 7 8 9 10

For my wife Louise, my fellow soldier in the war against the vicissitudes of life, and my fellow participant in the occasional triumph.

With special thanks to my New York literary agents Richard Curtis and Sarah Yake, and to Todd Bottorff, Stephanie Beard, Ryan Smernoff, and Amanda Chiu Krohn at Turner Publishing, for shepherding this work from concept to bookshelf.

CONTENTS

Atlas ix

Illustrations xiii

Introduction 1

I.   A Bolt of Lightning Changes Everything 3

II.   Caesar's Uncle Takes Power, Pompey on Trial 11

III.   Caesar the Priest, Pompey the Boy General 17

IV.   Caesar in Jeopardy, Pompey Becomes Great. 29

V.   Caesar Hides, Pompey Triumphs 39

VI.   After Sulla, Pompey & Caesar on Opposing Sides 49

VII.   Crassus the Property Developer & Cicero the Lawyer 61

VIII.   Sneaky Sertorius versus Persistent Pompey 65

IX.   Pesky Spartacus Terminated by Crassus and Pompey 71

X.   As Caesar Weeps, Pompey Conquers the East 81

XI.   Cicero Rules, Caesar's Star Rises 103

XII.   Pompey's Triumphant Return, Caesar Imperator in Spain. 119

XIII.   Caesar, Pompey & Crassus Rule Rome. 131

XIV.   Caesar Begins to Conquer Gaul, Pompey Rehabilitates Cicero. 147

XV.   Caesar Subdues Gaul & Again Embraces Pompey. 165

XVI.   As Pompey & Crassus Rule, Caesar Invades Britain. 185

XVII.   With Two Deaths, Everything Changes 201

XVIII. The Revolting Gauls Pressure Caesar. 213

XIX.   This Means War. 231

XX.   Battle of the Giants. 237

XXI.   Both Assassinated 249

XXII.   Assessment. 255

        Notes 259

        Bibliography. 265

        Index 269

ATLAS

"The West," First Century BC

"The East," First Century BC

"The West," First Century BC

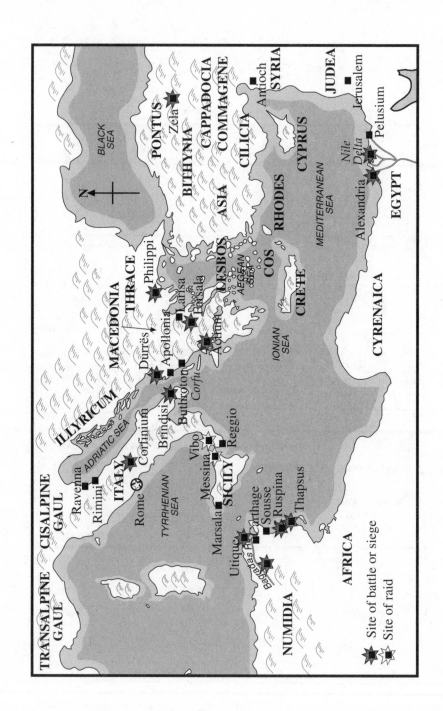

"The East," First Century BC

ILLUSTRATIONS

Bust of Julius Caesar (100-44 BC)

Bust of Julius Caesar as boy, from Leiden, Netherlands, 1st century BC

Portrait of Pompey the Great

Bust of Pompey (106-48 BC) c.60 BC

The first Roman, newspaper

Alesia Roman fortifications reconstructed. Burgundy, France

Murder of Gnaeus Pompeius Magnus

Bust of Marcus Tullius Cicero (106-43 BC)

Bust of Marcus Licinius Crassus (c.115-53 BC)

Bust of Cleopatra VII from c.30-40 BC

Bust of Mark Antony

Bust of Marcus Junius Brutus the Younger

Gaius Julius Caesar, Dictator of Rome, just months away from assassination.

Bridgeman Images.

Caesar as a teenager, around the time his father

died and Pompey became a boy general.

© *A. Dagli Orti* / © *NPL – DeA Picture Library* / *Bridgeman Images.*

*Gnaeus Pompeius, or Pompey, at twenty-three already a conquering
general given the title Great, called "the new Alexander the Great"
by his adoring Roman public and "Butcher Boy" by his opponents.
Luisa Ricciarini / Bridgeman Images.*

Pompey in his later years, called from his sickbed to
counter his former father-in-law Caesar.
Bridgeman Images.

Created by Caesar, the Acta Diurna, world's first newspaper, was posted on
bulletin boards in cities and legion camps throughout the Roman Empire.

*At Alesia in Burgundy, France, modern reconstruction
of Caesar's mammoth siege works, used to surround the
forces of rebel Gallic commander Vercingetorix.*

Pompey is murdered from behind by Egyptian assassins as he goes to step from a boat in Egypt. Said 1st century Roman poet Lucan, "If Brutus's deed was called wicked, what name should be granted to this crime?"

Bildagentur-online/UIG / Bridgeman Images.

Marcus Cicero, famed lawyer, writer, and orator, was Pompey's client and friend, and warned him of Caesar's ambitions for sole power. Pompey nonetheless "threw Cicero under the bus" to please Caesar. Bridgeman Images.

Marcus Crassus, successful property developer and banker, Rome's richest man, partner in power with Caesar and Pompey in the so-called First Triumvirate, who envied their military fame and tried to emulate them, with dire results.
Bridgeman Images.

Seductive, highly intelligent Queen Cleopatra VII of Egypt. At eleven she lived for a year in Pompey's house at Rome. At twenty-one she began an affair with the much older Caesar.

Pictures from History / Bridgeman Images.

*Marcus Antonius, aka Mark Antony, given his chance
to shine by a subordinate of Pompey, became Caesar's
loyal lieutenant when Caesar paid off his debts.
Alinari / Bridgeman Images.*

Marcus Brutus, thought to be Caesar's illegitimate son, pardoned by Caesar after he sided with the Senate against him, only to lead the sixty senators who conspired to assassinate Caesar, calling him a tyrant. Universal History Archive/UIG / Bridgeman Images.

CAESAR
VERSUS POMPEY

INTRODUCTION

This book tells the parallel life stories of Julius Caesar and Pompey the Great, as we see their lives and loves intertwined and interdependent, as they grew from rivals to partners, then from joint rulers to warring foes. One strove to preserve the Roman Republic, the other destroyed it.

Few people have had as many words written about them down through the centuries as Julius Caesar. A brilliant general who made the seductive Queen Cleopatra of Egypt his mistress, he has captured the imagination of playwrights, historians, soldiers, and emperors.

In comparison, little has been written about his ally, son-in-law, and eventual enemy Pompeius Magnus, or Pompey the Great, who crashed onto the Roman scene as a victorious twenty-three-year-old general and who, at the height of his career, was arguably more famous, more popular, and more successful than Caesar.

But history, they say, is written by the victors. That certainly was true in the case of Caesar, who was victorious over Pompey in battle and went on to become Dictator of Rome. His own well-written accounts and those sanctioned by the emperors who followed him painted Caesar as a man fighting for the underdog against the autocrats. Caesar's admirers in later times would include France's Emperor Napoleon, the Kaisers of Germany, and Italian dictator Benito Mussolini. By the twentieth century, noted American general Norman Schwarzkopf was describing Pompey as the rebel and Caesar as a champion of democracy. But was it so?[1]

Who was Rome's greatest general, statesman, and nation-builder? Caesar, or Pompey? Which one of them was in the right? Was *either* of them in the right? Was the five-hundred-year-old Roman Republic worth preserving? Or, considering the republic's flaws, and the flaws of its leaders, was democracy doomed and autocracy inevitable? Is this the future fate of today's great republics? Read this exploration of the parallel lives of Caesar and Pompey, and decide for yourself.

I.

A BOLT OF LIGHTNING
CHANGES EVERYTHING

O utside the Colline Gate in the Servian Wall, on the northern outskirts of Rome, rain beat down on rows of tents as a late-summer
thunderstorm lashed the city. Thunder clapped fiercely in the dark clouds
above. Striding around the camp in full armor, ignoring the rain, and dis-
dainful of the booming heavens was the forty-eight-year-old general commanding the tens of thousands of Roman troops quartered here.[2]

The Colline Gate was the most northerly of Rome's gates. North of it
rose the Pincian Hill, while west of it spread the full expanse of the Field
of Mars, a low plain of some 1.5 square miles, with the Tiber River on its
western boundary. The field took its name from the altar of the war god
Mars, which stood here, and, apart from a brief time when a king of Rome
took possession of it, the Field of Mars was public land, lying outside the
pomerium, the traditional boundary of the old city of Rome. Here on the
Field of Mars, so tradition held, the dying Romulus, co-founder of Rome,
had ascended to heaven in a dark cloud before the eyes of his assembled
warriors. Now, tens of thousands of Roman troops were encamped on
the eastern extremity of the Martian field. For, in this year 87 BC, Rome
was rent by civil war between the followers of the ex-consuls Marius and
Sulla.

For centuries since the overthrow of the last king of Rome in 509 BC,
the Republic of Rome had been governed by two elected officials, the consuls, who took their seats as presidents of the Roman Senate each January
and served for twelve months, after which a new pair took their place. In

January, 87 BC, the two new consuls taking the reins were Gnaeus Octavius and Lucius Cornelius Cinna. Both were ambitious men. Both had personally sworn loyalty to Lucius Cornelius Sulla, the dominating consul of 88 BC. In early 87 BC, Sulla had left Rome to take up the Senate appointment of commander of a Roman army that was being sent from Italy to counter the Pontic king, Mithradates VI Eupator, later to be labeled Mithradates the Great, who had overrun much Roman territory in the East.

Neither Octavius nor Cinna liked the other. And once Sulla left Rome, the pair was frequently in dispute, with Cinna going against his oath of support for Sulla, which he'd taken in a temple on the Capitoline Mount. Now, he openly proposed the recall from exile of Sulla's rival Gaius Marius. A consul six times, Marius was an experienced general who twice had defeated invading Germanic tribes and made major reforms to the structure, recruitment, and training of Rome's army. But Marius was a man who divided Romans because of his more recent underhanded tactics, which had led to his exile.

Increasingly, supporters of the consuls Cinna and Octavius were coming to blows in the streets, and within months there was a massive riot in the Forum, with the supporters of Octavius gaining the upper hand. In fear for his life, Cinna fled Rome. The Senate, at the behest of the remaining consul, Octavius, and against all convention and tradition, rescinded Cinna's consular appointment and removed his Roman citizenship, replacing him as consul with Octavius's ally Lucius Cornelius Merula.

Cinna had headed south, to the winter quarters of some legions encamped at Nola, outside Naples, who were there to put down unrest among the local Samnite tribe. With Cinna vowing to recall their revered former general Marius, these troops threw their allegiance behind him. From Nola, Cinna sent for Marius, who was cooling his heels in North Africa.

By the summer, Marius had arrived from Africa with a small force. Landing on the coast south of Rome, Marius recruited six thousand locals to create a legion, then headed north and sacked Ostia, the undefended port of Rome. As Marius next marched the fourteen miles up the riverbank to Rome, Cinna took his much larger army north to attack the city from above the Tiber.

The consul Octavius reacted by pulling together two armies. One of these forces, located at Rome, was commanded by Gnaeus Pompeius Strabo, a consul two years earlier. The other army, encamped in the north of Italy, was commanded by Gnaeus Caecilius Metellus Pius, commonly known as Metellus. Now in his early forties, Metellus had been a subordinate of Strabo in the past and was still outranked by him.[3]

As Cinna neared the capital, he dispatched part of his army under senators Quintus Sertorius and Papirus Carbo to attack the district of Rome north of the Tiber on and around the Janiculum, today's Gianicolo Hill. The Servian Wall ran around the bottom of the Janiculum, and a small fort flanked the hilltop gate. Traditionally, a signal flag atop the fort should have been hauled down at the approach of the Marian force, but the military tribune in charge of the Janiculum garrison was in Cinna's debt. The tribune opened the Janiculum gate to the Marians, allowing them to flood into the city's northern, pan-Tiber suburb.

In response, Octavius and Strabo rushed troops across the Tiber bridges and, in bitter fighting, threw out the Marian forces. But the victory came at a terrible cost—17,000 men under Octavius and Strabo were killed. Octavius then sent messengers hurrying north to instruct Metellus to hasten south with reinforcements, while Strabo and his surviving troops made camp on the Field of Mars. There, a fever quickly spread among Strabo's legionaries, just as it also took hold in the camp of Cinna's battered army several miles away. The Romans called this "quartan fever." It was malaria, which was rife in and around Rome in these times, and originated from mosquitoes inhabiting the marshes south of Rome. This malarial threat would only be terminated by the filling in of those marshes by the emperor Claudius in the first century.

On a humid September afternoon, as an electrical storm raged around him and his men lay in their tents, the arrogant Strabo, who himself had begun to show signs of illness, strode around the camp encouraging his troops to find the strength and the will for a new battle. Strabo was not a popular general. But he was a determined, aggressive, and effective one, and unbendingly loyal to Rome. Despite being a provincial, Strabo had sided with Rome in the Social War of 91 to 88 BC, when Rome's allies throughout Italy had unsuccessfully rebelled against her rule. Strabo was also enormously wealthy—the fact that he was the richest man in the Picenum region in northeastern Italy had earned him entry into the Roman Senate, then a high honor for a provincial.

Despite his wealth, Strabo had gained a reputation for greed. In 89 BC, as one of the year's consuls, he had defeated a large Italian army and taken the city of Asculum in his home region of Picenum following a siege of several months. After auctioning off the property of rebel leaders, instead of sharing the proceeds with his soldiers and the Treasury at Rome, which was the norm, Strabo had kept the lot. Being a fearsome figure, backed by thousands of troops from his native Picenum, no one in Rome complained. In fact, the Senate that same year awarded him a Triumph, with its spectacular victory parade through the streets of Rome.

But now, as Strabo defied the weather, and—the more religious believed—defied the gods, striding around his camp in the electrical storm, a bolt of lightning lanced down from the black sky and hit the general, knocking him from his feet. When his aides reached him, the general was dead.[4]

Inside Rome, few tears would be shed for Pompeius Strabo. Only barely tolerated by his allies and disliked by his own troops, he was despised by his enemies, among them the family of Gaius Julius Caesar. Young Caesar, who had turned thirteen that July, was firmly in the Marian camp—his aunt Julia, sister of his father, another Gaius Julius Caesar, was married to Gaius Marius, which made Marius Caesar's uncle by marriage.

In the well-to-do Caesar family home at Rome, there would be no loud or obvious celebrations at the news of Strabo's death—slaves might pass on news of such seditious joy to consul Octavius, for a reward. But, in their own quiet way, Caesar and his family would have enjoyed the news that Octavius's best general had been eliminated, which could only bode well for Caesar's Uncle Marius, now only a few miles away, and for Marius's objective of regaining power at Rome.

In contrast, in the camp outside the Colline Gate, another young man was grieving. Gnaeus Pompeius was his name, and he was Strabo's son. From the sixteenth century, British historians and playwrights including, in the seventeenth century, William Shakespeare, would Anglicize his name from Pompeius to Pompey, and it is by that name that we have come to know him.

Tall, slim Pompey would shortly turn twenty-one. He was not handsome in the classical sense. His eyes were small, his mouth narrow. His thick hair was brushed forward in something of an unkempt mop, over a forehead that would soon furrow. Yet his features were neatly in proportion; and in his boyhood, friends had compared Pompey to the pretty, all-conquering young Macedonian general Alexander the Great. Pompey hadn't taken the comparison to heart, but neither had he dismissed it—until enemies later made the comparison disparagingly, reminding the world that Alexander had died young and had a scandalous love life.

Like Alexander the Great, Pompey's military career had begun in his teens, at the age of fifteen, when his father Strabo was leading a Roman army against rebelling Italian tribes in the Social War. Later Roman general Velleius Paterculus tells us that Pompey joined his father's staff from the very day he officially came of age—during the Liberalis Festival in March, 90 BC, six months before Pompey's sixteenth birthday on September 29. "From the day on which he assumed the toga [virilis], he had been trained to military service on the staff of that sagacious general, his father," says Velleius. This had given Pompey "a singular insight into military tactics" and "developed his excellent natural talent," Velleius observed.[5]

A Roman youth was presented by his male guardian with the plain white *toga virilis* on the day of his coming-of-age ceremony, during the Liberalis closest to his sixteenth birthday. This signified his entry into manhood and assumption of the rights of Roman citizenship, which included the right to vote and to own slaves.

It's likely that Pompey's "toga party," hosted by his father, was held in Strabo's tented headquarters pavilion in a military camp. Probable attendees at the all-male party would have been Pompey's brother-in-law Gaius Memmius, his father's subordinate general Marcus Aemilius Lepidus, and other senior officers, as well as his father's freedmen such as Alexander, his financial manager. It would have been a lighthearted affair, with Pompey's own freedman servant Demetrius shaving his master's beard—which he had not been permitted to shave off until his coming-of-age. The young man's beard hair was then offered in a casket to the family's household gods. There would have been little to shave: even in his mid-twenties, Pompey would have difficulty growing a full beard when in mourning for a relative.

For more than three years since his toga party, Pompey had been serving at his father's side, most recently as a military tribune, an officer roughly equivalent to a colonel today. By the time of Strabo's death, Pompey would have commanded a cohort of 600 legionaries for ten months of the year. The military tribune of this era, typically aged in his early twenties but as young as eighteen, also took a turn with his legion's five fellow tribunes in sharing the rotating command of the legion for two months annually.[6]

Pompey was his father's heir, inheritor of his Rome mansion and vast estates in Picenum. But Pompey, now an orphan—his mother, of whom we know nothing, was dead by this stage—and still a humble company commander, was without a powerful patron to protect him.

The day following Strabo's death, Pompey, as the new front of his family, walked at the head of the funeral procession that would take his father's body to the funeral pyre prepared for him outside the city. Pompey had just one sibling, his elder sister Pompeia, who was probably living in the family home in Rome. Pompeia was then married to Gaius Memmius, who, like Pompey, was still short of senatorial age and held Equestrian rank. Like Pompey, too, Memmius would have been serving under Strabo as a military tribune. Because of their family connection, Pompey was close to Memmius, and trusted him.

As the black-clad funeral cortege made its slow progress, with professional mourners wailing and Pompey and his brother-in-law walking solemnly behind Strabo's bier as it was carried on the shoulders of family retainers, a vast mob of supporters of Marius suddenly descended on the procession. Outnumbering Pompey's party, the Marians grabbed Strabo's body from the bier and carried it away. Pompey, unarmed, struggled vainly to retrieve his father's body. He would never know what happened to it, would never be able to inter his ashes in a noble tomb beside the Appian Way, where all passersby could see it and remember Strabo, Rome's loyal general. It's likely that Strabo's corpse was cast into the Tiber by the Marian body-snatchers, to be washed downriver to the marshes or the sea without the benefit of funeral rites or cremation—the fate of other leading senators assassinated by followers of Marius.

Pompey would never forget this outrage by the Marians.

II.

CAESAR'S UNCLE TAKES POWER,
POMPEY ON TRIAL

Before the death of Strabo, and before the costly Battle of the Janiculum in which both Strabo and his son Pompey had taken part, Pompey had been in the camp of his father's army as Strabo set himself in Cinna's path, north of the Tiber. At the time, Pompey was sharing a two-man tent with another young military tribune by the name of Lucius Terentius. Over dinner in camp with his five fellow tribunes, Pompey had received a whispered warning that Terentius was going to stab him in his bed while he slept, as part of a larger uprising in which other men loyal to Cinna would set fire to his father's tent and raise an uprising in the camp.

Young Pompey had not visibly reacted to this warning. Instead, he had drunk more liberally than usual and acted in a very friendly manner toward Terentius. Finishing his meal and bidding his comrades a good night, he went to his tent. There, he lumped clothing and bedding in his bed to give the impression he was sleeping in it, then slipped out under the tent flap. Sure enough, Terentius later entered the tent and several times plunged his sword into Pompey's bed, before realizing that Pompey had escaped. Pompey had in fact gone to warn his father, who remained out of sight as the predicted uprising took place.

As Cinna supporters ran riot through the camp, tearing down tents and urging others to march with them to join Cinna, young Pompey tried to reason with them and restore order. Finally, he lay full length in the camp's main gate, and, in tears, dramatically implored the troops to either return to his father's authority or trample him to death. In the end, such was the esteem in which young Pompey was held, only eight hundred men, Terentius among them, deserted to Cinna's side. Some thirty thousand others heeded Pompey's call and remained loyal to his father, who subsequently withdrew the army to Rome, in time for the Battle of the Janiculum. We never hear of the budding assassin Terentius again.

In the wake of the death of Pompey's father, his rank-and-file soldiery was restless and reluctant to continue fighting for Octavius against the forces of Cinna and the famous Marius, which outnumbered them two to one. Octavius was desperately awaiting the arrival of Metellus with reinforcements from the north. When he learned that Metellus had reached the hill town of Alba Longa, just twelve miles southeast of Rome, Octavius arranged a meeting there. When Octavius arrived, he found Metellus's troops agitating for Metellus to take command from him.

With Metellus and his army remaining at Alba, Octavius scurried back to Rome and reported to the Senate, which humiliated him by calling on him to negotiate with Cinna now that he had lost one of his generals and lost the support of the other. When Octavius met with Cinna's delegates, they assured him that Cinna only wanted his citizenship and consulship restored; if Octavius agreed, all would be forgiven.

"I will not willingly cause anyone's death on reentering Rome," was Cinna's message to Octavius. Based on this, Octavius agreed to a cessation of hostilities, after which Strabo's former troops quickly swore loyalty to Cinna.[7]

The day before Cinna reentered Rome, Merula resigned from the consulship, paving the way for the Senate to restore Cinna's citizenship and consulship. Once he was back in his city house, Cinna's bodyguards proceeded to break into the Roman homes of dead and absent supporters of Octavius including Strabo and Metellus, looting them. Cinna did, however, keep his word to refrain from violence, and restrained his men from doing any physical harm to his opponents.

When Marius refused to enter the city until his exile of the previous year was overturned, the Senate swiftly complied. Greeted by crowds of overjoyed supporters, Marius now reentered Rome as a returning hero, and the Caesar family, among others, breathed a sigh of relief. But, unlike his colleague Cinna, Marius had given no undertaking to refrain from acts of revenge. As Marius crossed the pomerium, hundreds of former slaves of his personal bodyguard unit, the Bardyiae, flooded ahead of him, all lusting for blood.

The Bardyiae, led by Marius's officers including Gaius Censorinus, went on a killing rampage, murdering leading Sulla supporters, starting with consul Octavius and former consul Merula. Censorinus personally decapitated Octavius and sent his head to Marius. Octavius's general Metellus only escaped the bloodletting because he was at Alba. He fled Italy to Africa, where he had numerous wealthy clients. Other key Sullans were charged by Marius and Cinna with major crimes, all punishable with exile. Rather than face show trials and inevitable exile, losing all their property, fourteen senators, including six former consuls, took their own lives.

The young Pompey survived the worst aspects of this purge because he was quartered among his father's former troops; but as his father's heir he was charged by Marius with receiving the stolen property of the Roman Treasury. This was the loot from Asculum, which Marius reckoned Strabo should have given to the Treasury. Calmly and deliberately, Pompey, now twenty-one years old, prepared his defense. At several hearings, he appeared before Antistius, one of the year's eight elected praetors, or senior judges. Each praetor dealt with a different category of crime, with Antistius specializing in embezzlement.

Skillfully, Pompey proved that, while he had been with his father during the siege of Asculum, the proceeds from the auction following the siege had been stolen by Alexander, his father's Greek freedman. In the process, Pompey impressed all with an ability, dignity, and self-confidence that were considered well beyond his years.

One charge after another was dismissed, until just one remained—that Pompey had received Asculum-booty hunting tackle and books from his father. In answer, Pompey asked how he could be charged with possession of such goods when they had been stolen from his father's house, now his house, a spacious residence with extensive gardens, in the Carinae, or

Keels, Rome's most fashionable residential district, on the Esquiline Hill. And who had stolen these goods from his father's house? None other than Cinna's guards. As Pompey was able to prove, these guards had entered the city with Cinna and had gone directly to Strabo's house, broken in, and stolen every portable valuable on the dead general's property. It should be they, said Pompey, who were charged with possession of stolen goods!

This very likely brought sympathetic laughter from the crowded public gallery, for the case had raised the ire of supporters of the popular youth. The judge Antistius was certainly impressed. During the trial, he invited Pompey to dinner. There, he proposed that Pompey marry his daughter, Antistia. Without hesitation Pompey agreed, and a written marriage contract was drawn up and signed in secret by Antistius and Pompey. But the secret soon leaked, and after Antistius reconvened the court and announced that the judges were unanimously acquitting the young man of the final charge, good-natured cheers of "*Talasio!*" filled the courtroom. It was, you see, the custom at weddings for the guests to cry *Talasio* to bid the happy couple good fortune.

So Pompey was off the hook. Just a few days later, he and Antistia were discreetly married, and, as custom required, he carried her over the threshold of his home, his late father's vandalized house in the Keels, to the cheers and applause of wedding guests. We are told nothing of Pompey's bride. She would have been a teenager, Roman girls being permitted by Roman law to become engaged at twelve years of age and to marry from thirteen. Typically, when girls so young were married off, often to create a family alliance, their husbands refrained from having sexual relations with them until they were older. This seems to have been the case with Pompey and Antistia, for this marriage, which would last close to five years, would produce no children.

Not that Pompey lacked sexual experience. He had a mistress in his teens. All young Roman men of aristocratic birth were encouraged by their fathers to gain sexual experience with courtesans so they would know how to pleasure their wives once they married. This, they believed, was far better than for their sons to roam the streets in drunken bands of upper-class youths that frequented the common brothels, as Mark Antony would do in the coming decades. Conversely, the brides of aristocrats were expected to be virgins, unless they had previously been married.

Courtesans, instead of inhabiting common brothels with their partitioned cubicles occupied by whores who were usually slaves, were wealthy women with their own houses and their own slaves—their wealth being provided by rich clients. The woman who taught Pompey all about making love was Dora, a famous beauty who enchanted all who came in contact with her. Two decades before she took Pompey to her bed, another of her noble initiates had been none other than Metellus, the general whose failure to support Octavius had led to Octavius's downfall and death. Metellus had been so enamored with Dora that he raised a statue of her in Rome's Temple of Castor and Pollux.

Dora was in middle age by the time she took Pompey in hand but was still a stunning beauty. It would turn out that she fell in love with him, won by his youthful good looks, gentle manner, and kindness. In old age, she would recall that whenever he left her bed, she would give him the parting gift of a bite. And then one day Pompey's companion Geminius confessed that he had fallen for Dora. When Geminius asked Pompey if he could bed her, Pompey gave his permission, but he himself never again went near Dora. She was devastated and fell into a deep depression.

Pompey had a code of ethics when it came to women and propriety. His freedman Demetrius had a beautiful wife, and she seemed charmed by Pompey. So, while he retained Demetrius's services until the day he died, and remembered him generously in his will, Pompey always acted with brusqueness and lack of generosity toward the man's wife. He did this quite deliberately, to ensure that no rumor would grow that he was having an affair with his freedman's wife.

In 86 BC, with Marius once again elected to the consulship, sitting with Cinna for the year, Pompey reckoned he and his new wife would be safer back in his parents' home territory, surrounded by friends and retainers, and he returned to Picenum. There, in the northeast of Italy, he deliberately kept out of politics, concentrated on running his rural estates, and cautiously awaited the expected return of Sulla.

It was not that Sulla was a friend of Pompey or his family. To part Strabo from his troops and destroy his power, Sulla, as one of the consuls for 89 BC, had discharged Strabo's soldiers and sent them into retirement. This was because the stubborn Strabo had refused to swear loyalty to Sulla. But neither would he swear loyalty to anyone else. Right now, Sulla and his army were grinding down Mithradates's army in the East. But Pompey knew the day would come when Sulla returned to Italy, with his army. And then Romans would have to decide who to support. Would they stand with Rome's current brutal master Marius? Or would they follow Sulla, once a junior aide to Marius but now a general who had never been defeated? In choosing sides, sometimes in contradiction of family ties, a Roman noble was choosing his destiny.

III.

CAESAR THE PRIEST, POMPEY
THE BOY GENERAL

Just as Pompey had lost his father at Rome, in the second half of 85 BC, when he was fifteen, Gaius Julius Caesar the younger lost his father. The elder Caesar, a fifty-five-year-old senator, praetor, and former provincial governor, was putting on his shoes early one morning after rising from his bed when he suffered a major heart attack that took his life.

Young Caesar would be joined by Cinna, Papirus Carbo, and other leading Marians at his father's funeral. Caesar was known to friends and family as Gaius. In his own time he was never called Julius, his family's clan name. Upper-class Roman citizens had a minimum of three—first name, clan name, and one or more cognomens. The latter were frequently acquired in childhood, but they could also be added in adulthood as honorifics in recognition of significant service to the state, usually in war. Cognomens could be passed from father to son, as they were in the case of Caesar, which literally meant "head of hair" or "long-haired." This was ironic, as Caesar would in later years be very self-conscious about the fact he was balding.

Only when, much later, European historians and playwrights wrote about Caesar did he become Julius, a much easier handle than Gaius. In his own time, too, Gaius's last name of Caesar was pronounced Kaiser, which was why the emperors of Germany in the nineteenth and twentieth centuries became the Kaisers, as they sought to add some of the luster of Caesar's name to their reigns.

Caesar now became the youthful head of his family, which included his doting mother Aurelia, then aged in her forties, and his sisters, Julia Major, two years older than her brother, and Julia Minor, a year his junior. He was also responsible for his now-widowed Aunt Julia. For Caesar had lost his patron and chief protector Marius his uncle in January the previous year. Marius and Cinna had been elected consuls for 86 BC, but just seventeen days into the new consular year Marius had died, apparently from pleurisy. Despite Marius's death, the pro-Marius faction in the Senate, led by his protégé Cinna, continued to hold power, and Cinna had taken Caesar under his protective wing.

During this same year, Caesar is said to have had an affair with Servilia, half-sister of the future famous orator Marcus Cato, also known as Cato the Younger. Certainly, two and a half decades later Servilia would become Caesar's mistress, when she was described as being deeply in love with him. In 85 BC, Servilia was, like Caesar, only a teenager. She was also a married woman. Her husband was Marcus Junius Brutus, an up-and-coming Marian politician in his twenties. Despite her youth, by the end of the year Servilia would give birth to a son, Marcus Junius Brutus Jr. The boy would be raised as Brutus's son, but for the rest of Caesar's life and long after it the rumor would persist that Caesar was young Marcus Brutus's father.

The following year, during the Liberalis in March 84 BC, three months out from his sixteenth birthday, Caesar celebrated his coming of age. The toga party of the tall, lean youth was presumably hosted by Cinna, who successfully nominated him to become the high priest of Jupiter. This role traditionally went to youths, the sons of aristocrats, and added to the prestige of their families. But it also prevented the holder from any involvement in politics. This would have disappointed the ambitious Caesar, but would have been seen by his influential mother Aurelia as a way of shielding her vulnerable son from the dangers of political-faction conflicts.

Cinna went even further, contracting the young man to marry his own daughter Cornelia, who is believed to have been some three years younger than Caesar. To enable this, Caesar had to cancel a marriage contract arranged for him by his father when he was only a boy. The intended bride was a young girl named Cossutia. While her father Cossutius was only a member of the middle-ranking Equestrian Order, he was rich. This had clearly been the principal attraction of the projected union as far as the Caesars were concerned, while Cossutia would be marrying into a senatorial family and elevating her father's connections. In all likelihood, money changed hands to enable the cancellation of Cossutia's marriage to Caesar. Her family was no doubt also promised favored treatment by Cinna.[8]

The marriage of Caesar and young Cornelia soon followed, and they took up residence in the Caesar family's home at Rome, with Caesar having been willed the majority of his father's estate. Although it is clear that Caesar was fond of his young wife, she was then only fourteen and it is highly likely that it would be several years before they had sexual relations. It would be eight years before Caesar and Cornelia had a child.

From this point on, Caesar's life was restricted to carrying out his ceremonial duties as the high priest of Jupiter, which prevented him from using the oratorical skills he had developed under his boyhood tutor the freedman Marcus Antonius Gnipho. Among the other limitations imposed on Caesar as Jupiter's priest, he was not permitted to lay eyes on an army, to touch a horse, or to sleep outside his own bed for three successive nights or outside Rome for more than one night. This made him a virtual prisoner of Rome.

For the next few years, with Sulla still fighting Mithradates in the East, Rome continued to be ruled by the Marian faction. Several decades later, the noted lawyer and orator Cicero would characterize the two factions that dominated Roman politics at this time as the *Populares* and the *Optimates*, literally the populists and the good men, identifying Marius as a leader of the Populares because he had frequently used the popular assemblies to frustrate the edicts of the Senate to get his own way, even though he too was a senator. Sulla was considered by Cicero to be the leader of the Optimates, the "good men" who opposed Marius.

Later historians such as the nineteenth century's Theodor Mommsen, many of whose theories on ancient Rome have subsequently been proven to be hopelessly wrong, would take Cicero's labels to literally mean that Rome was divided into political parties like those of modern times. Some twentieth-century historians would even go so far as to describe the Populares as those who stood up for the rights of the ordinary man, while declaring the Optimates autocratic Roman nobles who wanted to keep power for the Senate and themselves. But this is incorrect. None of the political players of this period called themselves Optimates or Populares, or formed into political parties with opposing ideologies.

This labeling was merely a creative flourish on Cicero's part, designed to differentiate political divisions that were actually built on loyalties between clients and patrons, the foundation of the Roman social system. Mommsen and other unreliable historians totally overlooked these client/patron relationships that drove Roman business and politics.

While these labels would be borrowed from Cicero three hundred years later by the Roman historian Cassius Dio, first-century BC writers apart from Cicero didn't use them, and Julius Caesar never used the terms Optimates or Populares. The only thing men on both sides of the political argument had in common in the time of Marius and Sulla was a desire for personal preservation, personal advancement, and the pursuit of personal wealth and power. Rather than being like political parties, the Marians and the Sullans were more like Italian Mafia crime families, based on the two-way relationship between patron and adherents.

To succeed in Roman politics, it was necessary to ally yourself with influential patrons, who topped the metaphorical pyramid of power. But it was equally necessary to build your power base on a foundation of clients in the senatorial and Equestrian orders who owed allegiance to you and would do favors for you, in return for favors *from* you—such as giving male family and friends official posts, as well as supporting them in elections and in Senate debates, or lobbying colleagues to do so.

Caesar, by virtue of his family connection with Marius and marriage to Cornelia, was firmly in the Marian faction, now led by Cinna. Pompey, on the other hand, was not a client of either Cinna or Sulla. He was an outsider. Pompey had every reason to fear that Sulla considered him to be made from the same mold as his father—and was, furthermore, resentful of Sulla's treatment of his father. In which case, Sulla was likely to consider the young man an opponent. So, in Picenum, Pompey insulated himself from both sides of politics.

The time to test factional loyalties loomed when the news reached Rome in late 85 BC, just months after the death of Caesar's father, that Sulla, having outfought and outwitted Mithradates's army and navy in and around Greece, had brought Mithradates to terms that ended the First Mithradatic War. This meant that Sulla could be expected to return soon to Rome, with his army. Sulla's peace terms were humiliating for Mithradates. He was permitted to retain his own kingdom, Pontus, but was forced to give up two Roman provinces he'd occupied in Asia Minor and hand back two kingdoms he had taken from their kings. Furthermore, he had to hand over scores of his warships and tens of millions of sesterces in financial reparations to Sulla.

All through 84 BC, tension built in Rome as Sulla, in the regained province of Asia, rested and rearmed his forces and built his war chest. Late in the year, he sailed for the Balkans with 1,200 ships and his best troops. On hearing this, Cinna prepared for war, appointing Carbo his deputy. Marching from Rome, the pair assembled their forces at an Italian east-coast port, ready to preempt Sulla's return by catching him in the Balkans.

One convoy of Cinna's troops had already sailed for the Balkans when young Pompey arrived at the camp, having traveled down the coast from Picenum. After hearing of Cinna's military preparations, Pompey had come to offer his services. But he soon found false accusations being levied at him, apparently to the effect that he had come as a spy for Sulla. Remembering how close he'd come to being killed by Marians in an army camp years before, and fearing for his life, Pompey slipped away.

When it was found that Pompey had disappeared, some in the ranks were certain that Cinna had murdered the son of Strabo. Shortly after this, Cinna called an assembly to prepare his troops for embarkation. But rumors were rife. One held that the first troop convoy had been wrecked in a storm. And there was the accusation that Cinna had murdered Pompey. Then, when one of Cinna's attendants impatiently pushed a soldier to make way for his master, he sparked a riot among the unsettled troops. Cinna fled the assembly, but a centurion chased him down. Cinna, falling to his knees, begged to be spared, offering his valuable gold signet ring, which contained his personal seal.

"I didn't come to seal a covenant," growled the centurion, sword in hand, "but to be revenged upon a lawless and wicked tyrant." With that, he cleaved off Cinna's head.[9]

With Cinna's death, Carbo took command, sending word to Rome and Marius's twenty-six-year-old son, another Gaius Marius, to rally forces in the west to oppose a Sullan march on the capital. Meanwhile, Sertorius, another of Cinna's subordinates, left Rome. The Senate had appointed him governor of one of Rome's Spanish provinces, and Sertorius hurried away to take up the Spanish post on behalf of the Marians.

As for Pompey, he scurried back to the safety of Picenum to the north. Having seen that he was in danger in Marian ranks, he set about creating an army for his own defense. He began at the walled hill town of Auximum, today's Osimo. Twelve miles south of Ancona and not far from the Adriatic coast, Auximum had been a Roman colony and home to retired Roman soldiers for decades.

From a dais in the marketplace, Pompey addressed the people, calling on them to follow him. Two brothers of the Ventidius family, leading men of the town, had recently been speaking in favor of Carbo, so Pompey publicly banished them from Auximum. As the pair fled, other Marian supporters also quickly left town. The vast majority of the townspeople flooded to support the impressive young man.

Pompey subsequently went around all the towns of Picenum, ejecting Marians and levying an army from among the Piceni—in northern Picenum alone there were twenty Roman military colonies and towns with Roman municipality status. Over the winter of 84–83 BC, Pompey expended part of the fortune he had inherited from his father paying for the manufacture of armored vests, helmets, shields, swords, javelins, and the other equipment required by an army.

As his senior officers, Pompey appointed men who had been clients of his father, and as his centurions he personally chose men he could trust, many of them retired veterans who had served his father. Some of his draftees were also recalled veterans, but a number were raw recruits aged from seventeen, the vast majority of them young "rustics," farm boys made tough and strong by the outdoors life. According to the later Roman military writer Vegetius, it was rustics, not "soft" city dwellers, who made the best soldiers.[10]

That same spring, the twenty-three-year-old Pompey had raised an army of more than 18,000 men, all of them loyal to him first and foremost. He divided them among a small mounted unit and three infantry legions that he called his 1st, 2nd, and 3rd Legions, with each marching behind a silver eagle standard, symbol of Jupiter, king of the gods. The troops' young commander-in-chief was fit and athletic. A fine horseman, Pompey trained with his cavalry, showing great accuracy in throwing the javelin from horseback while galloping at speed. He also drafted non-combatants, slaves and freedmen, to handle his baggage train, which he equipped with mules, oxen, and carts, filling the carts with ammunition and provisions, all at his own expense.

In the spring of 83 BC, Sulla landed with five legions in the southeastern Italian port of Brundisium, today's Brindisi. He was joined in Italy by Metellus, who had deposed the Marian governor of Africa, gathered an army of veterans who had previously served him, and sailed to join Sulla. Metellus landed in the northeast, probably at Ravenna, and gathered significant forces to dominate Cisalpine Gaul, the then Roman province between the Po River and the Alps.

Two of Sulla's young staff officers, his thirty-six-year-old quaestor, or adjutant, for the past several years, Lucius Licinius Lucullus, and Lucullus's distant relative Marcus Licinius Crassus, would make names for themselves in the coming decades. Crassus in particular would play a significant role in the lives of both Caesar and Pompey. The thirty-three-year-old Crassus came from a distinguished consular family that supported Sulla, and his father and younger brother had been murdered by the Marians on the day Marius reentered Rome.

Avoiding the same fate by fleeing to Spain, Crassus had hidden out for eight months with servants in a seaside cave. Crassus later recruited 2,500 local clients of his father, sailed to Africa, and linked up with Metellus. Soon falling out with Metellus, Crassus sailed to Greece with his men, where he joined Sulla and his army just as Sulla was heading for Italy.

Once Pompey, back in Picenum, learned that Sulla was in Brindisi, he led his army out of Picenum, heading down the east coast, often over open country, with the intention of joining up with Sulla. He was in no rush. Moving in easy daily stages, he gathered more recruits and added supplies and regional support as he marched south.

Before long, a large Marian force appeared in his path to oppose him, led by senatorial commanders loyal to Carbo—the praetors Marcus Junius Brutus Damasippus and Gaius Carrinas, and legion commander Titus Cloelius. These generals, scornful of this boy who was still seven years short of senatorial age and yet had the temerity to think he could raise an army of his own, set up three camps encircling Pompey's force. But Pompey did not panic. Rather than divide his army, he formed his legions into battle formation in a single force, and, placing his cavalry in front of the infantry, with himself to the fore, he advanced against just one of the Marian armies, that led by Damasippus.

Hastily forming up his troops, Damasippus put his Celtic cavalry in front to meet Pompey's cavalry. Pompey promptly kicked his horse into a gallop and led his cavalry in a charge. He himself picked out the stout Celtic cavalry commander and rode straight for him. The pair launched into hand-to-hand combat, but within moments Pompey had dodged the spear thrusts of his opponent and sunk his own javelin into the man's body. The other Celts, seeing their commander topple from his saddle, turned and rode off, directly into Damasippus's infantry, causing chaos in their ranks. Damasippus's troops fell back in disarray, and when Damasippus frantically met with his two fellow generals to decide how to handle Pompey, the trio argued over what to do, with the result that all three Marian armies retreated—in different directions.

As Pompey, soon after this, continued his slow progress south, all the cities of the region sent envoys, vowing their allegiance to him. Before long, another Marian army appeared in his path, led by one of the consuls for the year, Lucius Cornelius Scipio Asiaticus. As Scipio formed his troops up in battle lines, Pompey did the same. But before a javelin could be hurled, Scipio's troops began hailing the men in Pompey's ranks as friends. As Scipio's troops went over to Pompey and were greeted with joy by Pompey's Piceni, the consul fled for his life. Now the young man from Picenum had a formidable army at his command, a force to be reckoned with.

Pompey's advancing army, now having left Picenum, reached a river where a cavalry force dispatched by Carbo stood in its path. Without hesitation, Pompey again led his cavalry in a charge. And once again he routed the opposition. This time, he and his mounted troops gave chase to the fleeing opposition riders, forcing them into rough, rocky ground that was impassable by horses. Here, the surviving Marian cavalrymen surrendered to Pompey.[11]

Up to this point, Sulla had been wholly unaware of the growing army of 30,000 men that marched down the coast to link up with him, an army led by a young tribune. When the first reports reached him of Pompey's approach, Sulla, anxious to incorporate this force, and fearing that Carbo would throw everything he had at Pompey to halt him, set off north from Brindisi at the double to "save" the youngster and his army before it was too late.

When couriers informed Pompey that Sulla was approaching, he ordered his troops into parade order. Instead of tramping along in loose, strung-out formations with baggage poles on their shoulders and standard-bearers to the rear, Pompey's men formed up for review, behind their standards in neat ranks and files. This was the impressive sight that met the astonished Sulla as he rode up. Noting how young and strong Pompey's rustic legionaries appeared, Sulla dismounted.

Pompey also dismounted. It was impossible not to recognize Sulla. He was a singularly distinctive man, square-jawed and ruggedly handsome, with red-blond hair and blue eyes. As his staff followed, he began walking toward Pompey, who strode forward to greet the general.

"Hail, *Imperator*!" boomed the massed voices of Pompey's legionaries behind him, orchestrated by their officers. This rare and sought-after title was traditionally given to a Roman general by his troops after a great victory. Sulla had been hailed Imperator by his own troops three years earlier, following his defeat of Mithradates's forces in several battles in Greece, but Marius and his supporters had prevented the Senate from giving the customary confirmation of the title.

The call brought a smile to the face of Sulla, and, to the surprise of his staff and Pompey's proud recruits, as Sulla and Pompey came together Sulla returned the compliment by calling out "Hail, Pompeius, Imperator!"[12]

The pair embraced, and from that day forward Pompey was one of Sulla's most valued generals, with Sulla greeting him by rising from his chair, an honor he granted few others. As they dined together that first night, Sulla offered to send Pompey and his legions to Cisalpine Gaul, to serve alongside, but not under, Metellus. This was because Metellus, despite commanding large forces, was sitting on his backside and doing little to inhibit the Marians. Pompey briefly resisted this posting, saying he would only do so if Metellus, his superior in age and rank, agreed to it. Letters were exchanged with Metellus, who advised that he had no objections to the young man serving as his equal. And so Pompey and his legions retraced their steps, marching up the east coast to Cisalpine Gaul.

Pompey went with specific orders from Sulla to force the timid Metellus into aggressive action. Sulla, having taken Crassus's 2,500 Spanish recruits into his own army, ordered Crassus to enlist recruits for him in central Italy. When Crassus asked for a bodyguard, Sulla bluntly refused. So Crassus attached himself to Pompey's army for the march north, and

Pompey got to know the man who would become one of his partners in power in years to come.

Sulla, meanwhile, marching via the west coast, set off with 40,000 men to advance on Rome.

IV.

CAESAR IN JEOPARDY, POMPEY
BECOMES GREAT

At Rome, the young Gaius Julius Caesar, high priest of Jupiter, in 83 and 82 BC heard reports of the defeats of the Marians by Sulla and his generals Metellus and the upstart Pompey, and could only fume that he was prevented by his post from joining the fight against Sulla.

In November, 83 BC, the first great blow to the Marian cause came at the Battle of Mount Tifata, on a spur of the Apennines. There, despite leading an army of 100,000 men against Sulla's 40,000, Gaius Norbanus, a Marian consul for the year, was routed by Sulla before Norbanus's consular colleague Scipio could reinforce him. Norbanus fell back to Capua, then retreated to Cisalpine Gaul to link up with Carbo, who was fighting off Metellus and the lively Pompey. Meanwhile, the consular army led by Scipio went over to Sulla. Scipio himself was captured in his camp, but Sulla let Scipio and his son go free. Sulla's fortunes were in the ascendant; but with significant Marian forces still arrayed against him, both sides hunkered down for winter.

At Rome, Carbo and Gaius Marius Jr., first cousin of young Caesar, were elected consuls for 82 BC, and Marian supporters including Caesar would have hoped for a reversal of fortunes this year. By the spring of 82 BC, Sulla resumed his advance on Rome and in April went into battle against young Gaius Marius at Sacriporto, east of Rome. Marius, still in his twenties, was no Pompey. He lost 28,000 men, to twenty-three men lost on Sulla's side.

With his seven thousand remaining men, Marius hastily withdrew to Praeneste, a hill town in the Apennines famous for its Temple of

Fortune and resident oracle, just twenty-two miles east of Rome. With him he took all the gold from Rome's Treasury. As he retreated, Marius vindictively sent orders to Damasippus at Rome to call a meeting of the Senate and then assassinate four senators he considered insufficiently loyal—and, more particularly, too close to Sulla's general Pompey. One was Carbo's cousin. Another was Quintus Mucius Scaevola, the Pontifex Maximus, young Marius's former father-in-law.

Scaevola managed to escape and flee to the Regia, official residence of the Pontifex Maximus, high priest of Rome, which stood beside the Temple of Vesta. On being pursued, he retreated to the temple itself, hoping the Marians would observe its sanctity. But the sword-wielding assassins forced their way in and killed the high priest in the temple vestibule. His body was then carried to the Tiber and unceremoniously thrown into the swift-flowing waters. Carbo's cousin was murdered in the Senate House itself. A third victim was Pompey's father-in-law Antistius the praetor, whose wife was so devastated by the news of her husband's murder that she took her own life, leaving their daughter Antistia, Pompey's wife, parentless.

Sulla, pressing his military advantage, followed Marius to Praeneste and besieged it. Once he had encircled the town with entrenchments and cut it off from supply, he left his subordinate Quintus Lucretius Afella in charge with part of his army, leading the rest of his troops to Rome.

To rescue young Marius, Carbo sent eight legions under his deputy Censorinus to break the siege of Praeneste. But young Pompey had Sulla's back. Anticipating Carbo's move, he intercepted Censorinus on the march. Pompey, while accompanied by Crassus, had previously routed a force led by his earlier opponent Carrinas on the Spoleto plain, at the foot of the Apennines, killing three thousand Marians. Censorinus's troops would have been aware of this when Pompey unexpectedly appeared before them at Sena Gallica, today's Senigallia, twenty miles north of Ancona on the Adriatic Coast. The reputation of the young general from Picenum having preceded him, and although Pompey was outnumbered, one of Censorinus's legions retreated while survivors of the other seven deserted en masse to Pompey.

Censorinus himself fled back to Carbo with just a handful of men. With Pompey in his path, Carbo retreated east, until, at Faventia in the vicinity of Bolognia, he was forced into battle by the waiting Metellus, and soundly defeated. Carbo sailed off to Sicily with a fleet. His comrade Norbanus, consul from the previous year, fled to Rhodes, where he committed suicide as the Rhodians debated whether they should hand him over to Sulla.

At Rome, Censorinus combined with Damasippus and Carrinas to defend the city against Sulla's advance. Their army was bolstered by rebel Italians from Samnium in central Italy and their southern neighbors the Lucanians. Both peoples had opposed Rome in past conflicts, with the Samnites even allying with the Carthaginian general Hannibal when he unsuccessfully attacked Rome. The Samnites and Lucanians had attempted to break through Sulla's lines at Praeneste; but, driven back, they had turned toward Rome to join the Marians there. According to Velleius, writing decades later, the real intention of the Samnite leader Pontius Telesinus, a likely ancestor of Pontius Pilate of biblical fame, was to destroy Rome, which he hated.

By November 1, 82 BC, the civil war had come to Rome's doorstep. At 4:00 in the afternoon, outside Rome's Colline Gate, the site of the death of Pompey's father five years earlier, Sulla led his army against the Marians. Sulla himself commanded on his right. When his left buckled under Marian attack, Sulla left the inexperienced Marcus Crassus in command on his right and hurried to the left. Despite Sulla's best efforts, he was forced to withdraw and find respite behind the walls of his marching camp.

Many of Sulla's men from the left wing fled east to Sulla's army outside Praeneste, where they assured Afella, the Sullan general commanding the siege, that Sulla was dead, and urged him to retreat. But Afella refused to believe it, and held his ground.

Crassus, on the Sullan right outside the Colline Gate, sent messengers to Sulla in the marching camp, asking what he should do—come to Sulla's aid, or withdraw? Sulla replied that he should do neither, urging him to go on the attack, against the Marian center. Hours later, in the night, Crassus arrived to tell Sulla that he had crushed the Marian center, with survivors fleeing in disarray. This astonished all who heard it. Up to this point, apart from briefly fighting alongside Pompey at Spoleto, Crassus had done nothing more than recruit troops. Now, displaying the qualities of a general, he had kept his men together and led them to victory.

Rome was now Sulla's, and the following day he entered the city as its conqueror. When captured Marian commanders were brought to him, he had them beheaded on the spot. Their heads were then sent to the besieged Praeneste and paraded around the Sullan entrenchments on the end of spears, in full view of Marian defenders.

Among these executed generals were Damasippus, who had fled from Pompey when the young general was first marching to link up with Sulla, as well as his colleagues Censorinus and Carrinas. The head of Censorinus, the man who had delivered Octavius's head to Marius on a spear, was now also on a spear. Also decapitated were Lamponius, leader of the Lucanians, and Telesinus the Samnite commander—captured seriously wounded in a field.

Faced by the indisputable evidence of the defeat of the Marian generals at Rome, the disheartened people of Praeneste surrendered. At the time, Gaius Marius Jr. was digging a tunnel beneath the town wall. When informed of the display of heads and the town's surrender, there, in the tunnel, Caesar's cousin took his own life, as did the brother of Samnite leader Telesinus. Young Marius's head was sent by Afella to his commander at Rome, where it was displayed in public.

At Rome on November 3, Sulla issued a list of men whom he now proscribed as enemies of the state. Under his edict, these men were subject to immediate execution if found in Italy. Scipio, consul of the previous year, was on the list, even though Sulla had let him go free. Anticipating this, Scipio had fled to Massilia, today's Marseilles in the south of France, where he would live out the rest of his life.

Another of the proscribed men was eighteen-year-old Gaius Julius Caesar. His appointment as high priest of Jupiter was annulled by Sulla, and the house at Rome he'd inherited from his father, along with all his other property, was confiscated. Initially, because Caesar had not actively opposed him, Sulla did not order the youth's death. But he did order Caesar to divorce his wife Cornelia, daughter of his late arch-opponent Cinna. On principle, Caesar refused. So Sulla confiscated Cornelia's dowry.

Meanwhile, Sulla's young general Pompey hurried from Cisalpine Gaul to Rome to congratulate his patron, who had a task for him. Several parts of Rome's empire were in the hands of men who opposed Sulla. In Spain, Sertorius had ejected the governor loyal to Sulla, allied with the locals, and made himself ruler of the entire Iberian Peninsula. Now aged fifty, like Hannibal Sertorius had lost an eye in battle, and he was a charismatic figure who won over local tribal chiefs who were fearful of Rome. His success attracted other leading Marians to Spain to fight beneath his standard. Sertorius would have to be dealt with, but Sicily was Sulla's first priority, primarily because its granaries contained much of Rome's grain supply for the coming year. To keep the Roman populace fed and onside, Sulla gave Pompey the job of removing Carbo and his Marian supporters from power on the island.

In return for being given this important responsibility, Pompey was required by Sulla to divorce his wife Antistia and marry Sulla's stepdaughter Aemilia, making Pompey Sulla's son-in-law and, in the eyes of many, his chosen successor. Aemilia was not only already married, to a young man named Manius Acilius Glabrio, she was heavily pregnant by her husband. But that didn't matter to Sulla.

Following orders, Pompey divorced Antistia—to be legal, a Roman divorce only required a written declaration from one party. Antistia is known to have lived for at least another decade and a half, most likely supported financially by Pompey. Aemilia divorced her husband, and she and Pompey married. All this occurred quickly and quietly. Once the nuptials had been completed, the twenty-four-year-old Pompey sailed for Sicily with an army to carry out his new father-in-law's bidding. As his deputy,

Pompey took along his brother-in-law Gaius Memmius. Technically, the commanders of this army were both mere military tribunes. Shockingly, within weeks of marrying Pompey, who was now off campaigning for her father, Aemilia died in childbirth while delivering Manius Acilius Glabrio's child, at Pompey's house on the Esquiline.

While Pompey was launching his Sicilian operation with tens of thousands of troops, young Caesar, along with his wife, mother, and aunt, was now depending on relatives for a roof and sustenance at Rome. Those relatives included Caesar's sisters, married by this time to patricians, members of noble families. Refusing to be cowed by Sulla, Caesar put himself forward as a candidate for one of the priesthoods filled by annual election. Sulla said nothing publicly, but behind the scenes he prevented Caesar's candidacy from proceeding. Caesar's wise and wily mother Aurelia now used her family connections to have a case made to Sulla by his clients that her son Gaius was a mere boy, posed no threat, and should be spared a death sentence.

Sulla replied by complaining that the people speaking for Caesar were clearly blind to the fact that the youth was not to be trusted, adding, "There are many Mariuses in this fellow Caesar."[13]

When Caesar learned of this, and despite suffering from malaria at the time, he quickly took himself from Rome and went into hiding in the countryside of central Italy, taking along plenty of cash to pay his way as he and his servants regularly moved from one house to another.

In Sicily, Pompey made rapid progress. Carbo had been welcomed by the Marian governor, Marcus Perpenna Vento, known as Perpenna, a slimy man who would prove a serial betrayer. As soon as Pompey arrived in Sicily, Perpenna fled the island with his troops, abandoning Carbo and heading by sea to join up with Sertorius in Spain. As Pompey based himself in western Sicily, at Lilybaeum, today's Marsala, Carbo was in hiding on the island of Cossyra, today's Pantellaria, southwest of Sicily and closer to the coast of North Africa than to Sicily. Fearful of Pompey, the people of the island handed Carbo over to his troops. In chains, Carbo was taken to Pompey, who without hesitation had Carbo tried as a traitor and then immediately executed.

Methodically, Pompey moved from one Sicilian city to another, executing some leading Marians but accepting pledges of loyalty to Sulla from most local leaders, acting with "great humanity" in the words of his Greco-Roman biographer Plutarch. Pompey even defended some men accused of being secret Marians when members of his own party called for their deaths for reasons of personal enmity, even smuggling some men out of Sicily to protect them. Even so, for the few executions Pompey did authorize, his enemies dubbed him the "Adolescent Butcher," or "Butcher Boy."[14]

At Himera in northern Sicily, Pompey was preparing to punish the city's leaders when one man bravely came forward and offered to take all the blame to save his countrymen. Pompey was so impressed that he pardoned the lot. His clemency also extended to the ordinary people—on hearing that his troops were using their swords indiscriminately against locals in towns and villages they passed through, he ordered all swords sealed in their scabbards until he called for them to be drawn. Only one Sicilian city, Messina, was harshly treated by Pompey, after its leaders refused to recognize his authority, citing an old grant of rights from Rome.

"What?!" Pompey exclaimed. "Will you never cease tediously spouting laws to us who have swords at our sides?" Steel being more persuasive than rhetoric, the civic leaders of Messina quickly changed their position.[15]

Having secured Sicily within weeks, Pompey received the Senate's commission to invade the province of Africa and retake it for Sulla. Another Marian leader, Gnaeus Domitius Ahenobarbus, had taken control of the province, allying with a Numidian prince, Hiarbus. Leaving brother-in-law Memmius in charge in Sicily, Pompey, sailing with six legions, 120 warships, and 800 transport vessels, landed half his force at Carthage, the provincial capital, and half at Utica along the coast. Ahenobarbus commanded 27,000 troops, but 7,000 of them, attracted by young Pompey's reputation, immediately went over to him.

But now Pompey's campaign was delayed by a treasure hunt. As they were making camp, some of his troops stumbled on buried treasure.

Booty was the principal motivation for Roman legionaries, who dreamed of retiring from the army wealthy men. And now the rest of Pompey's troops wanted their share of the loot, being convinced that the field where the camp lay was teeming with gold and silver buried by the Carthaginians, who had ruled this land before being conquered by the Romans a century earlier. So, ignoring their officers, all began to dig.

Instead of punishing his men, Pompey let them dig. Every day, he strolled among the thousands of diggers as they labored, stopping to talk and joke with his perspiring men at their holes. After many days of fruitless digging, the soldiers came to their senses. Going to Pompey, they begged his forgiveness, saying their fruitless labors had been their punishment.

"Lead us where you please, and we will follow!" they cried.[16]

Now, with his men cemented behind him, Pompey went after Domitius Ahenobarbus, finding his quarry camped outside Utica. Early one morning, he lined up his army for battle on the edge of a ravine outside the city. On the far side of the ravine, Ahenobarbus formed his units in battle lines, but, outnumbered more than two to one, he waited for Pompey to make the first move. Rain lashed both armies for much of the day, with neither side making a move. Late in the day, Ahenobarbus ran out of patience and ordered his troops to withdraw to their camp.

Seeing his opponent's men pulling back in disorder, Pompey instructed his troops to charge. Dashing across the ravine, they caught the other side unprepared and butchered them. Ahenobarbus himself reached the safety of his walled camp. Pompey's victorious troops now gathered around him and hailed him Imperator.

But Pompey refused the honor, for the moment. Pointing to the earthen walls of Ahenobarbus's camp, Pompey said to his men, "I cannot by any means accept that title so long as I see the camp of the enemy standing. If you wish to make me worthy of the honor, you must first demolish that."[17]

With a roar, his troops surged around the enemy camp and assailed its walls, soon breaking into it. Ahenobarbus was killed as, by day's end, the camp was destroyed and only three thousand of Ahenobarbus's 20,000 troops were still alive to surrender. Some of Pompey's men, knowing that Pompey had been compared to the all-conquering young Macedonian general Alexander the Great in his youth, now additionally hailed him Pompeius Magnus, or Pompey the Great. But he brushed this off as mere exuberance.

Following his emphatic victory, Pompey marched into Numidia, defeating Ahenobarbus's native ally Hiarbus and restoring the previous king, Hiempsai I, to his throne, as an ally of Sullan Rome. In the process, Pompey captured a number of war elephants used by the Numidian usurper. Forty days after Pompey had landed in North Africa, his work was done. On rejoining his fleet at Carthage, he found written orders from Sulla awaiting. Sulla commanded Pompey to leave one legion in Africa, to be commanded by a new governor, and to send the remainder back to Italy, to go into retirement in Picenum. Pompey himself was instructed to return to Rome alone as soon as his replacement arrived.

The 1st Legion had become like Pompey's personal bodyguard unit. From the day he raised it in Picenum he had kept it close, and it had served him devotedly. As a result, the men of the 1st were unhappy about losing their founder and commander. Pompey soon heard mutterings of discontent in his camp, with the legion warning their general not to trust Sulla, and not to return alone to Rome. He well knew that the paranoid Sulla wanted to deprive him of his troops so he would pose no military threat on returning to Italy. But, while inwardly aggrieved by his father-in-law's action, Pompey again displayed the patience that would serve him well throughout his career. For now, he would bide his time and follow orders.

While speaking to his men at an assembly from the camp's reviewing stand, explaining that he would be returning to Rome without them, he was met with loud resistance. His men, refusing to be parted from him, demanded that he continue to lead them. In tears of frustration, he left the dais. But soldiers followed him to his tent and dragged him back. There, for hours, he argued with thousands of unhappy soldiers, until finally his patience gave way, but not his resolve.

"I swear," he declared, "I will kill myself if you try to force me to continue to lead you."[18]

This calmed the waters for the moment, and Pompey was permitted to retire to his tent. Nonetheless, discontent festered in the ranks of the 1st Legion. Sulla had paid spies in Pompey's camp, just as he had spies on the staff of his other senior commanders and in the very streets of Rome, to report on all that was said and done by his friends as well as his foes. Those spies sent exaggerated reports to Rome, saying that Pompey's troops were in open rebellion against Sulla and demanding Pompey lead them to Rome to claim power for himself.

"I see, then," Sulla responded with a sigh on reading these reports, "it is my destiny to contend with children in my old age." The children he referred to were Pompey and the late Gaius Marius the Younger, both of them young generals still in their twenties.[19]

Pompey now boarded ship to sail home to Italy, without his troops. He could only guess what sort of reception he would receive from Sulla. Still, no one would be able to accuse him of disobeying orders. Apart from his personal staff, he took along a herd of captured African war elephants, together with their native handlers. The beasts sailed to Italy in converted cargo ships that normally carried army horses.

For Pompey knew his Roman history and the story of the Carthaginian general Hannibal, who, the previous century, had ferried African war elephants to Spain and then crossed the Alps from Gaul into Italy with them, in his failed campaign to conquer Rome. And here now was a young Roman general bringing elephants from Carthage to Rome, emulating Scipio Africanus as the conqueror of Africa. As Pompey would have hoped, the delicious irony of it all would not be lost on the Roman people.

V.

CAESAR HIDES, POMPEY TRIUMPHS

While Pompey was campaigning in Sicily, in the Sabine Hills of central Italy northeast of Rome, bordering on Picenum, the young Julius Caesar moved from one house to another, paying the householders to shelter him. But one night he fell into the hands of Sulla's soldiers, who were out looking for absconders from Rome like him. Caesar was able to bribe the centurion in charge to let him go. The bribe, of 48,000 sesterces, was the equivalent of several years' salary for the centurion.

By this time, Sulla had been appointed Dictator of Rome by the Senate. And, despite their earlier siding with the older Marius, the plebeians of the Popular Assembly ratified Sulla's dictatorship. In the past, a Dictator had been appointed to lead Rome in times of crisis for a maximum of six months. Against all precedent, Sulla's appointment had no end date.

As Dictator, Sulla was sole ruler of Rome. He could make and unmake laws, make official appointments, and unilaterally impose death sentences. His authority could be exercised throughout Italy and Rome's provinces, with the realistic exception of areas still in the hands of pro-Marian leaders, which, at the time of his appointment, included Spain, Sicily, and Africa. With the defeats of Carbo and Ahenobarbus, Pompey swiftly also brought Sicily and Africa under Sulla's control.

Caesar heard of Carbo's death at the hands of Pompey while still in hiding in the Italian countryside. Finding Italy too hot for him, Caesar decided to flee to the East, and headed for an Adriatic port. As he sailed as a paying passenger in a cargo ship bound for Bithynia in Asia Minor, he vowed to friends that he would one day return to Rome to avenge himself on Sulla and Pompey for the deaths of his cousin young Marius and his family's friend and patron Carbo.

Bithynia was a Black Sea kingdom in today's northern Turkey ruled by King Nicomedes IV, a client of Rome restored to his throne by Sulla following the peace treaty with Mithradates. The report would spread that, to win the king's support, Caesar went to bed with him once he landed in the kingdom. The writer and orator Cicero, who came to know Caesar well, claimed Caesar was conducted into Nicomedes's bedchamber by the king's attendants to find Nicomedes awaiting him on a golden couch and wearing a purple shift. "So this descendant of Venus lost his virginity in Bithynia," says Cicero. Certainly, Nicomedes became Caesar's firm friend, and Caesar would support the interests of Nicomedes and his family in Rome.[20]

Back in Rome, Caesar's mother had been tireless in her efforts to have her boy removed from Sulla's proscription list. Aurelia had a connection, probably via a relative, to the Vestal Virgins, the six priestesses of the goddess Vesta. The most senior and revered priestesses of Rome, the Vestals took a thirty-year vow of chastity on entering the order, and were responsible for ensuring that the Eternal Flame at Rome's circular Temple of Vesta was never extinguished. The Vestals were appointed from among Rome's most distinguished families. Fabia, a current Vestal, was the half-sister of the future wife of Cicero, while Licinia, a vestal since 85 BC, was the cousin of Marcus Crassus. Now, at the request of Aurelia, the Vestals petitioned Sulla to release young Caesar from proscription.

Aurelia also used family connections in the Senate to lobby for her boy. One of her advocates was her brother Gaius Aurelius Cotta, who had gone voluntarily into exile at the beginning of Marius's purge of opponents. He had only come back to Rome in 82 BC with the return of Sulla, and was accordingly in Sulla's favor and had his ear.

Another of Aurelia's advocates was the praetor Marcus Minucius Thermus, who remained steadfastly loyal to Sulla even though his brother was a Marian. In late 81 BC, Sulla appointed Thermus to govern the province of Asia, commencing the following spring, and Thermus proposed that he take Caesar onto his gubernatorial staff. Thermus, the Vestals, and Cotta harped away so persistently and annoyingly on Caesar's behalf that Sulla finally threw his hands in the air.

"Very well, then, you win!" declared the Dictator to Thermus. "Take him! But never forget that the man whom you want me to spare will one day prove the ruin of the faction which you and I have so long defended."[21]

So, word was sent to Caesar of his pardon, and he would join Thermus in Asia in 80 BC. Governors' wives and younger children traditionally stayed home in Rome during their overseas service, and Caesar had been an infant when his father had governed Asia, so he had never before set foot in the province.

Within days of the new year beginning, Sulla surprised allies and enemies alike when he resigned the dictatorship after making a number of legislative reforms. He nonetheless retained power, with Metellus and himself serving as consuls for 80 BC. The previous year, Sulla had further rewarded Metellus for his loyal service with appointment as Pontifex Maximus, a post for life. This role, as high priest of Rome, would later be appropriated by Rome's emperors—before, as Christianity took hold, they handed it off to the Christian bishops of Rome. As a consequence, an official title of the Roman Catholic Church's Pope, as Bishop of Rome, is to this day Pontifex Maximus, abbreviated to the Pontiff. The term Pope is a nickname, deriving from the Greek word *pappas*, meaning father.

On the subject of titles, in 79 BC Sulla formally went into retirement, adding a simple title to his name, Felix, meaning Lucky, his childhood nickname. For Sulla seems to have been grateful for a life in which he had been permitted to serve Rome and earn more glory than most in her history. Walking through the Forum now, he went without escort, encouraging his fellow citizens to talk to him and voice concerns they had with him, which they did. For while the public did not love him, they had come to respect him, especially now that he had voluntarily given up the dictatorship.

Sulla retired to his coastal villa outside the port city of Puteoli, today's Pozzuoli, north of Naples. There, he hosted heavy-drinking dinners with actors and entertainers, spending the remainder of his time writing his memoirs. But Sulla never entirely took his hand from the tiller of state. While the consuls had their authority restored to them, no major decision was made without Sulla's approval. And everyone knew it.

Thermus, new governor of Asia, arrived to take up his post in the spring of 80 BC to find that, not for the first time in their history, the people of the city of Mytilene, capital of the Aegean island of Lesbos, were rebelling against outside rule, taking charge of their city. With Lesbos forming part of his province, Thermus had the job of putting down the rebellion. Most annoyingly, the rebels were permitting Cilician pirates to use Mytilene as a base for raids against Roman shipping.

That summer of 80 BC, Thermus launched an amphibious operation against Mytilene, and Caesar joined the assault as one of Thermus's junior officers. Thermus commenced a siege of Mytilene, and before long his troops broke through rebel defenses and stormed the city. In this, his first taste of combat, the twenty-year-old Caesar distinguished himself by being awarded the oak leaf Civic Crown by Thermus, saving the life of a fellow Roman citizen, probably a fellow officer. The equivalent of America's Medal of Honor and the British Commonwealth's Victoria Cross, the Civic Crown was the highest decoration for valor that a Roman citizen soldier of any rank could receive. Some awardees later had a stone replica of their Civic Crown placed above their front door to advertise their award.

Thermus served a single annual term as Asia's governor. When he returned to Rome, Caesar, still wary of attracting Sulla's attention, remained in the East, out of sight and out of mind, through 79 BC.

This same year, Pompey returned to Italy from Africa and presented himself to Sulla at Puteoli. Word of Pompey's swift and comprehensive victories in Sicily and Africa had preceded his return. As Sulla was being told, the common people were excited by the young man's stunning successes, and wanted to see him, and cheer him.

The public also wanted to see his elephants. The last time that such massive, iconic beasts had been seen in Rome was in 99 BC, when they had featured in a spectacle held in the Circus Maximus, after which they had been slaughtered. Pompey's elephants were landed at Ostia and walked down the road a short distance to the coastal town of Laurentum—of which no trace remains today. Unlike his predecessors, Pompey saw a future for elephants in Italy, as participants in spectacles to entertain the masses. So, at Laurentum, Pompey's elephants became the foundation of a government-run elephant stud farm, with a procurator in charge. The following century, elephants from the Laurentum farm would be put on standby for the emperor Claudius's invasion of Britain, until it was realized that the rivers and boggy marshes in the invasion area of southern England would make elephant operations impractical.

When Pompey arrived at Sulla's coastal villa and approached his father-in-law amid a gaggle of staff and clients during his morning audience, the former Dictator rose from his chair to greet the victorious young general. This amazed onlookers. "Hail, Pompeius Magnus!" said Sulla, no doubt with a wry smile.[22]

Sulla had not only heard that Pompey's men had hailed him as Magnus; he himself was now addressing him with the very same title. More than that, Sulla went on to encourage others in the room to do the same.

Several years would pass before Pompey himself started using the title, but he was now emboldened to make a request before Sulla—the award of a Triumph for his African victories. He had witnessed his father taking a Triumph in 89 BC, and he reckoned his own achievements more than equaled those of Strabo.

The Triumph was an ancient Roman celebration of a general's victories over a foreign foe. Technically, at least ten thousand enemy had to be slain to entitle the general to the award of a Triumph by the Senate. The Triumph took the form of a victory parade through the streets of Rome, commencing on the Field of Mars and terminating at the foot of the steps that went up the Capitoline Mount to the Temple of Jupiter Best and Greatest—steps the triumphing general was expected to climb on his knees before conducting sacrifices and dedicating the spoils of his victory to Jupiter.

The triumphal parade's route was lined by the cheering public. It was led by the members of the Senate. Prisoners and war trophies followed, and then thousands of unarmed men from the victorious general's legions, singing bawdy and deliberately defamatory ditties about their commander. The triumphing general came last, driving a golden chariot normally kept in the Temple of Jupiter and drawn by four horses. Traditionally, a slave stood behind the general, whispering in his ear to prevent him becoming big-headed, that he was only a man, not a god.

Only recently, the Senate had voted Sulla a Triumph for his eastern victories against Mithradates, which he had yet to take.

Sour-faced, Sulla shook his head. "The law allows that honor to none but praetors and consuls," he coolly replied on hearing Pompey's request. He went on to remind Pompey that not even Scipio Africanus had asked for a Triumph for his defeat of the Carthaginians and their allies, because he had not been a praetor or consul. "And if you, Pompey, who have scarcely yet fully grown a beard, and are not of senatorial age, should enter the city in triumph, what a weight of envy would it bring, at once upon my government and your honor?"[23]

Pompey's expression must have revealed that he was unhappy at this, but he said nothing—at first. He would have known the ignominious fate of Afella, commander of the Praeneste siege who had sent the head of the younger Marius on a spear to Sulla. As soon as Sulla took charge at Rome, Afella had demanded a consulship. Sulla had resisted this demand, so Afella had paraded through the city with a vast entourage to win popular support. Sulla, watching from the Temple of Castor and Pollux, had sent a centurion of his bodyguard to meet Afella and kill him, which he did. Afella's outraged supporters had overpowered the centurion and dragged him to Sulla, who then set the man free and informed the crowd that the centurion had been operating on his orders.

Despite this knowledge, Pompey felt that he himself had been treated unjustly. As Sulla began talking with other guests, signaling that he was done with Pompey, the young general stood his ground and uttered a simple but meaningful analogy: "You should reflect on the fact that more men worship the rising sun than the setting sun."[24]

Sulla had not heard these words, but saw the amazed and fearful reaction of those who had. "What did he say?" Sulla irritably demanded. After one of his staff bent to repeat the words in his ear, Sulla paled, as he perceived precisely what Pompey meant—Sulla was the setting sun, and Pompey the rising sun. As Plutarch was to remark, it was immensely bold, and brave, of Pompey to speak like this, surrounded as he was by Sulla's adherents, and knowing Sulla's past reaction to the likes of Afella's ambitions. "Very well," Sulla now said, "let him Triumph. Let him Triumph!"[25]

There were many in Sulla's inner circle who thought it ridiculous that Pompey should Triumph. A leading opponent was Publius Servilius Vatia, a consul for 79 BC, who had himself celebrated a Triumph in 88 BC, when he held praetor rank. He was firmly loyal to Sulla, but on this one thing he could not agree with him. Servilius Vatia was not alone.

It was inconceivable to most of the Roman elite that this youth should be awarded a Triumph. For them to qualify, they first had to climb the *cursus honorum*, the strict civil service ladder that rose through military tribune to prefect, quaestor and on to senator, followed by a praetorship and then the coveted consulship. Apart from military tribune, Pompey had held none of these posts. Not only would he be the only member of the Equestrian Order to celebrate a Triumph, he would be the youngest triumphant ever. Over the Roman Empire's next five hundred years, no other Roman would exceed Pompey's achievement.

Yet Sulla had spoken, and no one dared oppose him. And so it was that, in the late spring of 79 BC, Pompey took his Triumph. But Sulla deliberately set out to blunt the public impact of the young man's achievement. He began by taking his own Triumph first. He followed it with a Triumph for Pompey's fellow general Metellus. After his triumphal parade, Metellus hurried away to Spain to take up Sulla's appointment as commander against Sertorius, the Marian general who held Spain.

To further annoy Pompey, having recalled the youngster's brother-in-law Memmius to Rome, Sulla appointed Memmius, who had by this stage reached the age of thirty, quaestor, or adjutant, of Metellus in Spain. This would take Pompey's very capable and loyal relative and right-hand man away from him.

To demonstrate his power over Pompey, Sulla this same year arranged a new marriage for him. Pompey's new bride, his third wife, was Mucia Tertia. She was the daughter of Quintus Mucius Scaevola, the Pontifex Maximus murdered by the Marians, and had previously been engaged to the younger Marius. Sulla, in marrying Pompey and Mucia, was sending a signal to remaining Marians, of his support for the family of Scaevola and contempt for his murderers. Pompey's relationship with his new wife seems to have been warm, and within the next few years she would become the mother of his children.

With Pompey's Triumph being the last of 79 BC, Sulla hoped the public would tire of Triumphs by the time the young man's day in the sun came around, and the celebration would fall flat. But as it turned out, the appetite of the Roman people for spectacle was only exceeded by their desire to see and applaud their all-conquering young general Pompey the Great.

On the day of his Triumph, Pompey met with two setbacks. He had brought four elephants up from Laurentum to draw his golden chariot through the streets of Rome. But, unusually for Pompey, he had forgotten a small detail: triumphal parades commenced outside a temple on the Field of Mars and then entered Rome proper via the Porta Triumphalis, or Triumphal Gate, which was only opened for triumphal parades. It was relatively narrow. A four-horse chariot could pass through, but not a chariot drawn by four hulking elephants. Pompey had to relent and use the traditional horse-drawn chariot.

Pompey's second problem was posed by his own troops. He had repatriated his 1st Legion to participate in his Triumph, and, as the parade assembled on the Field of Mars, Pompey was assailed by the same men who had defied him to dig for treasure in Africa. Loudly they demanded rewards for their service, or, they said, they would not march in the parade.

But Pompey would not bend to threats. "I would rather lose the honor of my Triumph than give in to you," he firmly told soldiers as they gathered around him.[26]

The troops, for whom participation in a Triumph was a once-in-a-lifetime experience, backed down. The two consuls for the year and the assembled senators witnessed this exchange as they prepared to lead off the parade. The consul Servilius Vatia, a chief opponent of Pompey's Triumph, was hugely impressed with the way the young man dealt with the situation. "Now," he said to colleagues, "I see that Pompey is truly great, and worthy of a Triumph."[27]

The Triumph went ahead, to a rapturous reception from hundreds of thousands of citizens, slaves, and visitors who lined the city streets and the Circus Maximus, through which the parade passed. In modern terms, Pompey was a rock star to the Roman people. Wearing the Triumphal Regalia of special tunic, cloak, and laurel-wreath crown, and driving his golden chariot, the young general smiled and waved to the adoring crowd.

Plutarch wrote that Pompey's ambition was for unusual honors, by achieving things that no other Roman had achieved. His tradition-breaking Triumph was only the beginning.

VI.

AFTER SULLA, POMPEY & CAESAR
ON OPPOSING SIDES

Caesar, ever wary of Sulla, remained in the East without an official post through 79 BC, staying behind when Asian governor Thermus returned home. There, in the East, Caesar heard of Pompey's Triumph, and almost certainly cursed his meteoric rise to fame. Caesar knew that celebrating a Triumph was a monumental thing, something that he himself would long for. In fact, in all the long history of the Roman Empire, little more than three hundred Triumphs were celebrated. But for a man so young to celebrate a Triumph must have galled the frustrated young Caesar.

It is likely that Caesar and Pompey had yet to meet, taking into account their ages (Pompey was 27 in 79 BC, and Caesar was 21), and opposing socio-political circles. Caesar had probably seen Pompey from a distance; and while Pompey was barely aware of his existence, Caesar had made a personal vow of revenge against him for his execution of Carbo.

Caesar needed a new post in the East, and back home his irrepressible mother had enlisted the help of Publius Servilius Vatia, the same consul for 79 BC who'd opposed Pompey's Triumph only to reverse his opinion and declare Pompey truly great. During his consulship, Vatia was appointed governor of the province of Cilicia, and he chose Caesar to join his staff there once he commenced his tenure in 78 BC.

As governor, Vatia would conduct a military campaign in Cilicia against pirates on the sea and against the local Isaurici tribe on land. After a grinding four-year struggle, Vatia would defeat the Isaurici, and on his return to Rome would be granted the title Isauricus. In the first year of the governor's tenure, Caesar helped organize the buildup of men, ships, and supplies for the operation, which would be launched the following year.

At Rome, meanwhile, Pompey had pointedly received no new appointment from Sulla. So he became involved in politics, in late 79 BC actively campaigning for the election of Marcus Lepidus as a consul for 78 BC. This was the same Lepidus who had served under Pompey's father. On Strabo's death, Pompey may well have inherited him as a client.

Despite Lepidus having always been pro-Sulla, the paranoid Sulla didn't trust him, seeing him as too self-serving. Sulla had put his weight behind another candidate, Quintus Lutatius Catulus. Paying a rare visit to Rome for the election, Sulla witnessed from a distance the declaration of the election results. To Sulla's great displeasure, Lepidus was elected. Sulla then saw a smiling Pompey, followed by a large crowd of admirers, depart the Forum and come toward him on his way home to the Esquiline.

"Well, young man," said Sulla to Pompey, "I see you rejoice in your victory. And indeed, is it not a most generous and worthy act that the consulship should be given to Lepidus, the vilest of men, in preference to Catulus, the best and most deserving in the city? And all by your influence with the people?" Sulla was being overdramatic. Catulus had also been elected, with the second-most votes. "It will be good, however," Sulla went on, "for you to be awake and look to your own interests, as you have been making your enemy stronger than yourself."[28]

The bitter Sulla moved on. He and Pompey never spoke again. And while Sulla remembered numerous men in his will, he removed Pompey's name from the list of beneficiaries. Sulla would die at his Puteoli villa the following year. While in the process of ranting that a corrupt official should be throttled to death, Sulla suffered a massive internal hemorrhage, spewing blood. The following morning, he was dead at the age of sixty. The indications are that Sulla, a heavy drinker who became increasingly liverish and irascible in his final years, died from liver disease.

It is likely that he knew he was in declining health when he resigned the dictatorship.

In the Senate it was moved that a lavish public funeral be granted Sulla, and that his ashes be interred in a tomb on the sacred Field of Mars, a rare honor. But, surprising fellow Sullans, the consul Lepidus, moving to sideline Pompey and take control of Sulla's faction, making it his own, spoke against both the funeral and the Field of Mars interment. Sulla, as it turned out, had proven to be a good judge of character. But now Pompey, who had backed Lepidus into the consulship, came forward and spoke on Sulla's behalf. Ignoring the strained relations that had existed between Sulla and himself toward the end, and the fact that Sulla had left him out of his will, Pompey backed Sulla's grand public funeral and Field of Mars interment.

Pompey's endorsement generated a wave of public and senatorial support for the measures, forcing Lepidus to back down. To ensure that Sulla's funeral arrangements went according to plan, Pompey personally oversaw the proceedings, guaranteeing that it went ahead in an honorable and secure fashion. The inscription carved on the former dictator's tomb was written by Sulla himself prior to his death: "No friend ever served me, no enemy ever wronged me, whom I have not repaid in full."[29]

On the governor's staff in Cilicia, Caesar learned via letters from family and associates at home that Sulla was dead. Those letters urged him to return to Rome, now governed by the consuls Lepidus and Catulus. Lepidus was in fact agitating for the cancellation of many of Sulla's measures and the pardoning of Marian exiles—Sulla had been right to distrust Lepidus, who was seemingly striving to destroy the dictator's legacy. So Caesar resigned and sailed for Rome on the next departing cargo vessel.

On Caesar's return to the capital, he reunited with his wife, mother, and other family members, offered his services for hire as a legal counsel, and presented himself to the consul Lepidus. But he was soon disenchanted. He lost his first court case, a prosecution against a former consul. And although Lepidus offered him advantageous junior government posts, Caesar turned down the offers. He was unimpressed by Lepidus, a man who, to Caesar's mind, showed no capacity to inspire or lead.

The political atmosphere at Rome proved much less rosy than Caesar had been led to believe. And it was no secret that Pompey disapproved of Lepidus's agenda, despite having backed his election. After several months back home, seeing trouble brewing, and deciding not to side with Lepidus, Caesar boarded ship to return to the East. He left his wife Cornelia pregnant—she would give birth to their daughter Julia by year's end.

Caesar's plan was to return to Rome once Lepidus had either swept aside the likes of Catulus and Pompey or had himself been swept aside. In the meantime, he headed for the Greek island of Rhodes, and Apollonius Molo, reputedly the greatest living exponent of the art of rhetoric. Caesar's plan was to take a course in rhetoric under Molo to polish his courtroom skills.

Winter had already set in when the ship carrying Caesar and several retainers among its passengers reached the Dodecanese island group in the Aegean, en route to Rhodes. Off the island of Pharmacusa—today's Farmakonisi in the southeast of the Dodecanese—the vessel was overtaken and captured by pirate ships. The Cilician pirates, of whom thousands were prowling the Aegean and Mediterranean, had no idea who Caesar was. Taking him to the island, they demanded a ransom of 480,000 sesterces for his release. Young Caesar scoffed, saying he was much more valuable than that, and would pay them 1.2 million sesterces, and the pirates permitted several of his freedmen to sail away and try to raise the money. Only his personal physician and two slaves remained with the young man.

For thirty-eight days Caesar remained with the pirates, acting more their guest than their prisoner. He joined in their exercises and their games. He called on them to be quiet when they were too noisy in their night reveries. He wrote speeches and poetry, and made his captors listen to him read his work aloud, calling the pirates illiterate and barbarous when they showed little liking for it. And with a smile, he would tell them that, one day, he would catch them and crucify them. The pirates laughed along with him, becoming quite fond of their amiable young prisoner.

The men sent to raise the ransom successfully borrowed the money in the Asian port city of Miletus. Returning to Pharmacusa, they handed the ransom over to the pirates, who made a fatal error—they let Caesar go free. On reaching Miletus, he put together several ships filled with armed men and sailed right back to Pharmacusa. The pirates had made a second major error; instead of putting out to sea, they had remained on the island, where they were easily found by Caesar and his men, and captured. Taking back the ransom money, Caesar conveyed the captured pirates to Pergamus on Crete, lodging them in prison. He deliberately chose Crete because it was then allied to Rome but not controlled by it; another twelve years would pass before Crete became a Roman province.

Seeking his captors' punishment, Caesar then traveled to Ephesus to see Marcus Junius Silanus, the new governor of Asia. Junius had his eye on the ransom money, and, trying to find a way to get his hands on it, he told Caesar he would think on the matter. Caesar, impatient to keep his promise to the pirates, sailed back to Pergamus, where, on his own authority, he had the Cilicians immediately crucified. And Junius Silanus could do nothing about it, because Crete was outside his jurisdiction. Caesar then resumed his journey to Rhodes, where he enrolled under Molo and applied himself to his studies.[30]

At Rome, the trouble Caesar had seen brewing erupted into civil war soon after he left. Lepidus, frustrated by opposition from Catulus, the Senate, and his past supporter Pompey, departed Rome and began raising an army in central and southern Italy with the support of Cinna's son Lucius Cinna, brother-in-law to Caesar. Lepidus drew to his standard remains of old factions, Marians and others who had suffered disappointment or loss at the hands of Sulla, including farmers whose land had been confiscated and given to retiring legionaries as a reward for their military service.

Meanwhile, Marcus Junius Brutus, a Tribune of the Plebeians in 83 BC under the Marians, held the command of a Roman army in Cisalpine Gaul. Brutus threw his support and that of his troops behind Lepidus. This was the same Brutus whose wife Servilia was Caesar's bedfellow. To support Lepidus, Brutus now crossed the Po River, which under Roman law rendered him an Enemy of the State, and advanced his troops into Italy proper, stationing pro-Lepidus garrisons at towns as he went.

The Senate, seeing the professional force led by Brutus as the more potent threat, and finding Pompey prepared to support the establishment against the usurper, offered the young general command of an army to deal with Brutus. Pompey accepted, and quickly marched north with the senatorial army, with his friend Geminius as one of his deputies.

Brutus, afraid of meeting Pompey on the battlefield, based himself with part of his force at the city of Mutina, today's Modena. Pompey easily subdued each of Brutus's garrisons before turning to Mutina. Surrounding the city, he put Brutus under siege, which lasted until Brutus's own soldiers became restive and sent to Pompey, offering up their commander. Negotiations began, and Brutus, given little choice, agreed to surrender in exchange for his life and a promise to never again take up arms against the Senate.

Pompey accepted Brutus's offer, and Brutus emerged from the city as his troops opened the gates. Sending messengers galloping to Rome, Pompey informed the anxious Senate that Brutus had surrendered, and that he had ended the war in the north without a battle. At the same time Pompey sent Brutus away with a mounted escort commanded by Geminius, to a town west of Mutina called Regium Lepedi, today's Reggio Emilia, which had strong familial links to Lepidus.

The following day, Geminius executed Brutus. Pompey again wrote to the Senate, this time informing them of Brutus's execution, saying that it had been on his orders, and claiming that Brutus had broken his word, although details of precisely what Brutus did would never emerge. Modern-day writers have speculated that Brutus attempted to exhort locals to rise up in support of Lepidus, but there is no way of knowing for sure.

The news of Brutus's summary execution was received with shock at Rome. Technically, Pompey had no legal authority to execute a Roman citizen and should have applied to a praetor for a death sentence to be imposed. Here, within months of each other, both Caesar and Pompey had taken the law into their own hands and ordered executions while not possessing the legal power to do so. Caesar's action would pass without drawing attention—the victims being pirates and noncitizens, and Caesar then being a relatively unknown figure. But Pompey's action became the topic of national conversation.

To Pompey's critics, this was proof that he was indeed the Butcher Boy; for decades to come, opponents would raise Brutus's death as a black mark against Pompey's name. With Pompey so well known for his kindness of heart—as the philosopher Seneca would point out the following century—Pompey's supporters would be at a loss to explain Brutus's execution. Nonetheless, Carbo's death in Sicily had shown that Pompey could be cold-blooded when he needed to be. There is a mysterious corollary to the execution of Brutus—his executioner Geminius, Pompey's longtime friend, is never heard of again.[31]

Meanwhile, with Pompey in the north, Lepidus and young Cinna had quickly descended on Rome with a ragtag army, where a senatorial force raised and led by Catulus fought them off in a battle at the Milvian Bridge on the Tiber, just to the north of Rome. Licking his wounds, Lepidus withdrew north, only to blunder into Pompey, who was rapidly marching south to come up on his rear with an army reinforced with Brutus's former troops.

Retreating to Cosa on Italy's west coast, eighty miles north of Rome, Lepidus hastily sailed for Sardinia, as young Lucius Cinna headed for Spain to join Sertorius. On Sardinia, Lepidus would before long die, from natural causes. His revolt died with him. For dyed-in-the-wool Marians, it seemed their faction had lost its last champion.

Following Lepidus's defeat, Caesar returned to Rome, reuniting with his family and holding his daughter Julia for the first time. Freed of the post of priest of Jupiter and its limitations, and through his family connections, Caesar was soon put forward to the Popular Assembly to be elected to the post of military tribune. He was older than the normal novice military tribune, but this was not unusual for the time. The upheavals of the past few years had kept a number of young men away from Rome and away from admission to the cursus honorum. Still, when the annual list of military tribunes was published, Caesar's name was close to the top, above that of young men from more famous consular families. Clearly, the plebeians saw potential in Caesar.

Normally, Rome's generals chose their legions' tribunes from this list; but Caesar, being related to both Marius and Cinna, was considered too thorough a Marian for Sullan generals in the field to even consider taking him into their armies. With his name remaining on the military tribune list for the year, he would stay at Rome, without a posting. Nonetheless, he was on the cursus honorum, the road to the Senate. It also brought him into the public eye.

From this vantage point, as low as it was, Caesar took a leaf from the book of his late uncle Marius and began vigorously supporting plebeian leaders of the Assembly, who were agitating for the restoration of the powers of the ten Tribunes of the Plebeians. This civil post, created as a means of preventing consuls from overreaching, had historically included the right to call meetings of the Senate and to veto the votes of the consuls. "The tribunate is a constitutionally sacrosanct and inviolate office with very great powers," the second-century Greco-Roman historian Appian writes, "so that tribunes on occasion imprisoned even consuls." But, seeing how Marius had manipulated the Tribunes of the Plebs of his day to his own advantage, Sulla had legislatively deprived the post of most of its powers.[32]

When the Senate met following the defeat of Lepidus, there was lavish praise for both Catulus and Pompey for so quickly dealing with the rebel. In this sitting, one senator, Lucius Philippus, proposed that Pompey be rewarded by being sent to Spain to help Metellus, who had been struggling vainly for two and a half years to defeat Sertorius and restore the Spanish provinces to Rome's rule. Metellus had gone to Spain confident of a swift victory, describing Sertorius as "Sulla's runaway slave." But it was like sending a hedgehog to catch a fox. It was never going to work.[33]

Sertorius had proven more than a match for the experienced but overly cautious Metellus. Enjoying the support of local tribes, Sertorius was able to hide in the northern mountains and use hit-and-run guerrilla tactics while in the main avoiding set-piece battles. Reportedly, he was able to call upon as many as 150,000 fighting men, vastly outnumbering Metellus. Some were the Roman legionaries he'd taken to Spain with him; others were locals to whom he granted Roman citizenship. He also had Mauritanian mercenary cavalry from North Africa, but most of his troops were lightly armed agile Spanish and Lusitanian tribesmen. Although the proud Metellus would not admit it, it was clear that he needed help.

Overwhelmingly, the Senate endorsed Philippus's proposal, granting Pompey the same proconsular powers as Metellus, ranking him as the equal of a consul and giving him the legal authority to impose death sentences. Pompey wasted no time in accepting the Spanish appointment. With an eye to the job, and potentially another Triumph, he had not disbanded his best legions, which were ready for action, blood, and booty.

To take away Sertorius's senior Roman officers, one of the Tribunes of the Plebs proposed an amnesty for leading Romans who'd fled to Spain to fight alongside Sertorius. If these men returned to Rome and gave their sacred oath to not seek public office again, the property confiscated from them by Sulla would be restored. Publicly, Caesar spoke in favor of this motion, which would benefit his brother-in-law, Cinna's son Lucius, brother to Caesar's wife Cornelia. The bill passed, and messengers were dispatched to Spain to pass on the amnesty offer.

Young Cinna was among those who took advantage of this offer and returned to Rome, regaining his property and throwing his moral support behind Caesar's career advancement. But several senators, including

Perpenna, who had fled from Pompey without offering a fight when governing Sicily for the Marians, remained with Sertorius in Spain.

For the Spanish operation, Pompey put together a 31,000-man army made up of five legions based around his original 1st, 2nd, and 3rd legions plus one thousand cavalry. Among his subordinate generals was Lucius Afranius. From a humble family in Picenum, Afranius had served under Pompey's father, from whom he was inherited as a client by Pompey. Afranius would remain a steadfast subordinate of Pompey through the years. Another of Pompey's commanders was Marcus Petreius, another native of Picenum and client of Pompey. Teenagers Gaius Cornelius and Decimus Laelius were among Pompey's tribunes.

Pompey's first child by Mucia, the boy Gnaeus Pompeius Magnus, was born that year. It was already the autumn of 77 BC when Pompey set off from Rome to join his army to march north. It's possible that as he departed, Pompey was unaware that he was leaving his wife Mucia pregnant with their second child: their daughter Pompeia Magna would be born the following year.[34]

After Pompey crossed the Alps, forging a new route to Gaul, he marched into an active local uprising in Transalpine Gaul. This Roman province took in today's southern France and would be renamed Narbonne Gaul during the imperial era. The locals chose the wrong time to rebel; Pompey's troops left a trail of carnage as they bloodily put down the uprising.

News of this would have warmed the hearts of Pompey supporters of all classes in Rome, as they relished the prospect of their twenty-nine-year-old hero going against fifty-year-old Sertorius in the spring, and delivering him a swift defeat, as the nimble wolf cub went against the wily fox.

Pompey and his legions wintered in the port city of Narbo Martius, today's Narbonne. Following the religious ceremonies that marked the commencement of the military campaigning season in March, 76 BC, Pompey marched his army over the Pyrenees and entered northeastern Spain, eager to show Metellus's men how Pompeian legions dealt with rebels, and spoiling for a fight with Sertorius. But Pompey and his overconfident legionaries were in for a shock.

VII.

CRASSUS THE PROPERTY DEVELOPER
& CICERO THE LAWYER

With Metellus and Pompey on campaign in Spain, Caesar was progressing his career at Rome. Being penniless, he borrowed heavily to reestablish himself in the capital. Unable to afford a house even approaching the grandeur of the Caesar family's mansion confiscated by Sulla, or to live in an affluent area, Caesar purchased a modest house in Rome's Subura district. This lay in a valley at the bottom of the Esquiline Hill and was, as it happened, overlooked by Pompey's family mansion on the hill. The Subura, densely crowded, noisy and dirty, was a hotbed of crime. It was home to tradesmen, manufacturing workshops, brothels, and the poorest of Rome's residents. From the Forum it was reached along the Argiletum, a narrow street lined by booksellers and cobblers' shops.

It's likely that the men who loaned Caesar money to buy his house and cover the living expenses of his family included relatives, but numerous Roman businessmen became his creditors, despite his lack of collateral. One such creditor was Marcus Crassus. Even though Crassus had won the Battle of the Colline Gate for Sulla, he had learned from previous experience not to ask Sulla for appointments or rewards as Afella and Pompey had done. Crassus was well-read, and particularly well versed in the philosophy of Aristotle. But his personal philosophy at this time was simple, and basic: make money. Lots of it.

Crassus had returned to Rome with Sulla intent not only on rebuilding the wealth lost to Marian confiscation, but on multiplying it. It was said that Crassus was never content with his riches, that he could never be rich enough. It was as if the overnight loss of virtually everything to the Marians, and the subsequent time as a cave-dweller, had scarred him for life, and that the fear of loss drove his never-ending desire to accumulate an ever-increasing fortune.

Much of the Crassus family's first 72-million-sesterce fortune, largely confiscated by the Marians, had been made from silver mines, which were now restored to Crassus, the sole male survivor of his family. But once back in Rome, Crassus, while carrying out his duties as a novice senator, concentrated on making a new and much greater fortune, as a property developer. He began by buying cheaply when confiscated Marian property was auctioned off by Sulla in 81 BC. Taking a liking to a luxurious villa on the outskirts of Rome owned by his cousin Licinia the Vestal Virgin, he pestered her until she sold it to him. He was even charged with sexually seducing Licinia, and she of having sex with him in contravention of her Vestal vow of chastity—a capital offense. Both were acquitted.

Apart from building his own city mansion, a palatial house on the Palatine Hill, future site of the palaces of Rome's emperors, Crassus never built from scratch. That was too slow, and not sufficiently profitable. Instead of building and selling new residences, Crassus looked for houses and apartment buildings damaged by the house fires that were almost daily occurrences in Rome, and bought them cheaply. Cleverly, he also bought neighboring properties, whose owners were quick to dispose of them because of the fires and the disruptions that rebuilding would entail.

At a time when Rome had no public fire-fighting service, which was a century away, Crassus established his own private fire brigade. Staffed by slaves, it would rush with its buckets, mops, and ladders to a burning building. If the building was owned by Crassus, his firemen fought the fire. If the owner sold the burning building to Crassus on the spot, his firemen fought the fire. If not, Crassus's fire brigade went home.

To rebuild fire-damaged properties, Crassus created his own building organization, staffing it with hundreds of slaves and freedmen with such skills as architects, engineers, carpenters, stonemasons, and bricklayers, and used them exclusively to rebuild and maintain his fire-damaged properties. Once they were like new, he either sold these places at a handsome profit or, more often, rented them out. Within not many years, canny Crassus became the single largest owner of houses and apartments in Rome, and arguably her richest citizen, tripling the family fortune to more than 200 million sesterces. As one modern-day biographer of Crassus has characterized him, Crassus was the first tycoon.[35]

Once he was flush with cash as Rome's landlord, Crassus expanded into the money-lending business. Apart from the official Roman Treasury beneath the Temple of Jupiter on the Capitoline, Rome had no banking institutions. Instead, wealthy men, even wealthy freedmen, became moneylenders, often charging exorbitant rates of interest. Crassus now joined the bankers' ranks.

Rich enough to be his own man, neither a Sullan nor a Marian, Crassus ran with both the hare and the hounds, switching allegiance as it benefited him, and switching back again. He would lend to anyone, whatever their affiliation. Even though he knew that Julius Caesar had celebrated the Crassus family's fall from grace under his uncle Marius, Crassus would lend to him, too, giving him great satisfaction to have young Caesar in his debt and numbered among his "friends."

Living on hefty borrowings, Caesar, based amid the noise and squalor of the Subura with his wife Cornelia, daughter Julia, and his mother and aunt, progressed his legal career, conducting private prosecutions against leading men accused of corruption. He began to win cases, and to win praise as a fine public speaker, if one with a high-pitched voice.

Caesar particularly won the attention of another young lawyer who was making a name for himself for his oratory and legal expertise. This was Marcus Tullius Cicero. Born in the same year as Pompey, Cicero had served with Pompey on the military staff of the latter's father Strabo for three years. Unlike Pompey, Cicero disliked the military life. His eye was always on public speaking and the law, and from at least 83 BC he was regularly before the courts as an eloquent and persuasive defense attorney.

In 80 BC, Cicero had won one of his most famous cases, persuading the jury to acquit a senator accused of murdering his own father. To obtain the acquittal, Cicero had switched suspicion to a freedman who was a favorite of Sulla. Naturally, this hadn't endeared him to Sulla, and, in 79 BC, Cicero had decided it politic to depart Rome for Rhodes to resume his rhetorical studies under Apollonius Molo, the same teacher that Caesar had studied under. By 76 BC, following Sulla's death, Cicero was back in Rome and back in the courts, winning cases and observing Caesar from close range.

From the get-go, the astute Cicero could see how ambitious Caesar was. He would claim, decades later, that even then he could see that Caesar's ambition was for absolute power, although he disguised it well with good humor and affability. Watching Caesar adjusting his finely coiffed but thinning fair hair with a single finger as he spoke confidently in court, Cicero was to remark that no one could have imagined that any such man would one day seek to "subvert the Roman state."[36]

Then one day in the summer of 76 BC, around the time of Caesar's twenty-fourth birthday, news arrived from Spain that surprised Cicero and put a smile on the face of Caesar. Pompey the Great had suffered a humiliating defeat at the hands of Sertorius.

VIII.

SNEAKY SERTORIUS VERSUS
PERSISTENT POMPEY

After departing southern Gaul in the spring of 76 BC, by the beginning of the summer Pompey and his legions were approaching Lauron, a city located in the province of Nearer Spain on the central east coast. Sertorius had based himself in the mountainous central north, and when he learned of Pompey's arrival on the Iberian Peninsula he sent part of his army to intercept the young general while sending another force to harry Metellus, Pompey's fellow general, who was based to the south in the province of Baetica, also known as Farther Spain. Metellus had proven a reticent campaigner, fearing the loss of ports into which supplies were shipped to him, and which remained loyal to Rome.

Sertorius's plan was to deal with Pompey before he could link up with Metellus. Reaching Lauron before Pompey, he lay siege to the city when it closed its gates to him. When Pompey arrived, he encamped close to Sertorius's siege camp and prepared for battle. Learning that Metellus was marching north to join him, Pompey did away with his usual patience and set out to defeat Sertorius before he had to share the glory of victory with his older colleague. Sending a message into Lauron, Pompey urged townspeople to line the city wall and watch as he swiftly dealt with the rebels.

But when Pompey formed up his eager legionaries to do battle, Sertorius refused to take the bait and kept his troops behind his camp walls. A stalemate developed, with each side glowering at the other from their camp walls. Sertorius at this point had little fear of Pompey. Calling him

"Sulla's Student," he set out to teach his twenty-nine-year-old adversary a lesson in military tactics.[37]

There were two places where Pompey's troops could forage for water, firewood, crops, and fodder for their horses and cattle. Sertorius had his light infantry harass every attempt by Pompey's men to use the nearby foraging place, but allowed the Pompeians to forage farther afield unmolested. Then, at night, he secreted 1,200 infantry and 2,000 cavalry in a forest beside the distant foraging place.

At dawn the following day, some 5,000 Pompeian troops marched to the foraging area with a convoy of carts. Around 9:00 a.m., as men began making their way back to camp with loaded carts, those on sentry duty let down their guard and themselves went foraging. Now Sertorius's troops rose from their hiding places.

Surprised Pompeian troops streaming back toward camp were ridden down by 1,750 Sertorian cavalry from one direction, while their path to the camp was blocked by the other 250. Pompey, seeing his troops being cut down like chaff before the scythe, sent out an entire legion of six thousand men to rescue the foragers, only for Sertorius cavalry to circle around behind the legion, cutting it off. The legion, and its commander, met the same fate as the foragers. Pompey lost ten thousand men and his wheeled transport that day, while Sertorius lost hardly a man. "Thus," writes first-century Roman general and governor of Britain Sextus Julius Frontinus, "in addition to inflicting a twofold disaster, as a result of the same strategy Sertorius forced Pompey to be the helpless witness to the destruction of his own troops."[38]

Sertorius now learned that Metellus's army was approaching. While Sertorius disparaged Metellus as "the Old Woman" even though they were roughly the same age, he was wise enough to realize that he couldn't afford to be caught in a pincer between Metellus and Pompey, and he regretfully withdrew his army. Pompey was able to relieve Lauron, but his army had been cut by a third; and, like his army, his reputation had taken a beating. Nonetheless, Pompey learned to never again underestimate an opponent. He also learned to never again boast of a victory before he had it. And he learned to be as tricky as Sertorius.[39]

Pompey and Metellus duly linked up their forces; and, as they camped side by side, Pompey allowed Metellus to always set the daily password for both armies. The two armies parted, with their generals agreeing that Metellus would take care of Farther Spain while Pompey went after Sertorius's forces in Nearer Spain.

The following spring, Pompey regained the initiative and evened the score with Sertorius. On the coast not far from Lauron, near today's Valencia, Pompey did battle with an army led by Sertorius's deputy Perpenna—the same Perpenna who had fled from Pompey without a fight in Sicily. Taking a page from Sertorius's playbook, Pompey let Perpenna think his troops were retreating, and when Perpenna's men broke ranks and gave chase, they ran into an ambush.

Pompey's legions delivered him a stunning victory. Ten thousand Sertorian troops were slaughtered. Perpenna himself escaped to rejoin Sertorius. Buoyed by this success, Pompey readied to take on Sertorius himself, as a smarting Sertorius marched to deal with his young opponent. Near a Roman fort on the bank of the Sucro River, today's Jucar in the Valencia region, Sertorius committed to a set-piece battle against Pompey.

In the late afternoon, Sertorius led his left wing against Pompey's right, where Pompey himself commanded. Sertorius's men broke through Pompey's lines, and Pompey, on horseback, found himself surrounded by opposition troops. A one-on-one sword battle with an enemy foot soldier ensued, and in the same instant both men struck the sword arm of their opponent.

Striking from above, Pompey's blade cleaved off the soldier's hand at the wrist. Pompey only suffered a minor wound to the arm; and as the man reeled away without hand or weapon, Pompey quickly dismounted and set his horse running free. As he hoped, the horse, draped with gold decorations, distracted the enemy. As Sertorians fought each other to claim the horse, Pompey ran from his distracted opponents, linking up with Lucius Afranius's legions on his left, which had broken into Sertorius's camp and were looting it.

The battle ended in a draw, with, once again, Metellus's army hurrying up to save the day and Sertorius's men melting away to avoid being caught between two senatorial forces. Sertorius withdrew to Huesca, his mountain stronghold. "If this old woman had not come up," Sertorius subsequently complained to his subordinates, "I would have whipped that boy (Pompey) soundly, and sent him to Rome."[40]

The following year, in the spring of 75 BC, at Italica, north of today's Seville in southwest Spain, Metellus won a victory against Sertorius's second-in-command Lucius Hirtuleius, who lost 20,000 men and fled to join Sertorius in the northeast. Metellus's men hailed him Imperator for this victory.

Following the battle, the armies of Metellus and Pompey joined up on the banks of the Douro River in central Spain, and Pompey congratulated his colleague for his success. The two generals then sent their men foraging on the Plain of Saguntum, never expecting Sertorius to attack their combined force.

But attack is what Sertorius did, against his better judgment. His local allies, tiring of the drawn-out war, pressed him to make an all-out attack on both Roman generals while he had them in the one spot. If not, they said, they would go home. The battle commenced at noon, and lasted until well into the night. In desperate fighting, Hirtuleius, Sertorius's best and most reliable commander, was killed along with thousands of his troops. Metellus was wounded by a spear. Pompey lost 6,000 men. But worse, Pompey lost his brother-in-law Gaius Memmius. In the end, Sertorius retreated back into the mountains.

While the battle failed to produce total victory for either side, it was a strategic victory for Pompey and Metellus, for from this day forward Sertorius would avoid facing them again in a set-piece battle. With some of his allies now disenchanted and deserting him, Sertorius would continue a harassing guerrilla war against his opponents. At the same time, he set his sights beyond Spain, all the way to Rome. News had reached him that his mother had died at the capital, and Sertorius was homesick. Letters also reached him from senators at Rome, who assured him that if he were to come to Rome, where he had many Marian admirers, he could take absolute power as sole ruler of Rome.

As attractive as this prospect was, Sertorius was wily enough to know that he would have to prepare the ground before such an ambition could be achieved. He needed to draw Rome's attention and resources away from Spain. And he knew precisely how to achieve that when, in early 74 BC, Nicomedes, king of Bithynia and Julius Caesar's close friend, passed away. In his will, the king left Bithynia to Rome, and the Senate voted to make the kingdom Rome's newest province. On learning this, Sertorius sent envoys to Pontus, to Mithradates, the ambitious king humiliated by Sulla.

Sertorius proposed that if Mithradates wanted to invade his neighbors, he would support him by sending a contingent of Roman legionaries led by one of his Roman officers, the former praetor Marcus Marius, to train and lead them. In return, he asked for seven million sesterces and a fleet of forty Pontic warships to carry his troops to the East. Mithradates accepted.

By the summer of 74 BC, Mithradates was on the march. Sertorius's man Marcus Marius, landing in Asia with his troops, took the Roman governor by surprise and occupied the province, ostensibly for Sertorius. This allowed Mithradates himself to invade the neighboring Bithynia by land, without any Roman interference from Asia.

The consuls at Rome for this year were Marcus Cotta, maternal uncle of Caesar, and Lucius Lucullus, one-time quaestor of Sulla, both of them firm Sullans. When, late in the year, existing and former consuls drew lots to decide who would take up the provincial governorships for the following year—the Senate having returned to this democratic republican practice previously suspended by Sulla—Cotta drew Bithynia. Lucullus wasn't happy with the province he drew, and swapped it for Cilicia. This was quite deliberate, because the new year's governors of Bithynia and

Cilicia were tasked by the Senate with dealing with Mithradates, and Lucullus, who had earlier combated Mithradates's armies alongside Sulla, was up for the fight and the rewards that would accompany victory.

In the spring of 73 BC, Lucullus landed in Cilicia with one legion of new Italian conscripts. Joining it with two existing legions already based in Cilicia, he went to war on land against Mithradates and Marcus Marius from the south, while his colleague Cotta arrived with a fleet to attack Bithynia by sea. Very quickly, Cotta was in trouble and bottled up, requiring Lucullus to come to his rescue. This war was destined to last for nine years, and, like a wildfire out of control, would consume country after country as it spread across much of the Middle East. But it would not save Sertorius.

IX

PESKY SPARTACUS TERMINATED
BY CRASSUS AND POMPEY

The year 73 BC produced a perfect storm as far as Rome was concerned. In the West, Pompey, Metellus, and their legions were still tied down combating Sertorius's guerrilla fighters in Spain. In the East, Lucullus had initially proved a skillful commander in the fight against Mithradates. Taking to the water with Cotta's fleet, he had defeated Marcus Marius's Pontic fleet off the island of Lemnos. Marius himself swam ashore from his sinking warship and was captured, after which Lucullus had him decapitated. But Roman forces in the East would be vastly outnumbered when the Pontic king allied with King Tigranes of Armenia, spreading the conflict. And while the war raged in the East, Rome found that it had a new war on its very doorstep.

That summer, at Capua, north of Naples, a revolt of two hundred slaves in a gladiatorial barracks saw seventy-two gladiators succeed in escaping and basing themselves on the heights of Mount Vesuvius. Their leader was a Thracian named Spartacus. Aged around thirty and a former noncitizen auxiliary soldier in the Roman army—almost certainly commanding a Thracian cavalry unit—he had fallen foul of Roman law and been condemned to slavery. Following their breakout from Capua, Spartacus and his colleagues raided farms and towns throughout the region. Freeing slaves as they went, they quickly built a slave army numbering in the thousands.

Initially, the Senate assigned one of the year's praetors to lead a force of three thousand men to deal with the slave revolt. These troops were almost

certainly from the Praetorian Guard, a standing military police force at
the capital, which, as their name implies, were commanded by the praetors. Spartacus quickly destroyed the praetor and his force, after which
the Senate dispatched another praetor to raise new recruits and a third
to march with a further three thousand Praetorians to tackle Spartacus.
This latest force soon met a similar devastating fate, with the praetor in
command killed by Spartacus while relaxing in a bath in a country villa.[41]

Another of the eight praetors for the year was forty-two-year-old
Marcus Crassus, banker and property developer. With alarm growing at
Rome, Crassus wrote to the Senate, urging it to recall Lucullus from the
East and Pompey from Spain to lead the war against the slaves. But time
being considered of the essence, the two consuls, Lentulus and Gellius,
neither of them men with sparkling military records, were called on by
the Senate to immediately conscript new legions and lead them against
the rampaging slave army, now numbering tens of thousands of men. Far
from being a rabble, the slaves were disciplined and well led, for Spartacus
had divided his followers into companies, appointed officers over them,
and trained them like Roman legionaries.

It was now that Rome had a little luck. When Spartacus wanted to
march out of Italy and return to his homeland, he fell out with his two
deputies, Celts who wanted to remain in Italy and amass booty. The deputies took more than half the slave army with them, only to suffer humiliating defeats by the consuls and lose their lives. But Spartacus was not
done for. In central Italy, he led his remaining men in routing those same
consular armies, and then did the same to legions that marched down
from Cisalpine Gaul, with their governor, to deal with him. The way
north out of Italy was open to Spartacus, but, unaccountably, he turned
back south into Italy, to loot and pillage some more.

The bloodied consuls retreated to Rome, where the anxious Senate
debated how to counter Spartacus. The praetor Crassus had by this time
regretted having recommended that Lucullus and Pompey be recalled, for
he now saw an opportunity for himself. Although he had little interest
in soldiering, Crassus believed that if he stepped in and led the defeat of

Spartacus, he would have to be offered the consulship. With the consulship came power. And with power came money.

Besides, Crassus was envious of Pompey. He had resented the honors that Sulla had paid the youngster. Crassus had won the Battle of the Colline Gate for Sulla. Yet, to his mind, he had never received his just reward, while people bent over backwards to praise Pompey. As far as Crassus was concerned, Pompey wasn't so great. Once, when Crassus was in conversation with a colleague, young Pompey had approached, and the other fellow had said, "Here comes Pompey the Great."

To which Crassus sarcastically asked, "How *big* is he?"[42]

So now Crassus proposed to the Senate that he lead the campaign against the slaves the following year, 72 BC, even offering to put his own money into equipping them. The Senate accepted his offer.

In Spain, Pompey had remained on the offensive, grinding down Sertorius's outstations and isolating him in the mountains. Pompey's fellow general Metellus was not even bothering to campaign. Leaving Pompey to keep up the pressure on Sertorius, Metellus even wintered in Transalpine Gaul in 75–74 BC. His excuse was the need to take personal command of two new legions being sent by the Senate.

These reinforcements came at the request of Pompey, who had written to the Senate that he had expended most of his personal fortune in raising and maintaining his own legions, and it was time the state supported his efforts to regain the Spanish provinces. For the first time, in his communications with the Senate from Spain, the young general signed himself Pompey the Great, which he would continue to do for the rest of his life. Overwhelmingly, the Senate approved his request for support.

For the most part, Metellus remained in camp, hosting long, luxurious dinners. He did post a reward of 2.4 million sesterces and 20,000 acres of land for any Roman who betrayed Sertorius, and this, indirectly, would lead to Sertorius's downfall.

On hearing of this reward, Sertorius became paranoid, replaced his Roman bodyguard with Spaniards, and increasingly sidelined his Roman officers, creating a tense atmosphere at his mountain headquarters. Confident that he could do a better job than his chief, his general Perpenna decided that Sertorius must go. Other senior Roman officers fighting for Sertorius, frustrated by their declining fortunes under the one-eyed general, sided with Perpenna. One night at dinner, while several of them held Sertorius down, Perpenna and the other Roman officers stabbed Sertorius to death.

Driven by a self-belief that wasn't supported by ability, Perpenna, believing he could defeat the young upstart Pompey, led the Sertorian army back down from the mountains to do battle with him. Like boxers feeling each other out with probing jabs, the two armies skirmished for nine days. And then Pompey played a trick on Perpenna, the very same trick he'd employed to defeat him several years earlier, for, in Pompey's judgment, unlike himself Perpenna was a man who never learned from his mistakes. With Pompey's cavalry pretending to retreat in disorder, Perpenna's troops fell for the ruse and gave chase. Led to where Pompey's legions lay in wait, they were ambushed and slaughtered.

Perpenna himself was found hiding in some scrub. Dragged to Pompey, he yelled that he had secrets to reveal, hoping to bargain for his life. He had incriminating letters from senators at Rome, he said, men who had encouraged Sertorius to take power at Rome. Disgusted, Pompey had Perpenna executed, then burned the letters without reading them, for which later Roman historians would praise him.

Most of the surviving Romans who had assassinated Sertorius fled to North Africa. One would die alone in a Spanish cave, friendless, penniless, hunted. With the Spanish tribal leaders who supported Sertorius coming to Pompey and suing for peace, Pompey would remain in Spain into the following year, reorganizing the administration of the two Roman provinces while cementing peace deals with the locals who had supported Sertorius. As for wild Lusitania, some of whose tribes had fought alongside Sertorius, it was outside Pompey's brief, and he would ignore it.

The region, which roughly covered today's Portugal, would remain outside the empire for some time to come.

In reorganizing Roman Spain, Pompey produced a region that would remain steadfastly loyal to Rome for centuries to come and would provide her best legionaries from among the Roman citizens of the two provinces. In doing so, Pompey displayed an eye for detail and a talent for administrative organization that would characterize the coming years of his career. And no one would accuse him of trying to profit personally from his success in Spain. Not only did he prevent his troops from looting Spanish property, promising them retirement and land instead, he would ask the Senate for just one reward for himself: another Triumph.

When Pompey did march from Spain with his legions in the late winter of 71 BC, he paused in the snows at the summit of the pass through the Pyrenees to erect a stone monument to his campaign. The inscription on that monument simply declared that Pompey the Great had restored 876 cities and towns in Spain to the rule and protection of Rome.

The reason for Pompey's return in winter with his experienced troops was a recall by the Senate, which, in desperation, had also recalled a Roman army then in Thrace, Spartacus's homeland, to support Crassus against Spartacus. Led by Marcus Lucullus, younger brother of Lucius Lucullus, the general commanding Roman forces in the new war against Mithradates in the East, the legions in Thrace had just brutally put down an uprising by a local tribe. That campaign would subsequently earn Marcus Lucullus a Triumph.

Crassus and his new legions were having limited success against Spartacus, and only then after Crassus had resorted to decimating his own units for cowardice in battle. Decimation, meaning to reduce by one tenth, involved one Roman soldier in ten being chosen by lot, after which their comrades were required to beat them to death with clubs. The performance of Crassus's remaining troops markedly improved once their general had made them more afraid of him than of the enemy.

But then, once Crassus had succeeded in bottling up Spartacus and his slave army on a peninsula in southern Italy over the winter of 72–71

BC, Spartacus had managed a surprise breakout before winter ended. With the slaves on the rampage again and now cautiously trailed by Crassus, the Senate was losing patience with his campaign of attrition, and expectations grew that the all-conquering Pompey would swiftly finish off Spartacus.

It didn't take long for Spartacus's men to learn that Pompey was on the way; and when the younger Lucullus landed his troops at Brindisi, the slave army found itself sandwiched between Lucullus to their southeast and Pompey advancing from the north. When Spartacus's followers demanded a decisive battle against the Roman commander they considered the weakest, Crassus, Spartacus initially opposed the idea. But realizing that his men were bent on attacking Crassus with him or without him, he relented, and the slave army swung on Crassus's tailing legions and lined up for battle in a river valley in central Italy.

As the slaves offered battle, Crassus couldn't believe his luck. Seeing his opportunity to eliminate Spartacus before Pompey arrived and stole his thunder, he commanded his army to form up in battle order. For Spartacus, this was do or die. Killing his horse, saying that if victorious, he would have plenty of Roman horses to choose from; and if not, he would not be needing a horse, he led his army in a charge against Crassus's legions, personally aiming for Crassus himself.

In the face of the charge, Crassus's men stood firm, and Spartacus was cut down and killed. Leaderless, Spartacus's followers were quickly routed by Crassus's legions. Thousands fell. Five thousand fled north. Another six thousand were made prisoners. Crassus marched these prisoners to Capua, starting point of the slave revolt, and symbolically crucified all six thousand alongside the Appian Way from Capua to Rome.

In the foothills of the Apennines, the fleeing five thousand slave soldiers ran headlong into Pompey and his legions as they marched south. With Pompey ordering no prisoners taken, his legionaries waded into slave ranks with swords flashing, killing every last man. When Pompey shortly after arrived outside Rome, news of his destruction of the last rebel force had preceded him, along with his report to the Senate in which he'd said Crassus had killed the slaves, but he had ended the war. Agreeing with him, and to the fury of Crassus, the populace hailed Pompey as victor over Spartacus.

A grateful Senate awarded Pompey and Metellus Triumphs for terminating the Sertorian War. And as Pompey and Crassus encamped their legions outside Rome and refused to disband them, both men stood for election to the consulate of the following year, even though only Crassus was technically qualified to stand, having achieved praetor rank. To win plebeian support, Pompey promised the Tribunes of the Plebs that, if elected, he would restore their old powers, the powers removed by Sulla.

When Crassus saw that Pompey had massive support from all levels of society, he compromised. Coming to Pompey's camp, he shook hands and promised to work with him. Disbanding his legions first, Crassus sent his men home. In return, after Pompey also disbanded his legions and subsequently spoke before the Popular Assembly leading up to the elections, he said he would be honored if Crassus was elected to serve with him. This guaranteed that, when the elections were held later that year, both Pompey and Crassus were elected consuls for 70 BC.

By the time he became a consul, Pompey would do something on a personal level that his enemies would declare shameful, and which his friends would have considered a masterful act of political maneuvering. Sulla, in excluding Pompey from his will, had made his longtime quaestor Lucius Lucullus guardian of his children, a duty that Lucullus had diligently performed ever since. With the excuse that Lucullus was tied up in the East in the war against Mithradates, Pompey assumed the guardianship of Sulla's children. He then promptly married Sulla's sixteen-year-old son Faustus Cornelius Sulla to his own daughter Pompeia, canceling the engagement of Pompeia to Cato's brother to do it. As a result, young Sulla would become a willing and loyal client of Pompey, Cato would be enraged, and Lucullus would have another reason to despise his rival Pompey.

Once Pompey and Crassus sat as consuls in 70 BC, Crassus would join Pompey in supporting the restoration of powers of the tribunes.

The biographer Suetonius, early in the second century, would credit Caesar with initiating this reform, but Caesar was not in a position to do so. He was not even yet a senator. It was Pompey, supported by Crassus, who was responsible for this 70 BC initiative. And Crassus didn't prevent Pompey from allowing the election of two censors that year, the first time this had happened since Sulla eradicated the post. With their duties much like those of modern ombudsmen, censors traditionally served for eighteen months before replacements were elected. But on virtually nothing else would Crassus and Pompey agree during their consular year, and they would grow increasingly at odds.

On December 31, 71 BC, Pompey and Metellus celebrated a joint Triumph through the streets of Rome. As Metellus officially outranked Pompey, he would have gone first, but Pompey would have received a more rapturous welcome from the adoring Roman public, who hailed him victor in both the Sertorian War and the Slave War.

Metellus could only grind his teeth with indignation, and envy. Although he and Pompey had worked together in Spain and the young man had always paid him respect, Metellus had never forgotten how Pompey had outshone him in Sulla's eyes the last time they had fought on the same side. Over the remaining seven years of his life, the bitter Metellus would work against Pompey's interests in the Senate and put his support behind another young man with promise, a rival to Pompey who Metellus aimed to manipulate—Gaius Julius Caesar.

Once the new censors, both of them clients of Pompey, had taken their vows, the pair took their seats on a traditional judgment bench on the Rostra in the Forum for a special ceremony created for and by their patron Pompey. Very much a student of the history and traditions of the Roman Republic, Pompey knew that the Equites, members of the Equestrian Order, had traditionally taken part in a ceremony with the censors at the end of Rome's wars. Because Pompey was technically still only a member of the Equestrian Order, he now revived this ceremony for this occasion, and for himself.

The ceremony's history was this: At the termination of wars, each Equite, in times past Rome's most senior enlisted soldiers because they could afford to own a horse, had led his horse to the Forum to give an account to the censors of how and where he had served, and under which general. The censors then discharged them from military duty, honorably or dishonorably as the case may have been. Pompey now came into the Forum leading his horse and approached the two censors seated on the Rostra. The event having been advertised in advance, a huge, expectant crowd of Equites, commoners, freedmen, and slaves had gathered to watch the ceremony.

"Pompeius Magnus," said the senior censor once the crowd had hushed, "I demand of you whether you have served the full time in the wars that is prescribed by the law."

"Yes," Pompey replied in a loud voice, "I have served all, and all under myself as general."[43]

This brought an almighty cheer from the audience. The censors then declared Pompey discharged from his duty as a soldier of Rome, and rising from their judgment bench the pair escorted him to the Esquiline Hill and up its narrow, winding streets all the way to his front door in the Carinae. Behind them thronged the happy crowd, in their tens of thousands, cheering and applauding Pompey as they walked.

Standing back on the fringes of the adoring crowd would have been men who didn't admire Pompey so much. Many in the Senate mistrusted a man who attracted so much popular devotion. It's unlikely that many senators were present, but some couldn't stay away. No doubt Metellus had come to watch from a distance, and probably Crassus, too. And Julius Caesar, watching along with a friend of his, an eighteen-year-old boy priest by the name of Marcus Lepidus, son of the Marcus Aemilius Lepidus who had been driven out of Italy by Pompey following Lepidus Senior's failed coup attempt. For Lepidus, too, all this adoration of Pompey was sickening.

X.

AS CAESAR WEEPS, POMPEY
CONQUERS THE EAST

Julius Caesar turned thirty years of age in July, 70 BC. In the elections held in the second half of 70 BC, the year during which the thirty-six-year-old Pompey and forty-five-year-old Crassus were serving as consuls, Caesar, meeting the age qualification for a quaestorship with his July birthday, wasted no time in putting his name forward for one of the vacancies for quaestor that would arise in 69 BC. The post of quaestor, providing automatic admission to the Senate on its completion, was the most junior of Rome's judges. As a quaestor, Caesar would be entitled to one lictor, an official attendant who walked ahead of him bearing the *fasces*, the rods and axes that represented the power to punish and execute criminals. A praetor was allocated six lictors; a consul, twelve.

In practice, some quaestors were little more than administrative assistants. Several worked as assistants to the praetor running the Treasury. Each Roman army commander-in-chief in the field also had a quaestor on his staff, as his adjutant. Every provincial governor had a quaestor working for him, administering the province's finances and running army recruitment in the province, but also conducting court sittings, usually for minor crimes. The quaestor's length of service varied, and usually lasted as long as the posting of his superior, which might only be one year. On the other hand, depending on the circumstances, it could be much longer—Lucius Lucullus had served as Sulla's reliable and efficient quaestor for eight years.

Sulla was no longer alive to oppose Caesar's advancement. And as Caesar's chief creditor, Crassus would have been happy to see the young man in paid government employment at last, for Caesar was by this stage in debt to the tune of 4 million sesterces. When the quaestor's list for 69 BC was announced in the autumn of 70 BC, the name of Gaius Julius Caesar was on it. He was allocated to the future gubernatorial staff of a praetor for 70 BC, Gaius Antistius Vetus, to whom fell the 69 BC governorship of Farther Spain.

In the midwinter of 70–69 BC, as Caesar was preparing to travel to Spain with Vetus in the spring, Caesar's aunt Julia, the widow of Marius, passed away. In the Forum, Caesar delivered what Plutarch describes as a magnificent oration to his late aunt. In part, Caesar said of his aunt: "Her mother was a descendant of kings, namely the Marcii Reges, a family founded by the Roman king Ancus Marcius, and her father of gods— since the Julians, of which we Caesars are a branch, reckon descent from the goddess Venus. Thus Julia's stock can claim both the sanctity of kings, who reign supreme among mortals, and the reverence due to gods, who hold even kings in their power."[44]

In all his published writings and reported speeches, Caesar would never again invoke the gods, would never beseech their help or blame them for setbacks. Despite twice holding very senior priesthoods during his lifetime, Caesar was not especially religious, and in fact, according to Suetonius, "Religious scruples never deterred him" from anything.[45]

Caesar would observe the necessary religious obligations of his official roles, would perform sacrifices, and would generally give an ear to the omens portended by the augurs. But Caesar was apparently of the belief that the gods helped those who helped themselves; and even when the omens were said to be inauspicious, Caesar would rely on his own judgment first and foremost. It was a policy that would serve him well for decades, until the day it didn't.

Caesar organized his aunt's funeral procession, and boldly had busts of her late husband Marius carried behind the bier. The carrying of family busts in a funeral cortege was usual Roman practice, but this was the first time that images of Marius had been seen at Rome since Sulla had had all the man's public statues removed, twelve years before, when declaring him a public enemy. During Caesar's speech, some in his audience began to decry him for resurrecting Marius, but they were howled down by others who cheered and applauded Caesar.

To former clients of Marian leaders, Caesar was their new champion, the new leader of the Marian family. As yet he was not an influential man who could advance his supporters' interests. But some men, like Caesar, wear their future destiny wrapped around them like an invisible but fabulously rich cloak, a cloak that we occasionally catch a glimpse of in their younger days.

Not long after his aunt's funeral, Caesar's second wife Cornelia also passed away, apparently due to complications during premature childbirth. Again, a grieving Caesar delivered a powerful and affectionate homily, and, says Plutarch, this gained him a reputation with the general public as a man of tenderness and kindness of heart. When Caesar departed Rome for Spain, his daughter Julia, now aged six or seven, would have been left in the care of his mother Aurelia at his Subura house.

Caesar was to spend two years in Farther Spain with Vetus, based in the provincial capital Corduba, today's Cordoba, where two legions had been permanently based by Pompey to keep the peace. Vetus did nothing novel or adventurous during his governorship: he merely maintained the status quo in the wake of the tumultuous Sertorian years, which was all that the Senate asked of him. At Vetus's side, Caesar was an efficient quaestor. Vetus, clinging to the safety of the capital in these post-Sertorian War days, stayed put in his palace and sent Caesar around the province's cities sitting as judge in the regular sittings of the assizes circuit. This gave Caesar valuable experience, but he presumably longed for the power to achieve more.

While conducting the assizes in Gades, today's Cadiz, the thirty-one-year-old Caesar gloomily reflected on the career of Alexander the Great and his own career. Suetonius says this occurred after he saw a statue of Alexander in the town. Plutarch says that Caesar was reading about Alexander at the time. Tears began to run down his cheeks. When his staff asked him why, Caesar, wiping away the tears, replied, "Do you think that

I have not just cause to weep when I consider that Alexander at my age had conquered so many nations, and I have all this time done nothing that is memorable?"[46]

During this period, Pompey, having served his consulship in 70 BC, pulled back from a prominent role in government and spent time with his wife Mucia and his children, the seven-year-old Gnaeus and six-year-old Pompeia. He preferred life in the country to that in bustling Rome, the city that never slept, away from legislative business and away from the public.

Pompey was uncomfortable in the public arena. He was the exact opposite of his co-consul Marcus Crassus, who reveled in public attention. Crassus was a friend to everyone he encountered, high or low, and was frequently seen in the Forum, where he displayed a prodigious memory for names. When Pompey did occasionally appear in public through this period, it was with a massive entourage of staff and clients, which prevented ordinary people from reaching him.

By this time Pompey was Rome's most famous living general. And just as famous generals of recent times such as Eisenhower, Montgomery, and MacArthur wouldn't have been seen dead in the local bar or supermarket, Pompey spent most of his time at home, observing from afar the slow progress in the East of Lucullus against Mithradates and his ally Tigranes of Armenia. While Lucullus had two major victories over enemy forces in Armenia in 69 and 68 BC, he was unable to kill or capture his chief adversaries; and, with his troops becoming mutinous, he had pulled back.

At Rome, the common people were beginning to speak openly about sending Pompey to take over from Lucullus. But then in 68 BC, Cilician buccaneers were so audacious that they sailed into Ostia, the port of Rome, and burned and sacked the town and every ship in port. The public, protesting in the Forum, clamored for something to be done about the pirates. These brigands had been plaguing Rome for decades, but this was the last straw!

There was no one at Rome who would not have wanted to see the estimated 30,000 pirates removed from the seas. Not only did they threaten the security of Rome's imported grain supply, they seized thousands of travelers. Most of these prisoners, men, women, and children, were sold into slavery from the pirates' slave-dealing center on the Greek island of Delos. At its height, the Delos slave market was turning over 10,000 slaves a day. Those captives valuable enough to be ransomed were kept until friends and family paid up.

Leading Romans were frequently taken hostage when they were traveling, on land as well as at sea, just as Caesar had been years earlier. Only recently, the pirates had taken a Roman admiral hostage, releasing him for a paltry 48,000 sesterces ransom. But Rome was never a maritime nation and didn't possess a powerful fit-for-purpose navy, as it would in imperial times. The Republic's admirals were all generals who knew about fighting on land, not on the sea. The pirates had the upper hand.

Finally, in 67 BC, the Senate was formally called on to rid the seas of the pirates. The motion, by Tribune of the Plebs Aulus Gabinius, to appoint a single commander with massive resources and unlimited powers to counter the pirates, didn't name Pompey or anyone else for the job. But as Gabinius was a client of Pompey, few people doubted who was behind the proposal.

One of the two consuls for the year was Manius Acilius Glabrio, none other than the man Sulla, years earlier, had forced to divorce his stepdaughter Aemilia so that Pompey could marry her. Of course, having lost his wife to Pompey, Glabrio had every reason to despise him, and he persuaded his consular colleague Gaius Cornelius Piso to oppose any appointment for Pompey. The pair of them promoted fear among their fellow senators, that this was an attempted power grab by Pompey, and Gabinius was ordered from the Senate.

After Pompey's appointment was debated in the Senate, Pompey was told by one of the two consuls, almost certainly the vengeful Glabrio: "If you are ambitious to emulate the fate of Romulus, you will not be disappointed."[47]

One of the legends surrounding the death of Romulus, co-founder of Rome, was that he died after being torn apart by the members of his own Senate. Once this remark was widely reported, an incensed crowd of commoners mobbed the Senate House, and the offending consul was lucky to escape with his own life. While the vote on the measure was taking place, Pompey withdrew to the country so that he would not be seen to influence the vote. In the country, his wife Mucia would shortly give birth to their second son, Sextus.

With both consuls against it, just a single senator voted in favor of appointing Pompey—Julius Caesar, who had just returned to Rome—after his posting as quaestor in Spain—to take his seat in the Senate as a novice member of the House. Caesar's support for Pompey would have left many scratching their heads. This was the same Caesar who, not many years earlier, had vowed to see Pompey punished for the execution of Carbo. But, as Plutarch was to say, Caesar didn't support the proposal through any newfound love of Pompey, but to curry favor with the plebeians, who, he knew, did love Pompey.

As senators weren't paid for carrying out their duties, Caesar needed a new paying job, and he was after the votes of the commoners, planning to soon stand for the well-paid annual government appointment of Surveyor of the Appian Way, the highway that ran from Rome to the boot of Italy.

With the Popular Assembly firmly behind the idea of sending the people's hero Pompey against the pirates, and violence being threatened by the general public if they didn't have their way, the Senate at first considered appointing two commanders, but then buckled; after a fresh vote, Pompey was offered the job. To avoid attracting public attention, Pompey returned to Rome at night following the offer, and, feigning reluctance, accepted the job.

In a combined meeting of the assemblies in the city marketplace, the appointment was formally promulgated, and Pompey proceeded to negotiate an even larger deployment than originally proposed by Gabinius. He was given the power to levy up to 132,000 troops and 500 ships and their rowers, and his authority would extend throughout the Mediterranean and fifty miles inland. According to the Roman historian Appian, in the end he employed 270 ships, and with his largest warships—triremes with triple banks of oars—being capable of carrying some 200 soldiers in addition to their sailors and oarsmen, it's likely that he recruited some 50,000 soldiers for the operation.

Pompey began by carefully organizing the logistics for a campaign against the pirates that would launch in the spring of 66 BC. He first divided the Mediterranean into thirteen zones, assigning a commander with a battle fleet to each. He also set aside a separate fleet for himself. As his senior officers, answerable only to him, he appointed two quaestors as his adjutants and twenty-four senators who had previously commanded legions on land, deliberately choosing men who were not his clients and who were from the most noble Roman families.

As the fleets were readied, Pompey recalled many of his retired loyal legionaries, putting together a taskforce of experienced soldiers, who he put on his ships. Roman warships had always carried a small contingent of marines, but now soldiers accustomed to fighting on land would have to overcome seasickness, find their sea legs, and train for ship-to-ship operations away from land.

This same year, as Pompey was planning the fine details of his amphibious operation at his house in the Carinae, with orders flowing from the pens of his freedmen secretaries and subordinate officers, and messengers coming and going in a flurry of activity, his unlikely supporter Caesar married again. This was very much a diplomatic marriage. Caesar's new wife, his third, was Pompeia. She was the daughter of Cinna, Caesar's late patron, making her very much a Marian. But she was also a granddaughter of Sulla. So her bloodlines straddled both of the formerly warring families. For Caesar, it was a cold-blooded political move, and his relationship with Pompeia would never be close. The union would produce no children.

In the spring of 66 BC, Pompey launched his campaign against the pirates. He began by focusing on the Western Mediterranean. With his admirals scouring the seas and blockading pirate ports, Pompey led his own fleet in tracking down every pirate ship on the water. As soon as his ships overhauled a pirate vessel, they closed around it and his legionaries stormed aboard. Pirates fought, died, or surrendered in their thousands, and their ships were scuttled. In forty days, Pompey swept the Western Mediterranean clean of the buccaneers. Those not caught in his net fled to the Eastern Mediterranean, where, seeking security in numbers, they clustered in their last ports in Cilicia and the islands of the Aegean.

On hearing that Piso the consul was withholding supplies to his fleets and discharging his seamen behind his back, Pompey made a surprise return to Rome. Gabinius the tribune was all for calling for Piso's dismissal, but Pompey stayed his hand. He merely spoke with Piso, who, reminded that the public might tear to pieces a man who prevented Pompey from dealing with the pirates, meekly ceased his opposition.

From Brindisi, where his battle fleet awaited, Pompey again went to sea, launching his campaign against the pirates in the Eastern Mediterranean. There was soon a major sea battle, and a crushing defeat for the pirates. One after the other, the pirates' island fortresses fell as Pompey's fleets swarmed on them. And then Pompey invaded Cilicia itself with his sixty best ships, landing 12,000 troops and taking town after town as the pirates holding them surrendered en masse. In forty-nine days, Pompey cleared the Eastern Mediterranean of the pirate menace.

In a total of just eighty-nine days, Pompey had achieved his objective, sweeping the seas clean of pirates, sinking 1,300 pirate ships of all sizes, killing 10,000 buccaneers and taking 20,000 captive. He also freed one hundred and twenty towns and fortresses from pirate control. At the same time, large numbers of affluent hostages were released from pirate hands. Pompey took the rich hoards of pirate loot he captured and shared it with his legionaries and the Treasury at Rome. He sold the slaves he found at Delos, adding the money this garnered to the pile. And then he did something quite extraordinary. Instead of punishing the surviving pirates, he issued a blanket pardon, and turned robbers into farmers.

Pirate leaders had complained to him that they had been driven to piracy by successive Roman governors who did nothing to help the locals. These pirates had originally been farmers, but their farmland in the rugged interior of Cilicia had been marginal at best. So Pompey gave the Cilician pirates arable farmland around towns along the Cilician coast, and in the under-populated Greek mainland province of Achaea—on the condition that they give their oath to never turn to piracy again.

With the boost of new settlers, poor towns would soon grow and flourish. Pompey's policy would prove a complete success, with the Cilicians never returning to the sea as pirates. These men and their descendants would honor Pompey's memory for generations to come—one Cilician coastal town was even renamed Pompeiopolis after him.

Yet the Roman nobility found cause to criticize Pompey. At the end of the pirate campaign, on the island of Crete, once a major pirate base, the Roman governor Quintus Caecilius Metellus, who had conquered Crete for Rome in 69 BC with three legions and accordingly been granted the title of Creticus by a grateful Senate, still had one last pirate band under siege in a Cretan city. This Metellus was very well connected. A former praetor and a relative of Pompey's fellow general in Spain and now firm opponent, Caecilius Metellus Pius, and with two brothers also in influential posts, Creticus had married his daughter to the eldest son of Rome's richest man, Marcus Crassus, who, like Metellus Pius, was no friend of Pompey.

When Pompey's general Lucius Octavius arrived on Crete at the end of the campaign, bearing Pompey's pardon for all pirates, he entered the fray and instructed Metellus to cease hostilities. Metellus refused, drove Octavius from the island, and continued until he had killed every last pirate in the city.

At Rome, Pompey's name was again on everyone's lips. His stunning success against the pirates, so swift and so sure, had his working-class fans applauding with wonder and delight. It also had his rivals in the Senate accusing him of favoring thieves and cutthroats over Metellus, a noble Roman propraetor. To show Pompey who was boss, the Senate granted Metellus Creticus a Triumph for subduing Crete; he would take his victory parade in Rome four years later. More than a century later biographer Plutarch would also condemn Pompey for taking the side of pirates against a former praetor, even though Pompey was merely being consistent in his policy of a universal pardon for pirates.

While Pompey was dealing so decisively with the pirates, in Asia Minor Lucullus was struggling against Mithradates and Tigranes. The previous year, while Lucullus was busy fighting Mithradates's ally Tigranes in Armenia, one of Lucullus's generals, leading four legions, had been routed by Mithradates in the First Battle of Zela, after the king had surged back into Pontus behind Lucullus's back. Seven thousand Roman troops had perished at Zela, and Mithradates had regained the ascendancy.

So, this year, while Pompey was engaged with his pirate operations, a Roman commander of consular rank arrived in the East to assist Lucullus, bringing more troops. This was Glabrio, one of the two consuls of the previous year and Pompey's bitter enemy. But Glabrio, who had no military record and proved a coward, merely skulked in his headquarters in Bithynia, permitting Mithradates to swiftly regain more territory that he'd lost to Lucullus.

With the pirate campaign all but wrapped up, at Rome another Tribune of the Plebs now proposed that Lucullus and Glabrio be recalled, and that Pompey, while still retaining command of his existing fleets and their associated legions, be given total charge of the war against Mithradates and Tigranes, with the troops of Lucullus and Glabrio also brought under his command.

Quintus Catulus, the former consul who Pompey had helped put down the uprising of Lepidus following the death of Sulla, now turned against Pompey. Jealousy of an ally more talented and more popular than himself drove Catulus to convince many in the Senate that such an appointment would give Pompey as much power via the stroke of a pen as Sulla had obtained through war. Meeting in secret, scores of senators agreed with Catulus that they would speak against Pompey's latest appointment. When the time for debate came, Pompey was in the East, supervising the resettling of the pardoned pirates. In fact, it would later become apparent that he had not sought the post, and was unaware of the debate raging at Rome about appointing him.

As tradition dictated, the ex-consuls spoke first, and Catulus led the way by declaring that his fellow senators would be well advised to flee to the mountains should Pompey be given such power with the Eastern command. But, to Catulus's horror, not one of his colleagues kept their word and followed suit. Aware of a swell of public support for the measure, and with no evidence to suggest that Pompey would abuse his new powers, several former consuls spoke in favor of the appointment.

Then, before the Popular Assembly, one of the praetors for the year, the thirty-nine-year-old Marcus Cicero, whose career was going ahead by leaps and bounds, also spoke, eloquently and at length, in support of appointing Pompey, saying he was the only man capable of doing the job. Cicero even subsequently published his speech, which could be purchased from Rome's booksellers and was soon in many private Roman libraries.

By the time junior senators were given their chance to enter the debate, Julius Caesar also rose to speak in favor of Pompey's appointment. Again, Caesar had a personal motive for backing Pompey: that July, Caesar would again be seeking election, this time as one of the four aediles who took office in 65 BC. The aediles, officials on the next rung up the official ladder from quaestors, were responsible for the upkeep of Rome's public buildings and for organizing and administering the public games associated with the religious festivals that took place through the year. Those games involved chariot races and gladiatorial contests conducted on public holidays, and an aedile who organized particularly memorable games could expect to win wide support when he next stood for election.

The motion to appoint Pompey commander-in-chief in the East being passed and becoming an official decree, word was sent to the general that he now had charge of all Rome's forces in the East, with a command that covered a host of provinces, along with the task of defeating

Mithradates once and for all. While Pompey accepted the post, to the surprise of friends who hurried to congratulate him, he was not happy about being sent on campaign so quickly after completing his last massive operation.

"Oh, what a series of labors upon labors!" he grumbled, slapping his thigh. "The only way I will ever end my service as a soldier, let alone escape this invidious 'greatness,' and live at home in the country with my wife, would be if I was an unknown."[48]

Pompey was missing family life. He'd barely had time to get to know his one-year-old son Sextus, while his eldest boy Gnaeus was now eleven, a good age for father-and-son activities. Daughter Pompeia was ten, and already of an age to be betrothed to a noble's son for a future political marriage—in fact, Pompey promised her in marriage to a Servilius Caepio, although the union would later be called off so that Pompey could marry her to Sulla's son Faustus. This Servilius was possibly Gnaeus Servilius Caepio, brother of the Marcus Cato who would later prove an implacable adversary of Pompey. Cato's enmity would have been fired by the termination of this engagement, which Cato would have considered a snub to his family.

To complicate matters, reports were reaching Pompey at the time of his latest appointment that his wife of fifteen years was being unfaithful at Rome, in his own bed. Outwardly, he expressed his utmost trust in Mucia. But he must have been troubled by even the suggestion of impropriety, and would have much preferred to have gone home to spend time with his wife and pour oil on any troubled marital waters. Instead, his sense of duty, his lust for further honors, and his determination to outshine Lucullus kept him in the East to win the war that Lucullus had failed to win.

In planning this campaign, Pompey this time appointed his own clients to prominent posts. His chosen generals included the well-tested Lucius Afranius and the now-former Tribune of the Plebs Aulus Gabinius, promoted to legion command. As his quaestor and adjutant, Pompey appointed thirty-year-old Marcus Aemilius Scaurus. Son of a distinguished consul, Scaurus had become a client of Pompey when Scaurus's late sister Aemilia married Pompey. Even though Aemilia was now dead, the patron-client relationship between Pompey and Scaurus continued, as was the Roman custom. Among the military tribunes on his staff, Pompey included his young son-in-law Faustus Sulla.

Pompey began the campaign by sending proclamations to all governors, legions, and allied kings in the areas covered by his new command, instructing them to join him. At the same time, he canceled all the awards and initiatives that Lucullus had made in the region. Plutarch believed that this was done by Pompey to belittle Lucullus because there was longstanding enmity between the pair. Perhaps it was, but Pompey had every reason to suspect that Lucullus would disobey the Senate's recall and attempt to hang on to his command, as indeed he did. In that case, Pompey was preempting obstruction from the man he was replacing by disempowering him.

At the same time, Pompey sent emissaries to Mithradates, proposing a peace deal in which Mithradates would return to his own kingdom and surrender all that he had garnered over the past few years, including thousands of Roman legionaries who had deserted from Lucullus's army and gone over to the rebel king. This approach gave Pompey time to organize his war machine; but at the same time, if Mithradates came to the party and signed an armistice, it would save Pompey, and Rome, considerable time, treasure, and blood.

Perhaps to buy time, perhaps because he was daunted by Pompey's reputation, Mithradates, who was nearing seventy years of age by this time, responded positively to his approach, at the same time duplicitously sending friendly solicitations to Phraates III, king of Parthia, seeking an alliance. But Pompey was one step ahead of him. He had contacted Phraates, offering a treaty of friendship. More afraid of making an enemy of Pompey than of offending Mithradates, the Parthian king rejected Mithradates's approach and entered into a treaty with Pompey.

A peace agreement now seemed in the cards, for Mithradates sent emissaries to discuss a truce with Pompey, only for the Roman deserters in the king's army to threaten Mithradates, to prevent themselves from being handed back to Rome, which would only execute them. So Mithradates ultimately backed away from peace. His war with Rome would continue.

Pompey had another problem to contend with. While his personal and political foe Glabrio returned to Rome, swallowing his pride and surrendering his command to Pompey, Lucullus was reluctant to hand over his command and his troops to his famous young replacement. So, having gathered his legions, Pompey marched into Galatia in the central north of today's Turkey and met with Lucullus, camping his army next to Lucullus's army.

The pair initially exchanged compliments, but Lucullus soon accused Pompey of being a vulture who fed off the victories of others. Pompey's patience gave way and, ordering Lucullus's legions—including the famous Martia Legion—to follow his army, he went on the offensive. Marching away into Lesser Armenia, where Mithradates was known to be operating, he left Lucullus with no troops and no choice but to go home.

Lucullus, when he arrived back outside Rome weeks later, formally petitioned the Senate for a Triumph for his victories in the East, as he was required to do by law. But on four occasions over the next three years, a junior senator named Gaius Memmius spoke against Lucullus's Triumph, and the Senate held back the award.

This Gaius Memmius wasn't Pompey's brother-in-law—that man had died in the Sertorian War. This senator was a client of Pompey with the same name as Memmius and, similarly, a connection through marriage with Pompey. For this Memmius had married a natural daughter of Sulla. It's unclear whether this Memmius opposed Lucullus's Triumph on instructions from Pompey, or did so simply to curry his favor. Certainly, on returning from the East, Pompey would speak in favor of Memmius's career advancement, which would include a praetorship in 58 BC.

Lucullus refused to be denied his Triumph. But, as a general could only be awarded a Triumph if he didn't cross the pomerium and reenter the city proper while he awaited the Senate's vote of approval, he stayed outside central Rome for the next three years.

It was very much in Pompey's interests to keep Lucullus outside Rome. This meant that the returned general could not sit in the Senate, where, jealous of his replacement in the East, he would have been a bitter opponent and a very vocal critic of Pompey—behind his back, while Pompey was away from Rome fighting her battles. Lucullus, considered one of Rome's richest men by this stage, would use those three years spending part of his vast personal fortune, much of it accrued while commander in the East, on lavish banquets—a "Lucullan Feast" became the Roman byword for extravagant, over-the-top dining.

Lucullus's cash splash was most obvious on monumental building projects, such as his vast, luxurious country villas, inland at Tusculum in the Alban Hills and on the coast at Naples. He would also develop the magnificent Gardens of Lucullus on the slopes of the Pincian Hill on central Rome's eastern outskirts—the Gardens would later come into the hands of Rome's emperors and remain today, in part, as the gardens of the Villa Borghese, above the Spanish Steps. Lucullus would be awarded his Triumph, but only in 63 BC, once Memmius ceased his opposition on Pompey's behalf.

Meanwhile, in Lesser Armenia, Pompey caught up with Mithradates's army, which was encamped on a mountain slope. Heavily outnumbered by Pompey, whose army is said to have numbered as many as 150,000 men once the troops of Glabrio and Lucullus joined it, Mithradates refused to give battle. So Pompey spent forty-five days besieging Mithradates's camp before the king broke out with his best men and fled for the Euphrates River, where he regrouped.

Pompey followed, and at midnight one night in 64 BC, in bright moonlight, he began an operation to encircle the enemy camp. As some of Pompey's troops moved in with the moon behind them, casting long shadows, Mithradates's troops attempting to fight them off were seen to badly misjudge the range, because of the shadows. Taking advantage of this, Pompey launched a full-scale attack, sending his legions against the enemy with the moon behind them. Mithradates's army was routed.

On horseback, the king managed to escape with just eight hundred cavalrymen. First trekking over mountains to Colchis on the Black Sea, in today's Georgia, Mithradates was deserted by all his followers but three. One of these was a young woman, Hypsicratia, the king's mistress, who dressed, rode, and fought like a man. With just these three companions, Mithradates entered the Bosporan Kingdom, today's Crimea, which was then ruled on his behalf by his son Maaspes.

When Maaspes opposed his father's plan to levy a new army locally, Mithradates murdered his own son and ordered mass mobilization in the Bosporan Kingdom. His grandiose plan was for a renewed campaign the following year with this new army, which would see him cross the Dardanelles to Europe and invade Italy behind Pompey's back.

Pompey had meanwhile come to the conclusion that Mithradates was a spent force, and turned aside to deal with Mithradates's ally and relative King Tigranes of Armenia, who was approaching seventy-five years of age but was still full of fight. Pompey invaded Armenia with the support of Tigranes's son, another Tigranes, who had for a time allied with the Parthians, whose king was his father-in-law, against his own father. At the same time, Pompey's general Afranius advanced against the Parthians with part of his vast army, frightening them into retreating back to their homeland, forcing the Armenian prince to ally with Pompey.

As Pompey marched on Artaxata, the Armenian capital, he drew local tribes into alliances. When one local force opposing him camped in a forest, Pompey, taking advantage of the prevailing wind, set fire to the forest. As the enemy fled the flames, they ran onto waiting Roman swords.

King Tigranes sued for peace, and, in the subsequent negotiations in Pompey's camp outside Artaxata, Pompey agreed to allow Tigranes to keep his throne, as long as he became a client-king of Rome and paid Rome millions of sesterces in silver. Pompey offered Tigranes's son regency over the Armenian province of Sophene and an assurance that he would succeed his father on the Armenian throne when the elder Tigranes passed away. But Prince Tigranes, impatient for power, wanted his father's throne then and there. This did not comport with Pompey's plans for Armenia, so he put the volatile prince in chains, to make a handsome addition to the Mithradatic War Triumph that Pompey intended taking on his return to Rome.

In the second half of 64 BC, the threat posed by Mithradates was terminated. Betrayed by his own son Pharnaces, and with the locals refusing to fight against the Romans, he found himself bottled up in the city of Panticapaeum, today's Kersh in the Crimea. Rather than be captured by Pompey and led through the streets of Rome in a Triumph, Mithradates determined to take his own life.

According to one ancient story, Mithradates poisoned his wife and daughters before unsuccessfully trying to poison himself. Another story had the king's two daughters voluntarily taking poison in solidarity with their father, and dying before he did. All sources agree that for years, Mithradates had been taking small doses of various poisons to build immunity against any attempt to poison him by those close to him. So when he now took poison, it failed to kill him. Lamenting his earlier precautions, Mithradates called on the chief of his bodyguard, a Gallic mercenary, to kill him with his sword, and the man obliged.

Pompey hadn't attempted to pursue Mithradates when he fled to the Caucasus. Instead, he used his fleet to blockade the Black Sea, preventing supplies from reaching the Bosporan Kingdom and turning the population against Mithradates. As this was happening, Pompey had left Afranius in the north with part of his army while he himself turned south, to expand Rome's provincial borders. He was camped near the desert city of Petra in today's southern Jordan, discussing an alliance with the king of Petra, when he learned of the death of Mithradates. In his marching camp, his men made a pile of pack saddles, and standing on these Pompey announced to his army that Mithradates was dead. His overjoyed troops proceeded to feast into the night in celebration.

The king's death would allow Pompey to reorganize Pontus to Rome's benefit. Using his Senate-conferred powers, he would unilaterally give the west of the country to Mithradates's son Pharnaces, permitting him to rule the reduced Kingdom of Pontus and the Bosporan Kingdom as

King Pharnaces II, with both states now being clients and allies of Rome. Pompey combined the east of the former kingdom with the neighboring Bithynia to create the new Roman province of Bithynia-Pontus.

On his march south, Pompey restored the royal family of Cappadocia to their throne after its king had three times been removed by Mithradates. Pompey made Cappadocia a Roman protectorate under King Ariobarzanes, who from now on paid Rome tribute and followed her directives. To prevent Pompey from annexing the wealthy city-state of Chalcis, midway between Damascus in Syria and Beirut in today's Lebanon, its ruler Ptolemaeus paid Pompey 24 million sesterces, which Pompey used to pay his legionaries. Chalcis also now became a Roman client and ally.

Pompey's deputies had already occupied Damascus, and he himself spent the winter of 64–63 BC in the western Syrian city of Antioch, close to the Mediterranean, setting in place arrangements to annex all of Syria as a province of Rome, with Antioch as its capital. This was the single largest Roman territorial expansion in the East ever to that time, and in the spring of 63 BC Pompey and his legions swiftly and forcefully added more territory to the new province of Syria by incorporating Coele-Syria and Phoenicia, taking in today's Lebanon.

This large, wealthy new province of Syria, separated from rival power Parthia in the east by the Euphrates, was the jewel in Rome's eastern crown. For centuries to come, it would be Rome's richest, most important province, its governor the highest-paid of all Roman provincial governors. With a number of legions permanently stationed in Syria and thousands of Roman legionaries retiring there, it would also be a major recruiting ground for new legionaries. Many of the legionaries stationed in Britain once it became a Roman province in the first century would be Syrians of Roman descent.

At the commencement of that autumn, too, back in Rome on September 23, Julius Caesar's niece Atia gave birth to a son by her husband the senator Gaius Octavius. Born at "Ox Head," the couple's small city house on the Palatine Hill, the boy took his father's name, Gaius Octavius. Three years later, after his father put down a slave revolt at the Italian town of Thurii, the boy would be given the cognomen of Thurinus, which he would discard once he was an adolescent. The boy, to be called Octavian by much later historians, would become Julius Caesar's favorite, and his heir.

That spring, once Pompey had consolidated Roman control of Syria, he found that, in the Jewish kingdom of Judea on the southern border of his new province, civil war was raging. The previous year he had sent his quaestor Scaurus to try to settle the dispute at the heart of the war, which was between two brothers, Hyrcanus and Aristobulus, members of the Hasmonean dynasty that had ruled Judea for eighty years. In their bid for supreme power, Hyrcanus had the support of the Jewish people, while Aristobulus had the support of the priests of the Sanhedrin, the Jewish faith's ruling body. But Aristobulus had been unhappy with the outcome of Scaurus's visit, with Scaurus favoring Hyrcanus, and wrote to Pompey seeking his intervention.

While Pompey was in Damascus, Syria, he summoned both Aristobulus and Hyrcanus. After they put their cases, Pompey said he would think on the matter of who should rule Judea while he dealt with the troublesome Nabataeans, the Arab peoples whose cities included Petra, and asked the brothers to wait in Damascus. Both agreed to do so, but Aristobulus broke his word and hurried back to Judea. This so annoyed Pompey that he marched into Judea with his legions.

Several times, Aristobulus met with the Roman general on the march, trying to forestall him with promises and protestations. At Pompey's camp at Jericho, Aristobulus promised to hand over a vast sum at Jerusalem. But when Pompey sent troops under Aulus Gabinius to collect the money, Aristobulus's guards would not admit them. Pompey's patience finally gave way, and, arresting Aristobulus, he marched on Jerusalem. When Aristobulus's followers barricaded themselves inside the massive Temple complex, Pompey had his troops surround it and commence building an earthen assault ramp against the wall.

Knowing that the Jews were not permitted by their faith to work on their Sabbath, Pompey waited for a Saturday and then launched his final attack on the Temple complex. His troops easily fought their way inside. Pompey's son-in-law Faustus Sulla, now a twenty-three-year-old military tribune, was the first Roman over the Temple wall. This highly risky act ordinarily earned a Roman soldier a bravery decoration, the Mural Crown, a golden crenellated crown, and Faustus may well have requested permission to lead the assault. Pompey himself became the first person apart from the Jewish High Priest, and the first non-Jew, to enter the Holy of Holies, the inner sanctum of the Temple of Solomon. Like another Roman general, Titus, one hundred and thirty-three years later, when he fought his way into the same Temple, Pompey found the inner sanctum completely empty when he walked in.

Unlike Titus, Pompey did not loot the Temple of its treasures. Respectfully, he left everything as he found it in the Temple, although he did level the city wall, punishing the Jews for resisting him. Installing Hyrcanus as high priest and ethnarch or governor of Judea, and a client of Rome, Pompey would take Aristobulus and his family back to Rome with him, to adorn his Triumph.

Pompey also proceeded to take a number of cities in the region that had been under the control of the Jewish Hasmonean rulers, rebuilding and returning them to the administration of their Greek residents. These cities, never a part of biblical Judea, had been founded long before by Greek settlers and were Greek in character, culture, language, and religion. Pompey took one group of ten of these Greek cities, including Damascus and Philadelphia (today's Amman, capital of Jordan), and put them into what he called the Decapolis, a loose league with shared interests. Apart from Damascus, seven of these cities were east of the Jordan River, two west of it.

These cities all commenced using a new calendar from that time forward. Our 62 BC became Year 1 in what the cities of the Decapolis called the new "Pompeian Era." Pompey also returned several Greek-majority cities along the Mediterranean coast to the administration of their residents, among them Gaza, Jamnia, and Joppa.

Clearly, Pompey thought his quaestor Scaurus a young man of talent, for with just the rank of proquaestor, Scaurus was left in charge by Pompey of the new province of Syria, as Rome's first governor, with two legions at his command, as Pompey himself headed north for Pontus to wrap up his eastern campaigns. At Amisus in Pontus, today's Samsun, Pompey found the embalmed bodies of members of the Pontic royal family awaiting him, sent by Pharnaces. Most prominent among these corpses was that of King Mithradates himself. Feeling, as the Roman historian Cassius Dio was to remark, "that his foe's enmity had been extinguished with his life," and refusing to look at the bodies, Pompey sent the remains to Sinope to be honorably interred in Mithradates's family tomb.[49]

There at Amisus, Pompey continued to redraw the map of Asia Minor, rewarding loyal kings allied to Rome such as Deiotarus of Galatia with additional territories. He also expanded the existing province of Cilicia inland and along the Aegean coast, allocating two legions from his army to the Roman governor of Cilicia as the province's garrison. He founded eight new Roman military colonies across Asia Minor, where legionaries could retire. And he instituted fair and reasonable new laws for the more than eight hundred cities he had brought back under Rome's sway, laws that would still be in force three centuries later. Finally, with the soldiering and administrative work done, come late 62 BC, Pompey sailed for home.

Taking his time heading back to Italy, Pompey lingered at various places en route including Athens, and also Mytilene on Lesbos. He so admired the Greek theater in Mytilene that he vowed then and there to build a theater modeled on it in Rome. In February, 61 BC, after four and a half years' absence, and having victoriously terminated what came to be known as the Third Mithradatic War and dramatically reshaping the

Roman East, Pompey landed back in Italy, at Brindisi. He was accompanied by the majority of his legions—those not being left in the East to garrison Roman territory—which came home sailing in seven hundred ships captured from the Cilician pirates. The troops brought with them booty, trophies, and prisoners from Pompey's eastern campaigns.

Word of Pompey's surprise winter return quickly reached Rome, and panic spread through the ranks of senators who had opposed Pompey's interests while he was away. Marcus Crassus was so terrified by the prospect of Pompey emulating Sulla by marching on Rome with his legions to take sole power that he gathered up his wife and children and fled the city—although some were to say that he had done this only to frighten his colleagues into sharing his dread of what Pompey might do. Another of Pompey's bitter opponents, Catulus, died this year, but there were hundreds of other conservative senators who, like Crassus, dreaded what Pompey might do with such military and financial power.

But then fresh word of Pompey's actions and movements reached the capital. To the astonishment of all, Pompey had paid off the legions that had returned to Italy with him, to the amount of 32 million sesterces, and, after a final assembly and emotional parting address, sent his troops back to their homes. He had gifted the captured ships to Rome. And he had commenced to walk up the Appian Way to Rome, accompanied by just his staff and senior officers, with thousands of ordinary people flooding to greet him and walk with him at each city he passed through along his route. For a man who had previously lacked the common touch, this was a master stroke in public relations, and his political foes would have no answer for it.

XI.

CICERO RULES, CAESAR'S STAR RISES

While the cat was away from Rome, the mice came out to play. With Pompey tied up on his eastern campaigns, a variety of ambitious men made aggressive and sometimes suicidal plays for power. Julius Caesar was among them.

Caesar won election to the post of aedile in 66 BC, the year Pompey terminated the pirate menace, and would serve in the post the following year. According to Suetonius (writing around AD 120 and quoting three earlier Roman authors including Gaius Scribonius Curio, whose relevant works have not come down to us), just days before Caesar was due to take up his aedileship in 65 BC he became embroiled in a plot to overthrow the government with three co-conspirators. One, says Suetonius, was Caesar's friend and creditor Marcus Crassus. The others were said to be Publius Sulla, nephew of Sulla the Dictator and brother-in-law and client of Pompey, and the senator Lucius Autronius.

Sulla and Autronius were elected in the summer of 66 BC to become the consuls for 65 BC; but before they could take up their appointments, they were disqualified on a charge of corruption and replaced as consuls by their chief accusers. So the pair plotted to take the consulship by force. The plotters supposedly planned to attack the Senate House, killing senators indiscriminately, and then install Crassus as Dictator and Caesar as his Master of Horse—traditionally the deputy of a Dictator. Once in power, so the story went, this pair would reinstate Sulla and Autronius as consuls. In due course, Crassus was said to have lost his nerve and failed to appear at the appointed time, after which the coup was called off.

Only Cassius Dio also mentions this coup plot, and the credibility of the story is dented by the gossip-driven Suetonius calling the disqualified consul *Lucius* Autronius—his name was actually Publius Autronius Paetus; Lucius was his son. Suetonius goes on to say that Caesar was also involved in a plot with Gnaeus Piso, a young nobleman appointed governor of one of the Spanish provinces. When Piso raised rebellion in Spain, Caesar was supposed to also do so in Italy with the help of the people of Liguria and Cisalpine Gaul. This plot was said to have ended with the premature death of Piso. No other account supports this tale, and it's unlikely that Caesar, although impatient and audacious by nature, would have been rash enough to become involved in such a plot without substantial military backing. Like many of Suetonius's stories, this one seems fictitious.

We do know that, once Caesar was an aedile, he went all out to impress the public with his munificence, and eclipsed all previous aediles. Not only did he spend government money on public games, stage plays, beast hunts, and religious feasts, as the job required. Determined to create the most magnificent games ever, he personally borrowed heavily and spent his own money on them.

Caesar's fellow aedile for the year, Marcus Bibulus, who co-produced some of these events with Caesar, was to reportedly complain that Caesar shamelessly took full credit for these shared productions. "The Temple of the Heavenly Twins (Castor and Pollux) in the Forum," said Bibulus, "is always simply called 'Castor's.' And I always play Pollux to Caesar's Castor when we give a public entertainment together."[50]

Caesar the aedile went overboard when scheduling a day of gladiatorial contests, which were traditionally a funeral celebration. To give him an excuse to stage his gladiatorial games, Caesar dedicated them to his father, who had died twenty years earlier. Caesar planned to put more gladiators in the arena on a single day than had ever before been seen, but news of this panicked members of the Senate. Fearing that Caesar might use all these armed men in a bid for power, they passed a law limiting the number of gladiators in the arena in a single day. Caesar still put on a show with 320 separate gladiatorial contests.

Again according to Suetonius, while an aedile Caesar attempted to have himself appointed to govern Egypt after King Ptolemy XII was deposed by his own people. When the Senate failed to appoint him, says Suetonius, in revenge Caesar used his aedile's powers to restore monuments to Marius's victories previously destroyed by Sulla. Plutarch confirms that Caesar did indeed restore these Marian monuments, in the Forum—but secretly, at night. When a large crowd of Marian sympathizers gathered outside Caesar's Subura house to praise him for the act, the Senate had all the confirmation it needed that Marius's nephew had been behind the brazen and illegal act.

The next time the House sat, Caesar was hauled over the coals for this, and he formally apologized to the House. On Senate orders, the monuments again came down. As for Ptolemy's overthrow in Egypt, that would not occur for another seven years, when Caesar was campaigning in Gaul, making Suetonius's story about Caesar's attempt to take control of Egypt while an aedile a total impossibility.

In the first half of 63 BC, two years after Caesar served as an aedile, he set his sights on further career advancement when Metellus the Pontifex Maximus died of natural causes. Caesar put himself forward for election to the now-vacant post, even though the role traditionally went to much more senior men.

Caesar's opponents in the election of the Pontifex Maximus were Catulus, the former consul, and none other than the former propraetor Servilius Vatia Isauricus, Caesar's onetime boss in Cilicia. The Pontifex Maximus had little power, but great prestige came with the role, making later election to the consulship more likely. Plus, unlike holders of the post high priest of Jupiter, the Pontifex Maximus had no restrictions placed on him. He could be involved in politics, could simultaneously hold other posts, and could travel.

Catulus, fearing Caesar's broad popularity, sent him a note offering a huge bribe to withdraw from the race. Caesar wrote back that he was prepared to borrow even more than that to win the election. He did just that, borrowing much more than he could afford to repay and then spreading cash around electors and election officials in a massive bribery campaign. It was common practice for all Roman political candidates to hand out bowls of food to voters, with the name of the man they were supposed to vote for inscribed in the bowl and revealed once it was emptied. But Caesar's bribery went far beyond these quasi-legal handouts.

On election day, Caesar's mother Aurelia conducted him out the door of his Subura home in anxious tears. Caesar embraced her, then said, "Mother of mine, today you will see me either High Priest, or an exile."[51]

What he meant was: if his bribery was discovered, he would assuredly be convicted in court, lose all his property, and be sent into exile a pauper. By day's end, Caesar had succeeded in bribing his way to the top. He even heavily outpolled Catulus and Isauricus in their own voting districts, a clear sign that the vote count was rigged. At thirty-seven years of age, somewhat younger than his opponents, Caesar was pronounced the new Pontifex Maximus for life.[52]

The responsibilities of the Pontifex Maximus were not onerous or time-consuming, and a house and servants came with the job. The foundations of this house, the Regia, show that it was not large, and had no outlook. But it was situated on prestigious real estate in the heart of old Rome, on the Sacred Way near the Forum, right next door to the Temple of Vesta and the quarters of the Vestal Virgins. This location was no coincidence, as the Pontifex Maximus was responsible for the safety and propriety of the Vestals. Caesar would move his mother and daughter Julia to his new residence with him, no doubt renting out his house in the Subura to help pay down some of his vast debts.

Caesar's success in this election meant that, just several months later, when the annual election for the praetors for the following year took place, Caesar put his name forward. His popularity ensured that he would again be successful, and he was duly elected. When the praetors-elect drew lots to see which portfolios would be theirs in 62 BC, Caesar drew the post of praetor inquiring into murder by blade or poison.

Within months of Caesar's latest electoral success, another attempted coup rocked Rome, and once again Caesar's name was linked to the plot as a likely co-conspirator. This was the year that Marcus Cicero achieved the heights of his political ambitions by serving as one of the consuls for 63 BC, and to him fell judgment of the accused coup leaders in what came to be known as the Catiline Conspiracy, led by Lucius Sergius Catilina.

Catilina, or Catiline as some later historians called him, was a former praetor from an old patrician family who, as a young man, had served as a junior military officer under Strabo, alongside Pompey and Cicero. Despite having married a niece of Marius, Catilina was a fanatical Sullan supporter. His reputation as an overly ambitious and unscrupulous man had been made during Sulla's proscriptions, when he handed over members of his own family for execution and then bought up their property cheaply.

Catilina had stood for the consulship in the elections of 64 and 63 BC, failing both times. His most recent consular election campaign had been bankrolled by Caesar and Crassus—this collaboration with a man who would be condemned for an attempted coup may have led to Suetonius's confused accusations against Caesar and Crassus, mentioned earlier.

Catilina was bitter at his back-to-back election defeats. He was particularly jealous of Cicero, his colleague in their youth, who had easily won the first consular seat at the most recent election. To add insult to Catilina's injury, the second consul elected after Cicero, Gaius Antonius Hybrida, was an ailing, heavy-drinking man of little consequence, and yet he had beaten Catilina, but only by a few votes. So the disgruntled Catilina began discussing taking power by force with Gaius Manlius, a former centurion in Sulla's legions who was dissatisfied with his rewards for years of military service.

As the conspiracy developed, several senators were brought into the plot, with secret meetings taking place at the house of Marcus Junius Brutus, a relative of Caesar's alleged illegitimate son Brutus. But Marcus Junius Brutus was not one of the conspirators. While he was away from Rome on government business, his wife Sempronia had embraced Catilina's plot—with "masculine daring," according to the writer Sallust (Gaius Sallustius Crispus), who was a teenager at the time. A beautiful, intelligent, and promiscuous woman, Sempronia provided Brutus's city house for Catilina's planning meetings.[53]

By the autumn of 63 BC, the retired centurion Manlius had left Rome and based himself north of the capital in today's Tuscany, where he began recruiting an army from poor farmers and dissatisfied army veterans who, like him, felt they had not been well enough rewarded for their service. In early October, the first word of the emerging plot reached the ears of consul Cicero when Crassus and two other senators visited him at Cicero's then home on the Oppian Hill, bringing a letter accusing Catilina, Manlius, and several senators of conspiring to take power by force. According to Suetonius, the informant behind this letter was a Quintus Curius, who received a cash reward from the Senate for his information. According to Suetonius, too, around this same time Julius Caesar went to Cicero and similarly warned him that Catilina was up to something.

Evidence then emerged that two assassins were going to attack Cicero at his house on the morning of November 7. When the assassins arrived, they found Cicero's front door firmly closed (doors usually remained open in Rome from dawn to dusk). At that moment, Cicero—who, in terror of assassination, had gathered an armed band of young Equite volunteers around him as his bodyguards—was convening an emergency meeting of the Senate in the Temple of Concord at the western end of the Forum.

Before the Senate, Cicero accused Catilina of heading the intended coup, providing details such as plans to kill the consuls and leading senators, and the setting of fires throughout the city. Catilina attempted to speak in his own defense, but was shouted down by fellow senators. Casting insulting comments Cicero's way, Catilina then declared he was exiling himself to Masillia, on the Mediterranean coast of Gaul. Hurriedly, he departed the Senate and the city, consigning his wife to the care of his patron Catulus, consul at the time of Marcus Lepidus's ill-fated attempt to take power by force.

Within days, word reached the Senate that Catilina had indeed gone north, but only as far as Manlius's growing military camp in Tuscany, where he had adopted the garb of a consul and put the ragtag rebel army on a war footing. Some twenty thousand men had gathered to support Catilina's bid for power, most of them mere peasants. Just one in four was armed. The Senate declared Catilina and Manlius enemies of the state and conferred on Cicero and his fellow consul Antonius Hybrida all the necessary powers to defend the city, including the levying of troops. Before November was out, Antonius led a small army from Rome to deal with the rebels, while Cicero directed defensive measures against saboteurs and insurrectionists in the city.

Sallust, who would later become one of Caesar's generals, wrote a contemporary account of Catilina's Conspiracy. He tells us that in Antonius's senatorial army marched a cohort of the Praetorian Guard, under the praetor Marcus Petreius. A native of Picenum and client of Pompey, Petreius had been an army man for three decades, serving first under Strabo and then rising through the ranks from military tribune through legate to praetor, commanding legions in the field. He would have served with Pompey in the pirate campaign, but Pompey had left him behind in Rome when he took up the eastern command against Mithradates and Tigranes, probably so that Petreius could achieve his praetorship and be his patron's eyes and ears at the capital.

At Rome, Cicero learned that Catilina had left two colleagues, Publius Cornelius Lentulus Sura and Gaius Cornelius Cethegus, in charge of coup preparations there. Lentulus was the stepfather of Marcus Antonius, or Mark Antony as Shakespeare was to dub him. Following the death of Antony's father by natural causes, Lentulus had married Antony's mother Julia, a member of the Caesar clan, making Antony a distant relative of Julius Caesar.

As Catalina's conspiracy continued to unravel, it was revealed that Lentulus had approached the Allobroges tribe, a longtime Roman ally in Transalpine Gaul, to participate in the coup, apparently by marching on Italy. It eventuated that the Allobroges' envoys had double-crossed the conspirators, bringing Cicero the letter from Lentulus to the chiefs of the tribe. In that letter, Lentulus had unwisely named the leading conspirators at Rome.

On Cicero's orders, Lentulus, Cethegus, and three others were promptly placed under house arrest, with a large weapons cache uncovered in the house of Cethegus. These men were held at the Rome residences of relatives or friends, with ringleader Lentulus held at the home of his relative Lentulus Spinther, then an aedile and working closely with consul Cicero to counter the conspiracy. Another four accused conspirators managed to evade arrest and escape the city.

On December 4, the day on which a mass escape attempt by the five arrested men was foiled, involving slaves and freedmen of the quintet, a low-ranking informer accused Marcus Crassus of being involved in Catilina's plot. But Cicero refused to believe the man, and had him arrested. The following day, the Senate debated the fates of the five leading conspirators. These men readily confessed to their involvement, and, one after the other, former consuls and praetors rose to condemn the plotters.

But when Julius Caesar's turn came to speak, as Pontifex Maximus and a praetor-elect now, he authoritatively and eloquently advocated a softer line. He questioned the rush to condemn the men, and suggested they be kept under house arrest in Italian towns nominated by consul Cicero until after Catilina had been dealt with, affording them a proper trial—before the praetor who investigated treason.

To many senators, this sounded fair and reasonable. Subsequent speakers including Cicero's impulsive brother Quintus and even some former consuls who spoke a second time came around to Caesar's way of thinking, until the intervention of Catulus and Cato the Younger. Both opposed any delay in condemning the men, saying a signal should be sent to other insurrectionists in the city.

Cato, in a blistering speech, accused Caesar of having an ulterior motive for defending the admitted traitors. Was he in cahoots with them? And would it not be easier for the accused to escape if they were held in rural towns, away from Rome? Cato demanded the immediate execution of the prisoners, before they escaped justice. Fired by Cato's words, the House overwhelmingly voted for the death penalty for all five accused.

Cicero, sitting as president of the Senate, ordered their immediate execution. It took place that same day, out of the public eye at the Tullianum, the small, mostly belowground city prison on the Street of the Banker, immediately below the Capitoline Mount. The normal method of official execution for Roman citizens was decapitation by sword, but garroting instead was reserved for enemies of the state. Plutarch would conjecture that it was Cicero's ordering of the summary execution of Lentulus, Mark Antony's stepfather, that gave birth to the mortal grudge that Antony would bear against Cicero for the rest of his life. As for the conspirators' female accomplice Sempronia, we hear nothing more of her.

Cato's accusation against Caesar was still resonating as Caesar was leaving the Senate session. Incensed by what they saw as Caesar's treasonous behavior, Cicero's young Equite bodyguards drew their swords and advanced on him, apparently with the intent of killing him on the spot. But one senator, Gaius Scribonius Curio (Curio the Elder), a highly respected former consul and general who had celebrated a Triumph, stepped in to save him. Curio's son, Curio the Younger, was then a leader among the Equite youth in Rome; and as the elder Curio threw his cloak over Caesar and ushered him away, with Caesar's few friends linking arms around the pair, the Equites held back and looked to the consul for orders. In response, Cicero shook his head, apparently fearing a violent reaction from Caesar's supporters among the commoners.

Shaken by this close call, Caesar wouldn't show his head in the Senate again until late December. With a large crowd outside, he spoke vehemently in his own defense. Subsequently, Cato, seeing an opportunity to dent Caesar's popularity with the plebs, introduced a new law granting a dole of grain to the poor. Quickly approved, this grain law increased public approval of the Senate and decreased support for Caesar, for a time.

Meanwhile, north of Rome, it had only taken a few days for consul Antonius's army to reach, and camp within, striking distance of the rebel camp of Catilina and Manlius. Antonius stayed put for the moment, awaiting the arrival of his quaestor with additional levies. When news of the execution of Lentulus and the others reached the rebel camp, many of Catilina's recruits fled, leaving a rump of three thousand resolute rebels facing Antonius, as the year came to an end.

At Rome, at dawn on New Year's Day, 62 BC, Julius Caesar, commencing his term as a praetor, appeared before the Popular Assembly and called on now former consul Catulus to appear before him and explain why he was taking so long to complete the Senate commission to restore the Capitol, which had been damaged by fire, and threatening to appoint another man to take on the job. Members of the Senate were at that moment escorting the new consuls for the year to the Temple of Jupiter to conduct sacrifices to inaugurate their consular year. Enraged that Caesar had gone beyond his legal powers as a praetor investigating murder, the Senate rushed as a body down from the Capitoline Mount and demanded a retraction and Caesar's resignation.

Caesar withdrew the proposal and went home. Casting off his praetor's robe, he dramatically declared that he was giving up his post, and giving up politics. When this was conveyed to a vast crowd of supporters that had gathered outside, they came close to rioting. Acting quickly, the new consuls reconfirmed Caesar's appointment as praetor, and in return he agreed to confine his activities to murder investigations. Not that he would please many Sullans in the Senate, because in the coming months Caesar would focus on prosecuting men who had years before brought in the heads of Marians proscribed by Sulla, charging them with the long-ago murders of those proscribed men.

In Tuscany as the year began, Catilina and Manlius learned that the Apennine passes had been sealed by the legions under the command of the Roman governor of Cisalpine Gaul, blocking their escape north. Deciding to do or die, the rebel leaders committed to battle. On or around January 3, 62 BC, their army and the army of Antonius met near Pistoria, today's Pistoia. Antonius, who had received his expected reinforcements, was suffering from a severe case of gout that prevented his ready movement; so, remaining in camp, he handed command of the senatorial army to Marcus Petreius.

As the rebels formed their battle line, Petreius placed his Praetorian Guard cohort, numbering 1,000 men, in the center of his line. The Praetorians were the only full-time professional soldiers at Rome, and the best troops that Petreius had at his disposal. He then gave the order for the charge, personally leading the Praetorians against the rebel center, which soon buckled. As rebels facing Petreius fell back, step by step, fighting all the way, the rebel line on each wing stood firm. But this meant that the wings were soon outflanked. Defiant rebels fell where they stood. Sallust was to say that every single one had frontal wounds, with none turning their backs to flee.

Catilina himself was found, lying out in front of his men on one wing, with dead senatorial soldiers all around him. He was still breathing, but died shortly after, cursing his adversaries. Catilina's revolt had come to a bloody and pointless end. Over the coming centuries, Catilina's name would be the byword among Romans for a foolish, doomed cause.

Some modern historians have dismissed Catilina's rebellion as being of no import—it was just a sideshow, they say. Yet Roman senators were executed, and thousands of rebels died. Had the rebels defeated Antonius in Tuscany, they would have marched on Rome, and possibly, with the help of fifth columnists inside, taken it. Importantly, too, Julius Caesar was officially linked to this plot to overthrow the Republic's elected officials, and within several years some senators would be expressing regret that Cicero's young bodyguards had not dispatched Caesar when they had the chance.

Caesar quickly strove to free himself of association with the conspirators, using his rank as praetor to halt an investigation by a commissioner appointed by Cicero to identify all who had conspired with Catilina. That commissioner had been handed two separately compiled lists of accused conspirators. Caesar was named on both.

One of these conspiratorial lists was provided by Curius, the informant who had written the letter to Crassus describing Catilina's plot. Caesar reminded Cicero that he had been the first to warn him of Catilina's plot, and urged him to move for the confiscation of Curius's bounty—which Cicero apparently did. As for the man who provided the second list, Caesar, sitting as praetor on the Rostra in the Forum, ordered him taken off to prison, then had his assets seized and auctioned off. He then sent Cicero's commissioner to prison, for having the temerity to indict a more senior magistrate—Caesar.

Consequently, the investigation came to nothing. Cicero, no longer a consul, could do nothing to protect his commissioner, and the new consuls for the year merely looked the other way, being content to let the Catilina affair be lost to history as quickly as possible. No one else tempted Caesar's retribution by volunteering his name as a plotter.

For the remainder of that year, Caesar did nothing remarkable or controversial as praetor. But in late December, as his term was coming to an end, he abruptly terminated his marriage to his wife Pompeia, in highly unusual circumstances. It happened like this. In December, the annual festival of the goddess Bona Dea, the goddess of fertility and chastity and mother of Bacchus the god of wine, was held in the Regia, Caesar's official residence as Pontifex Maximus. Another Bona Dea festival was held each May, but this second festival, applicable only to women, took place in the first days of winter.

Supervised by the Vestal Virgins, the secret rites of the ancient festival could only be witnessed by Rome's leading matrons, headed in this instance by Caesar's mother Aurelia and wife Pompeia. Men were banned from the house at the time the festival rites were being celebrated. It turned out that a thirty-one-year-old Equite by the name of Publius Clodius Pulcher was intent on breaking that ban.

His family name was Claudius, not Clodius—in full, he was Publius Claudius Pulcher. And he was a member of the noble Claudian line that would link with the Julians to produce multiple emperors early in the imperial era. Within several years he would change his family name from

Claudius to Clodius for political reasons, and it is as Clodius that history came to know him.

Clodius, the wealthy, spoiled, and hell-raising brother-in-law of the rich general Lucius Lucullus, was madly in love with Caesar's wife. Clodius's cognomen of Pulcher literally meant Pretty Boy. As this was a cognomen shared with his elder brother, both had clearly inherited it from a pretty-faced ancestor. Nonetheless, Clodius was a handsome fellow, and Pompeia had not rejected the young man's advances. Clodius was as eloquent as he was reckless, according to later General Velleius Paterculus, whose grandfather of the same name knew Clodius well. That grandfather was a client of Pompey, serving at one time as Pompey's prefect of engineers.

In a crazy bid to bed Pompeia, Clodius snuck into the Regia during the Bona Dea Festival dressed as a woman. Encountered by Caesar's mother, Clodius pretended to be Pompeia's maid Abra, who had admitted him to the house. Abra had either been paid by Clodius, or did it at the behest of her mistress. Despite Clodius's attempt to impersonate a woman, his deep voice gave him away. In horror, Aurelia raised the alarm. Closing the residence's doors, the women attending the ceremony searched the place for the interloper. Discovering him hiding in Abra the maid's room, they threw him out. Word quickly spread throughout Rome of the outrage, after the upset women had gone home to their husbands telling the story of Clodius's deed.

Caesar promptly divorced Pompeia and sent her back to her family. Clodius, not yet a member of the Senatorial Order, was charged by a Tribune of the Plebs with religious impropriety, and a hearing was quickly convened before the Popular Assembly. Caesar was among those called to give evidence.

"I have nothing with which to charge Clodius," Caesar declared when asked to testify against the accused.

"Then why did you divorce your wife?" asked the prosecutor, the Tribune of the Plebs.

"I wished my wife to be not so much as suspected," Caesar replied. In other words, any wife of Caesar, the Pontifex Maximus, had to be above suspicion.[54]

Commoners were in sympathy with Clodius, and public opinion was strongly for his acquittal. Rather than raise the ire of the ordinary people who elected them, the Popular Assembly's judges found that Clodius was not the man found in the Regia at the time of the Bona Dea Festival.

Within days, Caesar left town and headed for Spain. In that summer's ballot to determine which provinces the praetors would govern once their year in office came to its end, Caesar drew Farther Spain. This suited him admirably, being a province he knew well, having served his quaestorship there. But in order to leave Rome, he had been forced to ask for help.

Caesar's personal debts were enormous, and he had no capacity to repay them. Once he was no longer a praetor, his creditors could ask the praetor for financial crimes to order his arrest to prevent his skipping town and evading repayment, and then seek an order for the auction of his assets to clear his debts. As soon as it was learned that Caesar was preparing to leave town, his most impatient creditors came to his door, clamoring for payment.

Caesar persuaded Marcus Crassus to stand surety for what was owed to his most pressing creditors—close to a staggering 20 million sesterces. Caesar owed even more to less-impatient creditors. How much, we don't know. Crassus put up this financial guarantee for Caesar not through friendship but with a very personal political motive. Crassus knew that Pompey, having famously now wrapped up the Mithradatic War in the East, would be returning to Rome within the next year or so. And he dreaded what Pompey might attempt to do to punish him for his opposition ever since both had been consuls.

Caesar's star was rising, and he would be eligible for the consulship on his return from Spain. As a consul and then an ex-consul, Caesar would wield great power. And being so greatly indebted to Crassus, Caesar would be a man Crassus could manipulate. Or so Crassus believed. Besides,

Caesar's governorship would give him the opportunity to make good money in Spain, enabling him to reduce his debt to Crassus.

To be on the safe side, Caesar broke with convention and hurried from Rome while he still had days left to serve as praetor, giving him immunity from arrest as he hit the road for Spain, via Gaul.

XII.

POMPEY'S TRIUMPHANT RETURN, CAESAR IMPERATOR IN SPAIN

In February, 61 BC, as the winter snows still lay in the mountain passes to the north, Pompey the Great made his return to Rome, walking some 350 miles from Brindisi with a large following. When he was a day out from the capital, thousands of residents flooded out to welcome him and accompany him on the last stretch of the Appian Way to Rome's Servian Wall.

By this stage of his career, as far as the man in the street was concerned, Pompey was indisputably the most famous and popular living Roman. Julius Caesar's fame was growing too, but it was still much inferior to Pompey's. There was also the fact that the men's popularities derived from different sources. In modern terms, Pompey was a decorated war hero turned multi-award-winning movie star, while Caesar was a glib-tongued boxer going for the world-title belt, which still eluded him, while also having eyes on movie stardom in the future.

The third-century Roman historian Cassius Dio would say that, had Pompey chosen, his popularity was so great that he could now have easily taken sole power at Rome and no one could have resisted. But, says Dio, it was to Pompey's lasting credit that he remained loyal to Rome's republican traditions and institutions and ignored the temptation to make himself monarch of Rome.[55]

On arriving on the Field of Mars, Pompey sent a message to the Senate. As tradition required, he petitioned the House for the award of a Triumph for all his victories in the East, including the defeat of the pirates.

After everything that Pompey had accomplished for Rome over these past four years, of all her generals over the centuries, none deserved a Triumph more than he. Apart from conquering multiple enemies of Rome and creating new Roman provinces and vassal states, Pompey brought 480 million sesterces in silver, gold, and other booty home to the Treasury. And the ongoing annual tribute, or taxes, that he levied in these territories would increase the yearly income of the Roman Treasury by a staggering seventy percent, from 200 million to 340 sesterces per annum.

The Senate knew that Pompey deserved his Triumph. In fact, he could have claimed multiple Triumphs, one each for his victories over the Cilician pirates, over Mithradates, and over Tigranes. Then there was his conquest of Jerusalem. But Pompey was not greedy. A single Triumph would suffice for him. But a Triumph he must have. All Rome knew it, especially the hundreds of thousands of commoners now swelling around Pompey outside the city, cheering and applauding him—a force larger, and more vocal, than the army he had recently disbanded, says Plutarch.

You cannot deny a strong man his due, the Roman poet Lucan (Marcus Anneaus Lucanus) was to say when writing of Pompey and Caesar a century later. To deny Pompey his due now would be like putting a spark to a field of tall dry grass. The public would erupt and be unstoppable. So, despite the fact that many critics and jealous rivals of Pompey sat in the Senate, men like Crassus and Lucullus, the House promptly approved Pompey's latest Triumph, the third of his career.[56]

Once the date of the celebration was set for September 29, Pompey's forty-fifth birthday, which would give him seven months to organize a superlative spectacle, Pompey asked the Senate for a favor. This time he met with stiff opposition. By law, Pompey would have to remain outside the pomerium until his Triumph in September. While he himself professed no plans to run for consul in the next elections, he wished to support a client named Piso. So he asked the Senate to put that summer's election date off until October or November, to allow him to campaign for Piso in the city. Marcus Cato spoke vehemently against granting Pompey's wish, perhaps prompted by the fear that Pompey might himself run once it was granted, but certainly because it created a precedent. The Senate, falling in behind Cato, rejected Pompey's request.

Meanwhile, all was not well at home for Pompey. Although he had dismissed out of hand the accusations of adultery against Mucia while campaigning, when he was on his way home and still out of Italy he was confronted with incontrovertible proof of her guilt. While at war, Pompey had been presented with Mithradates's numerous captured concubines, beautiful young women, the daughters of princes and kings. He could easily have taken one or more to his bed. But Pompey was an upright man, and he sent the women home to their families, untouched and untainted.

All Pompey had been looking forward to after years of campaigning abroad was settling down in the country with his wife and children. Shattered, he sent the mother of his children a bill of divorce before he landed in Brindisi. For the rest of his days, Pompey would never speak of Mucia's infidelity, and would never name her lover—assuming that he even knew it. According to rumor, that lover was Julius Caesar.

So, to make Cato an ally by creating a solid family alliance, the now-single Pompey proposed that Cato marry the elder of his daughters to him and engage his younger daughter to Pompey's eldest son, the now-sixteen-year-old Gnaeus. Pompey clearly misjudged the depth of Cato's dislike and of Cato's apparent bitterness for the perceived snub when Pompey terminated the engagement of his daughter Pompeia to Cato's brother. For, while Cato's wife and sister wholeheartedly supported a marital connection with the famous Pompey the Great, and were indignant when Cato ignored their advice, Cato not only dismissed the dual marriage proposition, but he allied more closely with Lucullus in the Senate to oppose anything that Pompey supported.

Lucullus, apart from his longstanding political rivalry with Pompey and his humiliation at seeing Pompey achieve the crushing victories in the East that had eluded him, still held a bitter grudge against Pompey for the way he had gone behind Lucullus's back to marry his daughter Pompeia to Lucullus's ward, the son of Sulla. Lucullus would prove a malleable tool in Cato's hands, for Lucullus's mental health was in decline, as he was slowly claimed by what was called madness at the time but may well have been dementia or Alzheimer's disease. From this point forward, if Pompey had advocated a motion to thank the sun for rising each day, Lucullus and Cato would have opposed it on principle.

Forced to remain outside central Rome for seven months while he awaited his Triumph, and using a small proportion of his new eastern wealth, Pompey now acquired a country estate in the Alban Hills. There was probably already a villa on the site, but, taking up residence there with his daughter and two sons, Pompey immediately embarked on a massive building project.

Work would not be complete for three years, by which time Pompey's villa would stand three stories high, and the grounds would feature a nymphaeum in a cave dedicated to the Nymphs, plus a cryptoportico built into the hillside, as well as formal gardens, fountains, and marble statues. Those statues included two centaurs and a bearded Bacchus, god of wine and vegetation but also god of theater. Pompey installed a marble altar to the classical hero Hercules, the Greek Heracles, with whom the Pompeius family associated, having the altar carved with the twelve labors of Hercules.

Over the coming months, Pompey busied himself supervising the villa's builders and consulting with the host of officials and organizers involved in the staging of his Triumph in the early autumn. Apart from the betrayal by his now-former wife, Pompey, now at the height of his fame and fortune, is likely to have never been so content.

At Cordoba, the capital of Farther Spain, the staff at the governor's palace would have been surprised that their new propraetor, Gaius Julius Caesar, reached them even before the winter of 62–61 BC ended. Provincial governors routinely arrived to take up their posts in the spring, sometimes in the summer. But Caesar, impatient for action, had driven all the way by chariot, making the overland journey in twenty-four days, a record.

Because Farther Spain bordered lands occupied by hostile peoples, in this case the tribes of Lusitania, it was officially classified as an "armed province" and was garrisoned by Roman citizen troops. In 65 BC, the Senate had approved the mass enlistment of 35,000 new citizen soldiers in the two Spanish Provinces, and these men were allocated to legions that had traditionally been stationed in Spain for more than a century—the 5th, 6th, 7th, 8th, and 9th Legions. Some of these men, or their parents, had served under Sertorius when he controlled Spain and created a number of new Roman citizens. Such men took the last name of their benefactor. Typical of these men were the brothers Publius and Marcus Sertorius, legionaries of the 6th Legion at this time, men we know about from their later tombstones.

When Caesar arrived in Cordoba, the legions stationed in his province were the 8th and 9th, the 65 BC enlistments of which had seen no action of note during their time in service. Among the powers granted to Caesar by the Senate for his governorship was the ability, along with the funds, to levy ten new legionary cohorts in his province. He took advantage of this power to immediately raise a new legion of 6,000 local Roman citizens—6,000 men in ten 600-man cohorts being the nominal strength of Republican legions.

Caesar named the new unit the 10th Legion. Like the 8th and 9th, his new 10th Legion took the bull, a popular symbol in Spain, as its emblem. Ultimately, these three Spanish legions would form the nucleus of Caesar's armies for years to come, with the 10th his favorite unit. It would take several months to equip and train the new legion, with the unit's sixty centurions in eleven grades, men promoted from the 8th and 9th, imposing strict discipline on the raw recruits with lashes from their vine sticks. By May of 61 BC, Caesar's army of around 18,000 legionaries plus Gallic auxiliary cavalry was ready for action, and he led it north into Lusitania to go to war with the local tribes. There is no indication that those tribes had raided his province, but this would have been Caesar's excuse for a surprise "reprisal" attack.

At thirty-eight, a typical age for a propraetor, tall, lean, with an active mind that saw him writing prose and verse as he traveled, Caesar when he arrived seemed no better or worse than previous governors. But his thirst for military adventure and desire to emulate Alexander were soon evident, as he led his army from the front, never expecting his troops to go where he would not go himself, a quality that soon engendered the loyalty of his men.

Lying between the Tagus and Douro rivers, the territory of the Lusitani tribe, which gave the region its name, had been conquered and partly settled by the Romans in the second century BC, only to be recovered by the locals by the time of Sertorius. Caesar now invaded Lusitania in a swift campaign that lasted only a few months and required little in the way of strategy as he fought poorly led and poorly equipped native warriors. Driving the locals before them, Caesar's troops laid siege to fortified hill towns of the Lusitani and Gallaeci tribes. Soon storming over walls and sacking towns, they sold every man, woman, and child they took alive to the slave-traders trailing Caesar's army.

The Gallaeci, who lived in the northwest of today's Portugal and give their name to today's Gallaecia region, had a hill fort on the north bank of the Douro, near the mouth of the river and close to the port of Porto Cale established by the Romans in 136 BC. Port Cale gave its name to today's city of Porto, and the entire nation of Portugal. The hill fortress at Port Cale would have been among those stormed by Caesar's troops.

According to Plutarch, Caesar entirely conquered the Lusitani and Gallaeci, leaving their towns smoking ruins, and "subdued" the other ten or so tribes of the region, which would have deserted their homelands to flee to the mountains in the Iberian Peninsula's north. In pursuing those tribes, Caesar and his men marched all the way to the Atlantic coast of northern Spain.[57]

By the time Caesar and his legions returned to Cordoba after suffering minimal casualties and inflicting maximum damage on their opponents, killing at least 10,000 natives, they brought back their thousands of prisoners and booty of every kind—weapons, gold and silver, jewelry, clothing, household wares, stock. Caesar shared the proceeds of the campaign with his delighted troops and the provincial treasury. His troops were so pleased with their general that they hailed him Imperator—no doubt at his suggestion. And as Caesar had planned, his half of the loot would help pay off some of his huge debts back in Rome.

He spent the remainder of his gubernatorial year in Cordoba administering his province with good sense. He would leave Farther Spain to return home the following year with a fair reputation. Everyone knew that he had enriched himself while in the job, but it had not been at the expense of his own subjects.

It was in Cordoba, either during this posting or during his previous time there as a quaestor, that Caesar is first known to have suffered an epileptic fit. While epilepsy can develop late in life, frequently from age fifty-five, it typically begins early in childhood, between the ages of two and twelve. It's therefore likely that Caesar first experienced epilepsy in his childhood or adolescence. This is supported by the fact that when he was captured by the Cilician pirates, one of his few attendants was his personal physician, an unusual companion for a man in his early twenties. Not even Pompey, when his health declined in middle age, traveled with a personal doctor. It is possible that this physician had been attached to Caesar's party by his doting mother, because of a past history of seizures.

For that summer's election campaign for the consuls of 60 BC, Pompey placed his support behind his loyal general and client Lucius Afranius. But because Pompey was prevented by the law governing Triumphs to be in Rome to personally support Afranius, he had his extensive gardens on the Carinae opened up, and every one of the thousands of voters who flooded to see the gardens, and the "beaks" or prows of captured Cilician pirate ships with which the gardens were partly decorated, left with a cash donation from Afranius, provided by Pompey, and the request that they cast their ballot for Afranius. It worked. Afranius was duly elected, along with Metellus Celer.

Traditionalists such as Cato were outraged, declaring that Pompey had purchased the consulship for his lackey. Few listened to Cato's complaints. His fellow senators had come to consider him a sullen and interfering man, while Cato's distrust of Pompey had developed into the appearance of an irrational hatred.

By late September, Pompey's Triumph had been prepared, and recently retired men of his legions arrived outside Rome from their regional homes to join his parade. As tradition required, while they would march in their old unit formations and behind their old standards, they would do so unarmed and wearing simple white civil tunics. As they waited in their encampments, they began rehearsing the bawdy songs they would sing in the parade. So much material was gathered by Pompey for public display that his Triumph would run over two days. Even then, there was enough material for the Triumph to have run for another two days.

On September 29, with public and private business terminated for a public holiday, the population of Rome and thousands more people from outside Rome came dressed in their finest to noisily, excitedly crowd the triumphal route. That route started at the assembly point on the Field of Mars, passed through the now-open Triumphal Gate, wound around the packed Circus Maximus, then through city streets to the Gemonian Stairs at the foot of the Capitoline Mount. More than a million people would line the route, male and female, free and slave, watching, applauding, cheering, gawking in wonder at the parade, and preparing to throw flowers in the triumphant general's path as he passed.

As the parade set off, behind the hundreds of walking members of the Senate, all waving and smiling to their constituents, came displays mounted on horse-carts naming the many nations Pompey had conquered in the East, the enemies of Rome he had vanquished, and the nine hundred cities and thousand strongholds he had conquered or liberated there, as well as the new cities he had founded. There were statues of Mithradates and Tigranes—the statue of Mithradates was over twelve feet tall, made from solid gold, and it was followed by the king's throne and scepter. Hundreds more carts and countless litters carried by slaves participated in the parade, bearing treasures Pompey had captured in the East. They took hours to pass.

Pompey's thousands of happy soldiers marched by, singing their ditties. Then came senior prisoners, and hostages from monarchs Pompey had taken under his wing, all closely guarded. The chained prisoners included the chief Cilician pirates, seven surviving male and female children of Mithradates, and Aristobulus the Jew and his son Alexander, as well as princes, surrendered tribal chiefs, and generals such as Menander, Mithradates's cavalry commander. In all, there were 324 senior prisoners and hostages. Contrary to ancient custom, Pompey had none of them executed as the culmination of the parade. Hostages would have been sent to live with leading Roman families, while prisoners were lodged in the Tullianum prison.

Pompey himself came last of all in the parade, wearing the triumphal regalia of special gold-embroidered tunic with victory palm motif, the triumphant's cloak, and a crown of fresh laurel, symbol of victory, and driving a golden four-horse chariot embedded with precious stones. William Shakespeare, in his *Julius Caesar*, aptly describes the scene at Pompey's Triumphs, saying that the Roman people not only stood in the street, they climbed up onto walls and battlements, to towers and windows, onto roofs and chimney-tops, with their infants in their arms. "And there (they) have sat the live-long day," Shakespeare wrote, "with patient expectation, to see great Pompey pass the streets of Rome." And when the crowd made a universal shout of acclaim, it was so loud, says the Bard, that the very bed and banks of the Tiber shook.

Following the parade, after Pompey had carried out his ceremonial sacrifices at the Temple of Capitoline Jupiter, the public enjoyed an outdoor feast at tables and benches, a feast paid for by Pompey. And once the two days of triumphal parades were over, Pompey was able to concentrate on the building work that had commenced on the Greek theater he had vowed to erect at Rome, which, again, he would pay for entirely from his own purse.

Theaters were banned by law in old Rome. For centuries, the more stodgy leading citizens felt that theaters, or more precisely the material presented on their stages, corrupted the minds of the people, while actors were considered second-class citizens. Pompey disagreed. The benefits of cultural expression were, to him, the right of all Romans. Besides, his popularity and his legacy would be guaranteed by such a grand edifice.

Temporary theaters, built entirely from wood and usually pulled down after their festival use, had in the past been erected outside the city boundary. To circumvent the old law, the site Pompey chose for his permanent theater was on the Field of Mars, outside the pomerium. In addition to vacant land, there were four small temples already on the site, hundreds of years old. One, the only circular temple among them, was dedicated to Fortuna, goddess of fortune. Pompey had his architect incorporate all four into his theater complex.

The Theater of Pompey was, as he had promised, based on that at Mytilene on Lesbos. This was a Greek-style theater, with banks of marble seating in a half-moon facing the stage. While Mytilene's theater could accommodate 15,000 spectators, Pompey's would seat just under 23,000. Unlike most Greek theaters, whose seating was built into hillsides, Pompey's theater was freestanding, with massive exterior walls built on stone-and-concrete foundations and clad in handsome bone-colored marble. Although gladiatorial contests would occasionally be staged here, this was not an amphitheater. The Theater of Pompey was primarily for drama, comedy, mime, music, and public speaking contests.

In addition to the existing temples, Pompey erected a new Temple of Venus high atop the theater's banks of seating, joking that he had actually built a temple which just happened to have a theater attached. Sprawling theater gardens would be filled with fountains and the statues of noted actors. There was a massive covered arcade, off which opened large rooms where Pompey would display paintings, sculpture, and many of the larger trophies from his eastern campaigns, in the manner of a modern museum. Extending off the theater, a large vestibule, to be called the Curia of Pompey, would be used for official meetings. A larger-than-life marble statue of Pompey, painted in lifelike colors, would be the Curia's centerpiece.

The largest building project in Rome at the time, employing thousands of slaves, the Theater of Pompey would be officially dedicated within six years and fully completed within nine. For forty years it would be Rome's only permanent theater, and it would always be the Roman Empire's largest drama theater, becoming the model for new drama theaters throughout the empire. The complex would be open to the public, without charge, a gift to the Roman people from Pompey. It would be said that, despite the huge cost of construction, and the hundreds of millions of sesterces that Pompey donated to the Treasury, he came home from the East so personally enriched that he now outranked Crassus as Rome's richest man.

Pompey declined any new titles from the Senate as a result of his eastern victories, although Caesar and others had passed new titles for him in the Senate before he returned from the East, and new marble busts of Pompey produced at this time for private use boasted the inscription *"Gnaeus Pompeius Magnus Mithridatis Victor,"* or "Gnaeus Pompey the Great, Victor over Mithradates."

He did choose to accept the right to wear his triumphant's laurel crown at public games, the full triumphal regalia at horse races, and his general's scarlet cloak at all other times. These honors had been voted to him by the Senate the previous year, on the motion of Caesar. Again, Caesar had been currying favor with Pompey's huge plebeian fan base, which he wanted to make his own.

Otherwise, Pompey sought no formal personal recognition of his deeds. He reckoned those deeds spoke for themselves, along with the fact that in addition to having previously been the youngest-ever triumphant, he was now the first man in Roman history to have celebrated three Triumphs covering three different continents.

The year ended with an ancient ceremony that celebrated the fact that, unusually, no Roman soldiers anywhere in the Roman world were at that time at war with foreign foes. Rome was at peace. But not for long: Caesar would change that before long.

XIII.

CAESAR, POMPEY & CRASSUS RULE ROME

It was the summer of 60 BC by the time Caesar returned home from his gubernatorial year in Farther Spain. He'd awaited the spring arrival of his successor before heading back to Rome. Wintering in Spain, he had carefully crafted his intended political moves on his return. Plan A involved his petitioning the Senate for a Triumph and running for the following year's consulship. So, on his arrival outside the city, accompanied by a detachment of his troops from Spain, he sent a message to the Senate seeking the award of a Triumph for his Lusitanian successes. He also wrote to senators individually, seeking approval to run a consular campaign *in absentia* while he waited outside the city to take his Triumph.

Marcus Cato, at first thinking he was the only senator who Caesar had approached for help, and prepared to support anyone who was a rival to Pompey, spoke in the Senate in favor of Caesar's application. But then Cato learned that almost the entire Senate had received identical letters from Caesar. In a high dudgeon, Cato decided to draw the matter out, speaking in the Senate for an entire day without pause—a filibuster, in modern parlance.

Caesar, seeing the futility of pursuing his first plan against Cato's vocal and influential opposition, turned to Plan B. To him, while a Triumph would be nice, at this stage in his career it was the consulship he wanted most of all. Just as a modern-day movie actor might, as his career was beginning to take off, go after roles that earned him big money rather than awards so as to give him security for the future, Caesar plumped for the money-maker. Withdrawing his application for a Triumph, he entered

Rome, went home, and put forward his nomination for the consulship of 59 BC.

Once he made his candidacy public, Caesar shocked and surprised friend and foe alike by implementing a masterstroke of political maneuvering: his new plan was to unite the four most influential men in Rome, including himself, into a cabal that controlled its affairs. He began by convincing Crassus, who would bring his wealth to the partnership, that he should put aside his jealousy of Pompey and work with him, not against him, for mutual gain. He then approached Pompey, who would bring his well-placed clients, his extraordinary popularity with the ordinary people, and his money, to the group.

To seal the deal, knowing that Pompey was looking for a new wife and a political marriage, Caesar proposed that he marry Caesar's own daughter, Julia. The girl was only sixteen, but she had grown into a serene and beautiful young woman. Pompey was to fall head over heels in love with her, and although he was in his late forties, she would fall in love with him. Plutarch says of their devotion to each other once they were married: "The love displayed by this young wife for her elderly husband was a matter of general note, to be attributed, it would seem, to his constancy in married life and to his dignity of manner, which in familiar intercourse was tempered with grace and gentleness, and was particularly attractive to women."[58]

There was one small problem to overcome before Pompey and Julia could be married—Julia was already engaged, to Cato's brother Servilius Caepio, no less. To permit her marriage to Pompey, her father Caesar canceled this engagement, promising Caepio that he could again have the hand of Pompey's daughter Pompeia, who was now engaged to Faustus Sulla. Caesar seems not to have consulted Pompey on that, because, with Pompey intent on forging a link with the family of Sulla, Pompeia did indeed marry Faustus. This unfulfilled promise of Caesar's, involving Pompey, would have infuriated Caepio and added even more intensity to Cato's hate of both Caesar and Pompey.

Pompey was above all a pragmatist, and it didn't take him long to embrace the political union proposed by Caesar. Putting aside Caesar's past opposition to him, he saw the advantages of the arrangement in light of the fact that his influential opponents in the Senate currently had the upper hand, with every measure he proposed for consideration by the Senate being opposed on principle by his adversaries.

Lucullus and Cato also combined to ensure that none of Pompey's initiatives in the East—all the new provincial boundaries, alliances, and wise administrative reforms that Pompey had initiated while commanding there—was officially recognized by the Senate. They did this for no reason other than to frustrate and annoy Pompey, even though that recognition was in Rome's interest. Biographer Plutarch was to describe this concerted action by Lucullus and Cato as "an unworthy repulse," of Pompey and of what he had done for Rome.[59]

Hoping to ensure that Lucullus and Cato could not succeed in having Tribunes of the Plebs introduce bills that were against him or his interests, Pompey even courted the support of Clodius Pulcher and his Equite band, who had great influence over the ordinary people and the tribunes. But a partnership with powerful senators such as Caesar and Crassus was much more to his liking, and much more likely to achieve the results he desired. If each member of the group brought his clients and allies to the partnership, opponents such as Cato and Lucullus would be outnumbered and outvoted.

As a fourth member of the team, Caesar proposed Marcus Cicero, who had many admirers in and out of the Senate for his ability with words and high-minded ideals. But those ideals soon trumped political expediency. Although Cicero was a close friend of Pompey, when Caesar met with him Cicero balked at the idea of joining the partnership. Seeing that it had the potential to subvert the very cornerstones of the Republic if used for personal motives, Cicero would have nothing to do with it. Caesar took the rejection personally, and would never fully forgive Cicero.

In the end, three powerful men proved enough to make the plan work. The partnership on which Caesar, Pompey, and Crassus now shook hands had no formal name. Later historians would call it the First Tri-umvirate. This was because, seventeen years later, another group of three powerful men would inaugurate a similar power-sharing agreement, giv-ing it the name of the Board of Three (or Triumvirate) for the Re-Order-ing of the State. Historians would label it the Second Triumvirate, with its three members becoming known as the Triumvirs.

Caesar, Pompey, and Crassus met to agree on a joint agenda and goals. The first tenet of their agreement was that nothing any of them did in word or deed would be detrimental to the other two, or to their clients, while everything they did would be designed to advance the interests of the others. As a first step, Pompey and Crassus would actively support Caesar's bid for the consulship of 59 BC.

In return, once Caesar was consul, Caesar and Crassus would move and support official recognition by the Senate of all of Pompey's initia-tives in the East. They also agreed to throw their weight behind an agrar-ian bill drafted by Pompey. This bill met a promise Pompey had made to his troops as he sent them into retirement, but which the House had re-fused to countenance on his return to Rome. It provided for the creation of military colonies and free allotments of farmland to Pompey's retired soldiers as a reward for their service to Rome: grants of sixty acres per man became the norm.

The trio also agreed that, immediately following Caesar's consular year, he would take the provincial governorship of Cisalpine Gaul, and of Illyria in the Balkans, for five years. This suited Pompey, as it would remove Caesar from under his feet. Of course, none of this deal was made public. Details of the trio's secret agreement would only become clear with the passage of time. But it was soon obvious that the three were col-luding, as Pompey and Crassus very visibly supported Caesar's election campaign that summer.

Cicero was not the only noted friend of Pompey who hated the idea of their three-way alliance. Marcus Terentius Varro, the famous polymath and writer, considered by Petrarch to be one of the three great lights of Rome along with Cicero and Virgil, was a close friend of Pompey, and

Pompey championed his rise to the praetorship. Varro was to ridicule the alliance between Pompey, Caesar, and Crassus, calling it the Three-Headed Monster in a pamphlet about it. Nonetheless, Varro would shortly after this accept an appointment from Caesar as Pompey's nominee, and would subsequently throw his unyielding loyalty behind Pompey.

Caesar easily secured election to consul, winning many more votes than the second consul elected for 59 BC, Marcus Calpurnius Bibulus, a lackluster conservative who shared none of Caesar's popularity or agenda. On the first day of January, 59 BC, Caesar occupied the *curule* chair in the Senate as president of the House. Traditionally, the consuls took turns chairing sittings of the House, a month at a time through their consular year. Immediately, Caesar introduced his first bill. This was innocuous enough, and eminently pragmatic, requiring the recording and publication of parliamentary debates and proceedings of the People's Court.

This innovation probably came out of the fact that Cicero's chief secretary Tiro had invented a form of Latin shorthand. This permitted Cicero to dictate his writings to his secretaries, who recorded them onto wax tablets before transcribing them in longhand with pen and ink onto vellum or papyrus scrolls. These written records from the legislature and courts would become a valuable resource for lawmakers and historians.

This records bill passed without significant opposition, as did Caesar's next bill, reviving an old custom whereby, in the months that a consul was not sitting as president of the Senate, he would be preceded in the street only by a single attendant, not his twelve lictors. Again, there appeared nothing subversive about this, and it passed into law. But then Caesar introduced Pompey's agrarian bill, which proved to be a red rag to the opposition bulls in the Senate, who knew where the bill had originated.

Cato led the opposition to the bill with a filibuster. Caesar, as president of the House, impatiently terminated this by having Cato temporarily led off to prison by one of his lictors. Lucullus also vocally opposed the bill, until Caesar threatened to prosecute him, at which point Lucullus, now of unstable mind, suddenly became afraid and fell to his knees, begging forgiveness. Aggrieved by Caesar's bullying tactics, other conservatives in the House aggressively resisted the legislation in speech after speech, stating that this sort of bill should come from a Tribune of the Plebs, not from a consul, and that they were prepared to oppose Caesar with their swords if necessary.

"I cannot tell you how much it is against my will to be driven to seek support from the people," Caesar unhappily declared in response, coming to his feet. "The House's insulting and harsh conduct leaves me no other course possible than to devote myself henceforth to the people's cause and interest!"[60]

With that, Caesar stormed from the Senate House and strode out to the Comitium, the large, circular public meeting space next to it. Crossing the Comitium to the Rostra, the curved speakers' dais on the southeastern rim of the Comitium, Caesar was joined by Pompey and Crassus, and the trio stood before a massive crowd of commoners that included many of Pompey's retired soldiers, men who had come to Rome to see the agrarian initiatives enacted.

Caesar, with Pompey and Crassus on either side of him, called to the crowd "Do you consent to the bills I have presented?"

"Yes!" roared the crowd.

"Then, will you assist me against those who have threatened to oppose me with their swords?"

"Yes!" the crowd bellowed.

"And I," called Pompey, "will meet their swords with my sword, and my shield as well!"[61]

Again the crowd roared, even more loudly this time. And when the senators opposing Caesar heard of Pompey's declaration, some said it sounded like something a rash boy would utter, while others thought these more like the words of a madman. But Pompey's stance was as calculated as it was shocking. And shocking it was. To put it in modern context, imagine a newly elected president of the United States (Caesar) standing outside the White House with the world's richest man (Crassus) on one side of him and the world's most famous and decorated retired

general (Pompey) on the other, as they jointly railed against an obstruc-
tive Congress, and threatened armed resistance.

The following day, Caesar's fellow consul Bibulus attempted to delay
the passage of this agrarian bill. Going to the crowded Forum escorted
by his dozen lictors, two Tribunes of the Plebs, and Lucullus and Cato,
Bibulus publicly announced that he had overseen sacrifices to determine
the omens for the bill, and those omens were unfavorable. Many former
soldiers of Pompey were in the crowd, and, incensed by these delaying
tactics, they began to riot. In the melee, the two Tribunes of the plebs
were seriously injured, and all twelve of Bibulus's *fasces*, his rods and axes,
were broken. As Bibulus's battered lictors bustled him away, someone in
the crowd emptied a chamber pot filled with human excrement over the
consul's head.

The next day, Bibulus made a formal complaint in the House, accusing Pompey of being behind his rough treatment. But not a single senator dared to move a censure motion against Pompey with his soon-to-be
father-in-law Caesar sitting as president of the House. Bibulus was so
intimidated by his roughing-up that he stayed home for the next eight
months and played no role in government, only issuing occasional an-
nouncements about unfavorable omens, which were ignored. Lucullus,
equally intimidated, withdrew permanently from the Senate, claiming
that he had grown too old to contribute further. Cato, at least, attended
sittings of the House, but he did nothing more than repeatedly predict
the demise of Pompey and of the Roman Republic.

Caesar was now able to see his bills breeze through the House.
Firstly, Pompey's agrarian bill was enacted, allowing for the founding of
military colonies and the creation of a board of twenty commissioners,
whose members included friends and clients of Pompey such as Varro, to
oversee the distribution of land in Italy to veterans. As a result of this act,
20,000 former soldiers were settled in Campania south of Rome, around
the city of Capua, whose rights, as a military colony with its own elected
local senate, taken away during the Second Punic War 152 years earlier,
were restored.

Other veterans were settled around the city of Corfinium in Pompey's home region of Picenum, with a monument erected in Corfinium this same year hailing Pompey as the city's patron. More importantly, led by Caesar, Pompey's accomplishments in the East were officially ratified by the House, as they should have been long before.

Pompey, now satisfied that his legislative agenda had been enacted, withdrew from the public eye and let Caesar run the show. For the remainder of Caesar's consular year, Pompey traveled around the countryside with his young bride Julia, with whom he was besotted, enjoying the delights of country villas, gardens, and married life.

Several other bills introduced by Caesar during his consular year were innovative, and not the least bit as oppressive as critics such as Cato, Lucullus, and Cicero had feared. Yet, contrary to his claim to be all for the common man, apart from Pompey's bill giving land to ex-soldiers, none of the other legislation that Caesar brought forward improved the lot of the common man to any marked degree.

Caesar addressed every petition put to him, including a request for financial relief submitted by the "tax farmers," the Roman state's tax collecting subcontractors; but even then he told these businessmen to be more realistic in their bids when contract renewal came around. He certainly did nothing to decrease the gulf between the poor and the rich, of which Caesar was considered one.

Most of Caesar's legislation was eminently practical, yet little more than window-dressing. For example, Caesar fancied himself a skillful writer, which he would prove to be; and with writing, reading, and the dissemination of information in mind, one of his bills of 59 BC called for the creation of the world's first daily newspaper, the *Acta Diurna*—literally the Daily Acts. Inscribed by teams of literate slaves, these daily news broadsheets were posted on notice boards in the Forum at Rome and sent for display in every major town and city in the empire and also at the legions' winter bases. The *Acta* would come to contain official notices of new laws and decrees; senior appointments; war news; notable birth, death, and marriage notices; news of house fires in Rome; and even the results of the latest chariot races at the Circus Maximus.

Caesar's *Acta Diurna* would survive into the imperial period, only being discontinued in AD 222 when the emperor Constantine the Great created a new capital for the empire at Constantinople. Constantine, who hated Rome and rarely visited it in his lifetime—he was born, raised, and married in Gaul—deliberately closed or disempowered the city's long-standing institutions, including the *Acta Diurna*, to relegate Rome to backwater status.

Another of Caesar's bills of 59 BC involved something as mundane—but of importance to city management—as traffic regulations. Most of Rome's streets were narrow, while in the city's hillside suburbs they were often mere winding alleyways. At best, just a single cart or chariot could pass along them, with no room for passing. The city's streets were clogged from dawn to dusk, often with builders' carts delivering and taking away material from government building projects and private construction such as Crassus's housing redevelopments and Lucullus's gardens. So Caesar brought in a bill banning all wheeled traffic from Rome's streets until the hours of darkness. He excepted a single vehicle from these regulations, the four-wheeled carriage of the Vestal Virgins, for whom he, as Pontifex Maximus, was responsible.

As the new laws came into force, with all the night traffic crawling through the streets and with the accompanying rumbling of wheels, cracks of whips, and yells of animal handlers, the brothels, bars, and cafes of the city remained open late. As a consequence, Rome became confirmed as "the city that never sleeps," a label that would be appropriated by New York City in modern times. As in modern times, too, the nightlife attracted drunken revelers who partied until the sun rose. At the forefront of these revelers was a tall, handsome, curly-headed Equite, Mark Antony. His family claimed descent from Hercules, the Romanized version of legendary Greek hero Heracles, and many who knew him remarked that Antony looked a great deal like the statues and paintings of Hercules that abounded in Rome.

Antony turned twenty-four on January 14, just as Caesar was taking on the Senate and cowering his opponents with the help of Pompey and

Crassus. Antony's grandfather had been executed by Marius for supporting Sulla, while his father died while he was young. In his teens, Antony
had run with the Equite gang of Curio the Younger. In fact, it was rumored that Antony and Curio were homosexual lovers. Antony's family
had little money, so Curio had loaned him the cash for his hedonistic
lifestyle. But when Curio the Elder discovered that Antony owed his son
six million sesterces, he banned young Curio from having any further
contact with Antony.

So, Antony had found a new wealthy friend, joining the Equite street
gang headed by thirty-four-year-old Clodius Pulcher—the very same odi-
ous Clodius who'd been caught dressed as a woman in the house of Antony's cousin Caesar as he strove to bed Caesar's wife Pompeia, and who
now supported Pompey. Clodius was Antony's mentor in all things, including drinking, gambling, and debauchery. During the day, the young
Equites of Clodius's gang, sons of the Roman well-to-do, would make
trouble for conservative senators in the streets. To the horror of Cato,
they were even seen carrying Pompey through the streets in a litter, replacing the slaves who usually carried him around.

Before the latest consular elections in the summer, like Pompey, Caesar also became engaged to be married. His bride-to-be was Calpurnia,
daughter of the undistinguished senator Lucius Calpurnius Piso Caesoninus. Just seventeen years of age, Calpurnia was a plain, humble, and
shy girl, but she certainly must have appreciated the great honor to her
family that marriage to a sitting consul brought with it. She was to be
Caesar's last wife, and although the couple never had children together,
she would prove unbendingly loyal to him, ignoring his numerous affairs.
By this time, Caesar had resumed his childhood romance with Servilia,
mother of Marcus Brutus, and by most accounts she would remain Caesar's loving mistress for much of the rest of his life, until he replaced her
with Cleopatra in his later years.

Caesar's marriage to Calpurnia in the second half of this year would
again be a political union, converting the bride's father Piso from a severe
critic of both Caesar and Pompey into a client and ally. Piso's reward was

the promise that Caesar, Pompey, and Crassus would back him in the consular elections for 58 BC, and would make sure he received the job of governor of the province of Macedonia following his consular year. Piso duly won election, alongside Pompey's client and nominee Aulus Gabinius.

Through Caesar's consular year, Pompey's once great rival Lucullus resorted to even more expensive, exotic, and eccentric dinner parties. Pompey, joking to Crassus, called Lucullus "Xerxes in a toga," referring to the debauched Persian king of the fifth century BC. But Lucullus's mental health was steadily declining, and he was receding further from reality with each passing month. The man feted as one of Rome's greatest generals and one of her richest men would be dead within another two years.[62]

This same year, a campaign was originated by Clodius Pulcher with the objective of destroying Marcus Cicero. Ever since the pair had been engaged in legal battles in Clodius's younger days, Clodius had been Cicero's sworn enemy. Because of Cicero, Clodius had even been forced into exile in the East for a time, where he'd served briefly and disastrously under his brother-in-law Lucius Lucullus. By 59 BC, the wealthy Clodius was living in a house right next door to the mansion of Crassus on the Palatine Hill, the one that none other than his enemy Cicero had recently purchased.

Clodius resolved to have himself elected a Tribune of the Plebs, which would give him power to introduce legislation that was unfavorable to Cicero. But Clodius wasn't a plebeian by birth: he was a patrician from an old noble family. To attract plebeian votes, he paid to have himself adopted by a member of a plebeian family, a man younger than himself, then renounced his patrician status and changed his family name from Claudius to Clodius.

To become legal, this needed to be formally recognized in the Senate, but no member of the House was prepared to bring a motion in favor of Clodius, who, while popular with young Equites, had no friends in the Senate. As a consequence, his application sat gathering dust for months through Caesar's consulship.

Then, one day, Caesar, still unhappy that Cicero had rejected his invitation to partner in power with him, was informed that Cicero had spoken that day from the bench in a court case, lamenting the evils of the times. Caesar took this personally and, even though Clodius had tried to bed his wife in the past in the infamous Bona Dea Festival incident, Caesar surprised one and all by bringing recognition of Clodius's adoption before the House. Doing this just prior to the late afternoon adjournment, he rushed through approval of Clodius's adoption.

Clodius then stood for election as a Tribune of the Plebs for 58 BC, and with his popularity among commoners and the backing of Caesar, Pompey, and Crassus, he was easily elected. When he took up his powerful new post in January, 58 BC, he began well, introducing a popular new grain-dole bill. He then brought in a bill proposing that Rome annex the Mediterranean island of Cyprus, then an independent kingdom and dependency of Egypt, and make it a Roman province. This was approved in March, 58 BC, after which Clodius suggested that Pompey's man Gabinius, the current consul, be given the job of occupying and governing Cyprus the following year.

Because Gabinius didn't support the annexation, Clodius then proposed that Cato the Younger, vociferous opponent of Pompey, be given the job. Apparently seeing the opportunity for profit, Cato accepted. He would proceed to occupy Cyprus the following year, sending his nephew Marcus Brutus, Caesar's illegitimate son, on ahead as his advance man. The king of Cyprus, Ptolemy, brother of King Ptolemy XII of Egypt, would commit suicide rather than become a prisoner of the Romans, making Cato's task of taking Cyprus and emptying its treasury easy. When Cato eventually handed over Cyprus to a new governor and sailed home, it would be with tons of silver, only for half of it to be lost when one of his two ships sank in a storm.

Clodius continued with his legislative program by introducing a bill calling for the punishment of any man who executed a Roman citizen without the benefit of a proper trial. On the face of it, this would create a reasonable and equitable law, and the Senate approved it. But Clodius's intent was now revealed, as he launched a prosecution against Cicero for condemning to death the five admitted conspirators involved in Catilina's revolt, including the stepfather of Clodius's follower Mark Antony.

When Cicero turned to his allies for support, he ran into brick wall after brick wall. Crassus had never been a friend to Cicero, or vice versa, and he would provide no aid. The consul Caesar declined to speak in his favor, as did Caesar's new father-in-law Piso, who had been at the forefront of the move to execute the Catiline conspirators. When Cicero sent representatives to the Carinae house of his old friend Pompey, seeking his help, Pompey had the gates to his property closed and then slipped out a back door.

Later writers such as Plutarch would severely criticize Pompey for turning his back on Cicero, which was indeed a betrayal of a loyal friend. Pompey had two reasons: he was now allied to Clodius; but, more importantly, he was allied to Caesar, who wanted to bring Cicero down. And in return for the implementation of Pompey's agenda, what Caesar wanted, Caesar would receive.

The matter dragged on until, in May, Clodius announced that he intended bringing in a law denying Cicero fire or water within four hundred miles of Rome. The consuls for this year—Piso, Caesar's man, and Gabinius, Pompey's man—refused to intervene on Cicero's behalf. At the time, Caesar was encamped on the Field of Mars with the core elements of the military force he would take to Cisalpine Gaul as he took up his five-year provincial governorship, which, while Caesar had been consul, had been extended by a compliant Senate to also take in Transalpine Gaul.

Caesar's staff in camp with him included several senators who would become his legion commanders, and a dozen or more Equites, sons of clients and allies chosen by Caesar to serve as his military tribunes and prefects. Cicero went to the now-proconsul's camp, and, dropping to his knees in Caesar's pavilion, begged for his help. But Caesar replied that, as he was no longer consul, he was powerless to intervene. This was wholly untrue: in combination with Pompey and Crassus, and with friendly consuls in power, he could easily have constrained Clodius if he, Pompey, and Crassus had wanted to do so.

The same day that Clodius introduced his bill denying Cicero fire and water, Cicero fled Rome for Greece. Arriving at Thessalonica on May 29, he went into self-exile. Clodius, reveling in his victory, proceeded to have all Cicero's assets put up for auction. He himself purchased Cicero's Palatine mansion, then demolished it, building a temple to Liberty where the house, originally built by Crassus, had previously stood. To Clodius's chagrin, such was the popular sympathy for Cicero that not a single bid was received for his two rural villas at Tusculum in the Alban Hills and Formiae on the west coast of Italy.

As Caesar shortly after prepared to depart his camp outside Rome for Cisalpine Gaul, two sitting praetors demanded an inquiry into his consulship the previous year, alleging numerous illegalities. According to Suetonius, and only Suetonius, there was even an accusation current that, while consul, Caesar had put a man up to declaring from the Rostra that he knew of a plan to assassinate Pompey; but, when no one took his claim seriously, Caesar had the man poisoned to terminate the matter before the episode backfired on him completely.

One of the two praetors leading the call for an inquiry into Caesar's consulship was Gaius Memmius, who was connected to Pompey by marriage and had supported Pompey in the past. This connection would have troubled Caesar, although his new son-in-law Pompey would have assured him he had nothing to do with Memmius's action, and that he had no power to stop him. The other praetor was Lucius Domitius Ahenobarbus, son of a former consul, a client of Pompey, and a longstanding opponent of Caesar.

Caesar referred the praetors' demand to the Senate. Over three days, there were wordy speeches about the matter, but no senator had the courage to move for a prosecution to be launched against Caesar, knowing that he was just outside the city with armed troops. Caesar now set off for Gaul. To his great displeasure, a Tribune of the Plebs attempted to arraign him. Without halting, Caesar had an appeal made on his behalf to the entire College of Tribunes, on the basis that he was now absent on business of national importance and could not be delayed. A stay was put on the proceedings, for now. But the tribune was determined to pursue the case, and laid charges of similar offenses against Caesar's quaestor, who couldn't claim the same public-service indemnity.

As for Caesar, once he crossed the Po River into Cisalpine Gaul and assumed his governorship, under Roman law he was untouchable. Only if and when he set foot back in Italy proper could he be arrested on the tribune's charges. Caesar reasoned that a lot could happen in five years, the duration of his governorship, and by the end of his tenure those charges could well have been made to go away.

Meanwhile, Pretty Boy Clodius had turned against Pompey. He had grown to despise the semi-retired way of life that Pompey had adopted with his devoted wife Julia. Few Roman men treated their wives as equals—even Pompey had in the past treated his wives as a means to a political alliance. Fewer men still enjoyed the company of their wives in preference to that of men, or indulged their wives' female whims and desires, as Pompey now did. Even Plutarch, writing a century and a half later, was to describe Pompey's new lifestyle as "effeminate."[63]

With Pompey off the scene, Clodius began to mock him. On his authority as a Tribune of the Plebs, he had Prince Tigranes, the centerpiece of Pompey's last Triumph, released from the filthy depths of the city prison. Cleaning him up and clothing him, Clodius then took the prince with him everywhere he went. To see how far he could push his power, Clodius next launched prosecutions against several of Pompey's friends. This very quickly brought Pompey out of retirement, and he was in the audience when the charges against one of his friends were read publicly from the Rostra.

Clodius was there with his gang—which no longer included Mark Antony, who had fled to Greece, apparently to evade his creditors. Clodius secured an elevated position from which to watch the proceedings, and he began to heckle Pompey, shouting a series of offensive questions to his gang members. "Who is the dissolute general?" he began.

"Pompey!" roared his grinning followers.

"Who is the man who seeks another man?"

"Pompey!"

"Who scratches his head with one finger?"

"Pompey!"[64]

Unaccustomed to such public lampooning, Pompey withdrew to his house and never again entered the Forum while Clodius was tribune. In the Senate, Pompey's enemies chortled over Clodius's ability to so easily humble the famed general. Determined to restore respect and support in the Senate, Pompey took advice from friends. One counseled him to distance himself from Caesar and divorce Caesar's daughter Julia. He might have done the former had it been all he was advised to do, but under no circumstances would he divorce the wife he adored.

A fresh plan was then suggested to him. If he were to have Cicero brought back from exile, had all his property returned to him, and restored him to the Senate, Cicero, who was popular among senators, would become his firm ally and a fearsome adversary of Clodius. Pompey needed very little persuading of the wisdom and justice of this idea. Patiently, as always, and apparently without consulting Caesar or Crassus, Pompey set a secret plan in motion for Cicero's rehabilitation and Clodius's humiliation the following year, once Clodius was out of office.

XIV.

CAESAR BEGINS TO CONQUER GAUL,
POMPEY REHABILITATES CICERO

O n reaching Cisalpine Gaul in the spring of 58 BC, Caesar based
himself at the 140-year-old Roman military colony of Luca, today's
Tuscan town of Lucca, which sat beside the Serchio River on a fertile plain
just to the north of the provincial border, not far from present-day Pisa.
From there, Caesar began assembling an army much larger than the two
legions normally stationed in Cisalpine Gaul. This was partly for his own
protection against anything his enemies in Rome might attempt. But he
was also intent on going to war with Rome's northern neighbors, for glory
and for booty. To help him achieve this, the bills of the previous year giving Caesar his provinces had included the allocation of four legions, at
Senate expense.

Firstly, from Farther Spain, he had summoned the 10th Legion, the
unit he had personally raised three years earlier, ordering it stationed, officially, in Transalpine Gaul. Next, he summoned from Farther Spain the
two other legions he'd commanded there, the 8th and 9th. Plus he sent
orders for the 7th Legion, which was stationed in Nearer Spain, to also
join him in Cisalpine Gaul.

Caesar didn't stop there. He employed a clever piece of sleight of hand
to increase the number of his legions from four to six. To begin with, to
strengthen the now-depleted Roman garrisons in Spain, he appears to
have partially replaced the four Spanish legions now marching to join
him with the two legions normally stationed in Cisalpine Gaul, which
would have swapped stations with the Spaniards that spring, marching

over the Alps and the Pyrenees to effect the change. Caesar then took advantage of an existing law that enabled the governor of Cisalpine Gaul to raise two legions locally at Senate expense, giving him a total of six.

The units transferred by Caesar to Spain from Cisalpine Gaul would have been the 2nd Legion and the 3rd Legion. These were two of the three legions personally raised by a young Pompey in Picenum prior to his joining forces with Sulla at the commencement of Sulla's war, two decades earlier. Their ranks had more recently been filled with new recruits from Cisalpine Gaul, but these legions' roots and loyalties were with Pompey.

That spring, Caesar levied 12,000 recruits from Roman citizens in Cisalpine Gaul, creating his own new 11th Legion and 12th Legion. Although his recruiting officers could legally enlist recruits aged between seventeen and forty-six, these new men were, according to Caesar, in the prime of life. The known birth sign of one of these two legions, Gemini, tells us that Caesar commissioned it between late May and late June. To serve as their centurions, he most likely transferred experienced men from the Spanish legions.

As tough Spanish centurions led their training, Caesar's northern Italian Celtic recruits came to swiftly appreciate that these were *his* legions, and they were *his* legionaries. In the coming years, Caesar was to demonstrate the ability to remember the names of many, if not all, his hundreds of centurions, which would ensure strong personal devotion and loyalty.

By the summer of 58 BC, Caesar would have an army of 36,000 legionaries in six legions, 4,000 Gallic cavalrymen, and several thousand non-citizen Gallic auxiliaries. At more than 40,000 men, this was the largest Roman army to take the field since Pompey's eastern campaigns. As his second in command, Caesar chose Titus Labienus, a nominee of Pompey. A native of Picenum and almost certainly one of Pompey's clients, Labienus, who was a similar age to Caesar, had been a praetor the previous year, when Caesar was consul. Another of Caesar's senior officers was Publius Considius, a mature officer who'd been recommended to him, apparently by Crassus, as a first-rate soldier who'd served under Sulla and then under Crassus himself.[65]

As a favor to Crassus, Caesar had also chosen to take along Crassus's youngest son, Publius Crassus, as one of his officers. In his mid to late twenties, young Crassus was not yet a member of the Senatorial Order, and held the rank of prefect of cavalry. Irrespective of this, Caesar would soon recognize Publius's ability, within a year putting him in command of a legion.

Another of Caesar's young officers was Servius Galba, a relative of Pompey's late foe Catulus, who had died several years before this. Unlike the young Crassus, Galba, who had probably become a client of Caesar after the death of Catulus, had been elevated to the Senatorial Order, but only recently. The following century, Galba's great-grandson, another Servius Galba, would become the sixth emperor of Rome.

One of the military tribunes taken onto his staff by Caesar was his nephew and client Quintus Pedius, son of one of his sisters. Another young client of promise, Lucius Aemilius Paullus, was appointed one of Caesar's cavalry prefects. A quaestor the previous year, he was an avowed opponent of Pompey. His thirty-year-old brother Marcus Aemilius Lepidus, who would also soon join Caesar's staff, would become one of Caesar's most trusted lieutenants.

Yet another young client to join Caesar was Decimus Junius Brutus Albinus. Known as Decimus Brutus, he was a distant cousin of the Brutus believed to have been Caesar's illegitimate son. Caesar was to say he considered Decimus Brutus like a son, and it has been speculated that Caesar had an affair with Decimus's beautiful stepmother, the infamous Catilina co-conspirator Sempronia, via whom Caesar would have had close contact with Decimus when the latter was a boy. By the time Decimus was a teenager, he was running with Clodius's gang of Equites along with his best friends Curio the Younger and Mark Antony. Aged twenty-five now, he was given a cavalry prefect's commission by Caesar.

Of the young senators appointed legates, or legion commanders, by Caesar, one was his client Lucius Aurunculeius Cotta, a relative on his mother's side. Another was Servius Sulpicius Rufus, whose father was a friend of Cicero and supporter of Pompey, suggesting that the young man joined Caesar's staff on the recommendation of Pompey. The third was Quintus Titurius Sabinus; his affiliation is unknown, but he may have been a client of Crassus.

Serving as Caesar's prefect of engineers from the outset of his Gallic campaigns was Lucius Cornelius Balbus, a client and good friend of Pompey. A Spaniard and native of Cadiz in Farther Spain, Balbus had served efficiently under Pompey during the Sertorian War, after which Pompey had extended Roman citizenship to Balbus and his family, including his nephew, another Lucius Cornelius Balbus. In 71 BC, Balbus had come to Rome with Pompey, after which, as Pompey's client, he remained in gainful employment. Caesar had used him in Farther Spain in 61 BC, and now Balbus came to Caesar's staff with recent experience under Caesar and with Pompey's strong endorsement. Caesar, who would employ engineering as a weapon of war more effectively than any other Roman general, was to find Balbus a loyal and reliable addition to his team for years to come.

Suetonius says, in his biography of Caesar, "He now lost no opportunity of picking quarrels, however unfair and dangerous, with allies as well as with hostile and barbarous tribes, and marching against them." Caesar's first quarrel was with the Helvetii, principal tribe of Switzerland— for a time during the Napoleonic era, Switzerland came to be officially known as the Helvetian Republic. Caesar had received intelligence that the Helvetii and four allied Celtic tribes living on the Swiss Plateau had decided to migrate to south-central Gaul, and in late March they had begun to mass above the Rhône River near the town of Geneva, after which they intended coming down from the mountains to invade the southeast of present-day France.

Even while his recruiting officers were still drafting recruits for his two new legions, and with the excuse that he was protecting the Roman province of Transalpine Gaul, Caesar led his 10th Legion in marching quickly up into the mountains and to the Rhône, where his troops destroyed the bridge that crossed the river at Geneva. The 10th then threw up an earth wall sixteen feet high, extending it eighteen miles from Lake

Geneva to the Jura Mountains. This succeeded in holding up the Helvetii and their associates.

According to Caesar, once gathered, the tribes had taken a census of their people, which, in records written in Greek that he later captured from them, showed that more than 380,000 men, women, and children had assembled for the migration. These numbers have been thought by many since then to have been grossly inflated by Caesar. The practicality and likelihood of the Celts lugging around such records have also been questioned. There is no other occasion in ancient European history of Celts conducting such a census, in Greek. The Roman historian Livy would put the number of Helvetii and their allies involved at less than half Caesar's figure, while some modern historians suggest that the total was only between 20,000 and 50,000. Certainly, Caesar was a master propagandist, and his figures can often be doubtful.

Irrespective of their numbers, the Helvetii were intent on migrating. Caesar's prompt action had delayed, but not stopped, the tribes, as Caesar would have guessed. By the summer, they had found and followed an alternative route down into Gaul, using a massive column of thousands of wagons that trundled down into today's Burgundy in eastern France, between the Saône and Loire Rivers.

Gaul, all the way to the Rhine north of Transalpine Gaul, was divided among scores of sovereign Celtic tribes, some loosely allied to Rome but none answerable to her. Romans then called this region "Longhaired Gaul," as the men, as well as the women, wore their hair down to their shoulders.

The area entered by the Helvetii was the home of the Aedui, a tribe with friendly relations with Rome. The Aedui sent messages to Caesar, begging for his help, and this was all the invitation he needed to become involved beyond the borders of his provinces. The delay of the Celtic immigrants at the Rhône had given him time for the basic training of his two new legions; so, combining these with his existing Spanish legions, he set off to deal with the Helvetii in Aedui territory. Catching up with their wagon train, Caesar trailed it for days, often just five or six miles to its rear.

When the Helvetii created a sprawling camp at the base of a hill, Caesar saw an opportunity. Just after midnight, he sent his deputy Labienus with two legions via a circuitous route to climb the hill unseen from the rear, while he himself made a frontal approach with the main force. Sending Considius, Crassus's man, ahead with the cavalry, Caesar followed with his four remaining legions. Just after daybreak, when Caesar was only a mile and a half from the hill, Considius came galloping up in a panic, declaring that he had seen enemy troops occupying the hilltop.

"I recognized their Gallic arms and their helmet crests," Considius gushed.[66]

Caesar's later loyal personal assistant and future author Gaius Pollio was to candidly state that throughout his career, Caesar had a habit of failing to corroborate reports from a single source. Ironically, Caesar would accuse the tribes of Gaul of habitually doing the very same thing. Always fast to react, Caesar took Considius's word for it, and, fearing that Labienus and his men had been thwarted, or defeated, Caesar withdrew his legions to a defensive position on another hill.

Late in the day, Labienus and his legions arrived back, fully intact. It turned out that it was Labienus's men that Considius had seen on the hilltop. Labienus had waited all day for Caesar to arrive; and, when he did not appear, had withdrawn and gone looking for his commander. We never hear of Considius again, and it is likely that Caesar sent the man back to Rome.

After following the Helvetian column for another day, Caesar, running low on grain, turned away and headed for the Aeduian hill-fort capital, Bibracte, in today's Burgundy region in eastern-central France. Within decades, Bibracte would become a Romanized town of 10,000 residents with a forum and a basilica, only to be unaccountably abandoned during the reign of Augustus, with its people relocated sixteen miles away to the new city of Augustodunum, today's Autun.

As Caesar turned toward Bibracte, the Helvetii turned with him and began following the Roman column. Now putting prefect Lucius Aemilius Paullus in charge of his cavalry and sending him to harass and slow the Helvetii, Caesar selected a hill beside the Bibracte road where he placed the two green new legions and auxiliaries on the top, with the baggage. Stationing the four Spanish legions in three lines around the lower slopes, he prepared for battle.

With Aemilius Paullus and his outnumbered cavalry being chased all over the plain by wild Helvetian horsemen, the main Helvetian column arrived below the hill, where they lined up their wagons for their wives and children to watch the ensuing battle. The Helvetii then advanced in a massed phalanx, projecting long spears in front of them. The Spanish legions launched volley after volley of javelins at the Helvetian foot soldiers. Those missiles that didn't lodge in enemy shields bent on hitting the ground—via a design feature introduced by Marius when consul that prevented javelins from being thrown back. As the Helvetii were brought to a standstill, many throwing away shields encumbered with embedded Roman javelins, Caesar ordered the Spanish legions to charge.

The onslaught sent tribesmen reeling in retreat to another hill. As Caesar's legions gave pursuit, still in their regimented three lines, 15,000 warriors of the Boii and Tulungi tribes forming the Celtic rearguard swung into the Roman right flank. This encouraged the Helvetii on the hill to charge Caesar's front. While Caesar's first two lines dealt with the frontal attack, he turned his third line to face the flanking attack.

The fighting on the hill lasted all afternoon, with the Celts refusing to give ground until the survivors were finally driven back to their wagon laager, from where they continued to offer resistance until after dark. Finally, in the early evening, the fighting ended. Caesar estimated that 130,000 Helvetii of all ages and sexes had fled in the darkness. Six thousand escaping Helvetii warriors would be captured and killed in the coming days by local Gallic tribesmen. All the tribes' abandoned worldly goods, including their animals, wagons, and contents, fell into Roman hands. For Caesar's legions, which had only suffered moderate casualties, this battle would prove extremely profitable in terms of booty.

First spending three days to bury the masses of enemy dead, cremate his own dead, and collect booty, Caesar then followed hard on the heels of the remaining Helvetii. The Swiss soon sent envoys suing for a truce, and Caesar instructed them to halt and wait for him. When his marching legions caught up with the enemy, the latter now looking exhausted and defeated, the tribesmen disarmed and fell to their knees in front of the Roman general, begging for mercy.

Ordering the Helvetii to provide hostages to guarantee their future good behavior, Caesar also demanded escaped Roman slaves who had joined Helvetii ranks—among them slaves of prefect Aemilius Paullus, who had earlier escaped from Caesar's camp and joined the tribe, passing on information about Caesar and his army. Subsequently, the Helvetii wearily retraced their steps to the Swiss Plateau, on Caesar's orders repairing Gallic villages and farms they'd pillaged along their way into Gaul.

It was still summer, the height of the Roman army campaigning season, and Caesar didn't rest on his laurels. Reports had been coming in from the Aedui that Suebi Germans under King Ariovistus were advancing toward them. According to Caesar's information, the Suebi fielded 100,000 fighting men every summer. The tribe had been progressively migrating west from their homeland around the Elbe River, and three years earlier, allying with Gallic tribes the Averni and the Sequani, Ariovistus had brought many of his people across the Rhine, forcibly ejecting the Aedui from a third of their traditional lands. He'd settled 120,000 Suebi men, women, and children in this former Aedui territory. Rome hadn't opposed this movement of the Suebi. In fact, the previous year, while Caesar was consul, the Senate had formally recognized Ariovistus as a king of the Germans and an ally of Rome. Now Ariovistus was advancing into the territory of his own allies, the Sequani, to their consternation.

In early September, Caesar advanced toward the Germans, and after three days of forced marches his army occupied the Sequani stronghold of Vesontio, today's French city of Besançon, on a horseshoe bend of the Doubs River. From there, he sent Ariovistus messages demanding that he present himself to explain his latest movements.

As Caesar's troops mixed with the Sequani, they were told of the immense stature and terrifying martial skills of the approaching Suebi, and soon the talk around Roman campfires was all doom and gloom, with many of Caesar's men making and sealing their wills. Seasoned centurions warned Caesar that if he gave the order to go against the Germans, his daunted troops might refuse to budge.

So Caesar let it be known that if his other legions would not march with him, he would go against the Germans with just the 10th Legion, which, he said, would never fail him. This had a double effect. The proud men of the 10th declared they would indeed march wherever Caesar led them. And, with the element of competition thrown into the mix, the other legions, not wishing to be outdone by the 10th, declared they would also go wherever Caesar led. Now, when Caesar ordered his army to march, his men sprang to obey.

On learning that Ariovistus was encamped fifteen miles from the Rhine, Caesar established two camps within three miles of the enemy. Ariovistus, meanwhile, had been incensed by Caesar's summons. After harsh words were exchanged by letter, he agreed to a meeting to discuss terms—on a mound in a field, with both commanders only permitted to be accompanied by mounted troops. These men were to stay back three hundred yards while Caesar and Ariovistus came to the mound, accompanied by just ten men each.

Caesar, probably concerned that the German had corrupted his Gallic cavalry, or hoped to do so, instructed men of the 10th Legion to commandeer steeds from his Gallic troopers and escort him to the meeting—it would only be in the imperial era that each legion included a 120-man legionary cavalry squadron of its own. Men of the 10th joked that Caesar had promoted them to the Equestrian Order, and for decades to come the legion would carry the unofficial nickname of *Equestris*, meaning "mounted." Some 10th Legion veterans would even include the nickname on their tombstones.

The meeting between Caesar and Ariovistus took place in the second week of September, with the two cavalry detachments facing off across the mound. The Germans were unarmored, used smaller horses than the Gauls and Romans, and rode bareback. But their horses were tough and superbly trained: when their riders dismounted in battle to fight on foot, their steeds would stand perfectly still until remounted.

As the two mounted leaders conducted a long dialogue, each strove to persuade the other to withdraw from Gaul. Ariovistus told Caesar that he had received word from friends in the Roman Senate that they would be grateful if he killed Caesar. But he would be Caesar's loyal friend, he said, if given a free hand to do as he wished with the Gauls. Meanwhile, the king's ten mounted bodyguards attempted to provoke the legionaries of Caesar's bodyguard by throwing stones and javelins at them, which the Spaniards dodged. Caesar had to break off temporarily from the meeting to order his men not to respond. In the end, with neither leader prepared to back down, the conference achieved nothing, and each rode back to his own camp.

The following day, Caesar sent two envoys to continue the discussion. When Ariovistus took these envoys prisoner, Caesar knew the time for talking was over. The next day, Ariovistus moved his camp to Caesar's rear, blocking supplies and reinforcements coming to the Romans from Besançon. When Caesar's patrols captured several Germans, they revealed under questioning that their superstitious king believed he would be defeated if he engaged in battle before the full moon later in the month. What Caesar didn't know was that Ariovistus was awaiting reinforcements from beyond the Rhine.

Caesar set out to catch the enemy unprepared, physically and mentally. He came to be called a lucky general by his troops, and this would be one example of his luck—deciding to attack before the arrival of German reinforcements he knew nothing about. On September 14, forming his usual three infantry lines, Caesar ordered his troops forward in battle formation. As the Romans advanced on the enemy camp at a steady walk, the long-haired, bearded Germans, caught unawares, formed up in confusion in their seven clans. Caesar was to say that he faced 120,000 German warriors here, which is more than the number he himself attributed to the tribe each summer. Modern scholars suspect the number was probably around 60,000.

Nonetheless, Caesar's troops were significantly outnumbered, and the Germans were on average several inches taller than their Roman adversaries. Partly clothed with skins, and with their long hair tied up in the characteristic Suebian knot, most were armed with a small shield of wood and hide and a long spear. Forming up in clan phalanxes, the German warriors prepared to face the steadily approaching Romans while their 6,000 cavalrymen organized in the rear.

With Aemilius in temporary disgrace for having allowed his own slaves to defect to the enemy, Caesar placed Marcus Crassus's son Publius in command of his 4,000 cavalry and ordered him to wait while the legions did the initial work. Perceiving that the enemy was weakest on their left, Caesar, on foot, joined the 10th on his own right, with Labienus apparently commanding the Roman left. Caesar then ordered his first two lines to charge. Trumpets sounded, standards dropped, and 24,000 Roman infantrymen went forward at a run.

The Germans also charged, running so quickly that the Romans didn't have time to throw their javelins before the two forces crashed together. The 10th Legion soon had the better of their opponents, wrenching shields from German hands and pushing tribesmen back. But the Roman left was having a harder time. Caesar, on the right, couldn't see this, but young Crassus could, watching from his horse in the rear, and he boldly took it upon himself to order the waiting Roman third line to also charge, bringing up the cavalry in support. The arrival of these Roman reinforcements quickly changed the situation, and before long the entire German army broke up in disarray. Germans, on foot and on horseback, threw away their weapons and fled.

Publius's cavalry chased Germans all the way to the Rhine. Some Germans succeeded in swimming the river, and Ariovistus and his attendants commandeered a few local boats to also make their escape. But the remaining Germans were hunted down and killed, like wild beasts. Germans fleeing east of the Rhine ran into the Suebi reinforcements as they approached the river, and, caught in the wave of panic, those reinforcements also turned and fled. In the abandoned German camp west of the Rhine, the king's terrified pair of wives and his numerous daughters were taken prisoner. Already, Caesar could visualize the women being led in chains before him through the streets of Rome in his first Triumph.

With autumn just days away, Caesar's legions gathered their spoils of war and then pulled back, to build a massive camp not far from Besançon, where Caesar intended that they would spend a full six months of the autumn and winter before he led them on fresh adventures in Gaul the following spring. Leaving Labienus in charge of his six legions, Caesar returned to Cisalpine Gaul with a cavalry escort, intending to spend the autumn sitting in judgment in court cases as he fulfilled his role as chief judge in his three provinces.

———————————

B ack in Rome, the consul Aulus Gabinius had chosen his gubernatorial post for the following year: Syria. With Pompey's backing, the Senate would extend his appointment so that it eventually lasted three years. As Gabinius selected family members, clients, and friends to join his Syrian staff, he included his own son Gabinius Sisenna, and sent messengers to seek out Mark Antony in Greece, inviting him to also join him in Syria. As Gabinius was Pompey's man, it's likely that Pompey suggested that Antony be approached, to prize him from the grips of his patron and mentor Clodius, whose power Pompey was now methodically working toward destroying.

At first, Antony declined Gabinius's job offer. He claimed that he was too busy improving his education and his military skills in Greece just to become the lackey of Gabinius. But Antony, still heavily in debt, indicated that he might be induced to consider a military appointment, which would elevate him above civil law, freeing him from pursuit by debt collectors. Gabinius subsequently offered him a commission as a cavalry prefect, which outranked military tribunes and was the most senior army appointment Gabinius could offer an Equite like Antony. Gabinius also appears to have promised Antony command of all his cavalry in Syria.

Antony agreed, and from Greece he would join Gabinius in Antioch the following spring.

———————————

As winter began in late December, Caesar, in Cisalpine Gaul, was receiving worrying messages from Labienus in Gaul, warning of intelligence reports about the tribes of northernmost Gaul, the Belgae—from whom today's Belgians take their name. According to Labienus's information, the Belgae were preparing to march south the following spring to attack the Romans before the Romans attacked them. Caesar had his own spies among the tribes, who backed the Labienus reports.

Acting swiftly as was his habit, Caesar ordered two new legions levied among the Roman citizens of Cisalpine Gaul. Over the winter of 58–57 BC, 12,000 men of the province soon found themselves summoned from their homes to attend assemblies where they were allocated to Caesar's newly created 13th and 14th Legions. Caesar raised these new units on his own authority and without consulting the Senate, paying the cost of equipping these 12,000 new troops from his own funds, which had been bolstered by booty from the summer's multiple campaigns.

Once the two new legions were equipped and had completed basic training, Caesar would send them over the Alps into southern Gaul to join Labienus, marching there under the command of Caesar's young nephew Quintus Pedius, now promoted to prefect. Caesar, tied up through the winter and early spring conducting the annual assizes in Cisalpine Gaul, would not himself head for Gaul to join his army until the spring, arriving in time for the religious ceremony in late May that launched the Roman military campaigning season.

———————————

In Rome in January 57 BC, Pompey began his move against "Pretty Boy" Clodius, whose annual term in office as a tribune of the plebs had come to an end. To the surprise of most and the pleasure of many, Pompey appeared on the Rostra accompanied by Marcus Cicero's younger brother Quintus. Before a massive crowd of his followers, Pompey announced that he was supporting the overturning of Marcus Cicero's conviction in the Catilina case, and backing Cicero's recall to Rome. The crowd roared its approval.

Over the previous months, Quintus Cicero had obtained his exiled brother's agreement to Pompey's terms, and Quintus had given personal guarantees to Pompey that his brother would remain faithful to that agreement, would back Pompey to the hilt and champion measures put forward by him, and would refrain from opposing Caesar and Crassus. Based on these guarantees, which seem to have been financial, Pompey had then written to Caesar, giving his word that Cicero would be a faithful ally of the triumvirs if allowed to return to Rome. With this assurance, Caesar backed Pompey's plan to rehabilitate Cicero, and wrote to Cicero telling him so, offering him friendship and support.

Methodically, Pompey was laying the groundwork for Cicero's return. The new consuls Spinther and Nepos co-sponsored a motion for the overturning of Cicero's conviction. Spinther, a friend of Cicero and client of Pompey, had managed to persuade Nepos, a bitter opponent of Pompey, to back Cicero's rehabilitation. Whether money changed hands we will never know. For the time being, the Cicero initiative lay on the table; but like a boat launched into a steadily flowing stream, it would quickly gain momentum.

On January 23, primed by Pompey, a new Tribune of the Plebs for 57 BC, Titus Annius Milo, appeared on the Rostra to make an announcement about Cicero. Milo, a man of undistinguished background, would demonstrate a clear affiliation with the Sullan faction, marrying Sulla's daughter Fausta, a significant step up in class for him. In return for doing Pompey's bidding, Milo would see his career fast-tracked to a seat in the Senate, followed by appointment to the praetorship three years after the rehabilitation of Cicero. The following year, he would overconfidently run for consul. Predictably, that move would be opposed by Clodius, but it would also be opposed by Pompey, who must have considered such a run premature. Milo would nonetheless remain a Pompey adherent, and opponent of Caesar, for the rest of his life.

Clodius, aware that a move to rehabilitate Cicero was afoot, employed a band of gladiators to prevent Milo from making his announcement. But Milo was ready for him. As the gladiators appeared in the Forum and began to agitate against him and rough up the crowd, Milo ordered their arrest, and following violent scuffles the gladiators were temporarily hauled off to prison.

Each Tribune of the Plebs was assigned an officer to execute his arrest orders. Likely to have been a centurion from the Praetorian Guard, this officer, accompanied by Praetorian guardsmen, would have carried out these arrests. Milo would subsequently launch a criminal prosecution against Clodius for inciting violence. But, with none of the gladiators implicating Clodius, that would fall through.

With the gladiators removed, Milo announced that he was bringing legislation before the People's Assembly and the Senate proposing that Cicero be exonerated and recalled. When the Senate came to consider the matter, it was unanimous in voting for Milo's measure. Even Clodius's cousin Metellus Nepos, one of the two consuls for that year, who had gone from loyal Pompey adherent to his fierce opponent once Pompey retaliated against Clodius, voted in favor of Cicero's return. In the Assembly, just a single member voted against it: Clodius.

All this took place in the winter, while Caesar was moving around the cities and towns of Cisalpine Gaul conducting court sittings. Suetonius tells us that Caesar would have liked to have personally resolved the matter of the Egyptian throne, and to profit from it. And now he learned of talk at Rome of Pompey being sent to Egypt to restore the dethroned King Ptolemy XII. In early 57 BC, a motion had been put by a Tribune of the Plebs that Pompey be sent as ambassador to Egypt, with just two lictors for protection, to negotiate Ptolemy's return to his throne.

The Egyptian people had overthrown their king in June the previous year, driving him from his own country after a reign of twenty-two years.

Ptolemy was replaced by a pair of rulers, his eldest daughter Berenice IV and Cleopatra VI, the latter being either Berenice's sister, mother, or stepmother. King Ptolemy had fled to the Greek island of Rhodes with a few servants and his eleven-year-old second daughter Cleopatra VII—*the* Cleopatra.

From Rhodes, Ptolemy had written to the Senate asking for Rome's help in regaining his throne. His predecessor as king had actually willed Egypt to Rome in the event he had no surviving heirs, and even though Ptolemy had five children there were many in the Senate who slavered at the prospect of Egypt one day becoming a Roman province.

Pompey was known to be warm to the idea of being sent to Egypt as conciliator, but the House had voted down the tribune's proposal, with one of the consuls for the year, Lentulus Spinther, leading the opposition. Spinther, a Pompey man, gave as his reason for opposing the motion the Senate's unwillingness to put Pompey's life at risk with such a mission. Opponents thought that Spinther was angling for the ambassadorship himself the following year, in the expectation that King Ptolemy would reward him handsomely if he reclaimed his throne for him.

The one thing that continued to cement Caesar and Pompey together at this point was the woman they both loved—Julia, Caesar's daughter and Pompey's wife. But was that enough to assure Caesar that he had Pompey in his pocket, so to speak? Apparently not. According to Plutarch, while Caesar, in Gaul, seemed far distant from Rome and its politics, "in truth he was working craftily by secret practices in the midst of the people, and undermining Pompey in all political matters of most importance."[67]

As for Crassus, he was determined to continue covertly supporting everything Clodius did to oppose and antagonize Pompey. So it was that, as winter gave way to spring, two legs of the triumvirate were actively working to bring down the third. It was a self-destructive course; a three-legged table with only two legs cannot stand. But Caesar hankered for a table with just one strong, central leg—himself. And Crassus was too blinded by his jealousy of Pompey to see it.

It happened that while King Ptolemy was waiting on Rhodes for an answer from Rome, he had a meeting with Cato the Younger, who was there awaiting word from his nephew Marcus Brutus that it was safe to go to Cyprus and take up his governorship. Cato urged Ptolemy to return to Egypt, taking him along as representative of Rome, no doubt expecting to be well rewarded if he was successful in negotiating the return of the king's throne.

On learning that the Senate was vacillating, King Ptolemy was close to taking up Cato's offer and returning with him to Egypt. But members of his party convinced him that he would stand a better chance of success if he went to Rome and asked for the Senate to send him back to Egypt with a Roman army to restore his rule. It's not impossible that the young Cleopatra was among those who pushed for this course, despite her youth. Within a decade she would be displaying a learned interest in literature and science, and would fluently speak as many as four languages (she was the only member of her Greek-speaking royal family to bother to learn Egyptian, the language of their subjects).

So, once the Mediterranean sailing season commenced in the spring of 57 BC, Ptolemy and Cleopatra traveled from Rhodes to Rome. But once in Rome, the deposed king soon began to regret making the trip. He discovered that, for the aid he sought, he would have to apply to the Senate via the *praetor peregrinus*, the magistrate responsible for dispensing justice to foreigners. Worse, Ptolemy was made to stand in line outside the gates to the praetor's house, along with a gaggle of foreigners seeking their own hearings.

Ptolemy was thinking about giving up when Pompey heard of his plight. Pompey immediately housed Ptolemy and Cleopatra, apparently at his Carinae mansion, promising to progress the king's case with the Senate as best he could, when he could. At this point, Pompey was still engineering Cicero's return, after which he expected to be in a better position to secure Senate approval for his proposals.

So, for the time being, the king had no alternative but to wait. Ptolemy and Cleopatra would end up living under Pompey's roof for more than a year, as Pompey endeavored to persuade enough senators to throw Rome's support behind the king's restoration. Pompey's own difficult partner in power, Crassus, would have been among those who opposed anything Pompey proposed; and once Cato the Younger returned to Rome, he would also jealously and influentially oppose support for Ptolemy—who had turned down his earlier offer of help when on Rhodes. Pompey, wary, and ever patient, was having to play his cards with care.

CAESAR SUBDUES GAUL &
AGAIN EMBRACES POMPEY

In the late spring of 57 BC, while Cicero's restoration was fermenting at Rome, at the Besançon legion camp Caesar rejoined Labienus and his army, now eight legions strong, to combat the threat from the Belgae. With his legions following, he moved quickly with cavalry and auxiliary light infantry to the territory of the Remi, Roman allies, who gave their name to their capital, today's city of Rheims in the Champagne region northeast of Paris.

Earlier in the spring, the Belgae had slowly moved into Remi territory, and they now prepared to confront Caesar north of Rheims at the Aisne River. Although Caesar was to report that the Belgae could muster 260,000 men, it is thought that some 85,000 warriors from several Belgic tribes were encountered by his army. Seeing the Belgae disorganized, unprepared, and poorly led, Caesar didn't wait for his legions to arrive. Instead, he immediately went on the offensive, attacking with just his cavalry and auxiliaries. Reeling from this unexpected attack, the Belgae split into their tribal groups and fled for home.

This allowed Caesar's legions to come up and defeat them tribe by tribe. Sometimes Caesar would lay siege to their towns before accepting their surrender. Other times the tribesmen surrendered as soon as he appeared. Bloodlessly, Caesar conquered the Bellovaci, the largest of the Belgic tribes, as well as the Suessiones and the Ambiani.

Caesar's army now invaded the homeland of the Nervii, east of the Scheldt River. Originally from Germany, the Nervii were famously tough. They even banned the sale of wine in their territory, believing it made men soft. Boduognatus, king of the Nervii, convinced his neighbors the Atrebates and the Viromandui to join him in ambushing and looting a Roman army baggage train. Sixty-five thousand tribesmen participated in this plan, which was to take place as Caesar's army came to the Sambre River.

Normally, each of Caesar's legions marched with its own baggage train immediately behind it. Having received reports from his scouts that Belgae were active near the Sambre, Caesar combined all his baggage trains into one, with legions in front in battle order, and the two new legions as a rearguard along with a cavalry wing. This thwarted Boduognatus's plan, but the tribesmen, now gathered in a forest near the river, contrived a new scheme—attack the Romans while they were making camp.

On reaching the Sambre with the leading elements of his first six legions, and seeing Nervian mounted pickets on the far bank, Caesar sent his 3,000 cavalry across to deal with them. At the same time, he ordered his legions to commence building a camp on the slope of a hill on the riverside to protect the long, vulnerable baggage train when it arrived. The Nervian riders lured the Roman cavalry away from the river and into the nearby forest, where the Belgic foot soldiers lay in wait.

When sixty thousand yelling tribesmen rose from hiding, Caesar's surprised Gallic cavalry fled in all directions, leaving the Belgae to run unimpeded to the river. Splashing across in their thousands, the tribesmen attacked the Roman foot soldiers as they dug their camp entrenchments. Caesar galloped to the 10th Legion, which was on the left of his campsite under Labienus's command.

"My soldiers of the 10th," Caesar called from the back of his horse, "live up to your tradition of bravery, keep your nerve, meet the enemy's attack with boldness, and we shall win the day!"[68]

The men of the 10th roared a hurrah, and, as Caesar rode off to energize his other troops, the 10th formed battle lines with the 9th Legion. As the Belgae emerged from the river, Labienus led the two legions in a charge. Their momentum drove the tribesmen back into the water and to the far bank in a disorganized rabble. Labienus and his legions subsequently chased the Belgae all the way back to their vast camp in the forest, which the Romans seized.

On the Roman right wing, King Boduognatus and his Nervii had all but surrounded and cut off the 7th Legion and the less-experienced 12th Legion, with the 12th losing most of its centurions and standard-bearers. When Caesar rode up, he saw that the chief centurion, Baculus, was so badly wounded that he couldn't stand. Dismounting, Caesar grabbed a shield from the nearest man and led the defense. First rallying the 12th, Caesar called to tribunes and centurions of the 7th by name, ordering them to have their men join those of the 12th in forming a defensive square as the enemy surged all around them.

Meanwhile, as Labienus looked back to the Sambre from a hilltop in the forest, he saw that Caesar was in trouble. Keeping the 9th with him to deny the captured camp to the enemy, he ordered the 10th to cross back over the river with all speed to Caesar's aid. At the same time, the rearguard legions, the new 13th and 14th, began to arrive, topping the hill above the beleaguered Roman campsite.

Cavalry accompanying these arriving troops, men of the Treveri, a Germanic tribe living on the Moselle River, panicked on seeing Caesar surrounded. Convinced all was lost, the thousand Treverans turned and galloped away. They didn't stop until they reached their hometown, Trier, where they reported that Caesar was dead and his army wiped out. The fate of the wing's Treveran officers can only be imagined once the facts later became known; in the Roman army, desertion was punishable by death.

As the callow youths of the 13th and 14th watched in fear from the hilltop, the 10th Legion waded, literally, into the Nervian rear. Catching Boduognatus by surprise, the 10th cut down the enemy in droves. Before long, the 8th and 11th Legions, occupying the Roman center, were able to push their assailants back into the river, then swung to Caesar's aid. Fighting from behind mounds of their own dead and refusing to run, the

surrounded Nervii were massacred, and victory was Caesar's. Boduognatus disappeared, never to be heard of again, presumed dead. Caesar
claimed that barely five hundred Nervian fighting men survived the day.

It had been a close call, but Caesar's luck had held, again, with the
outcome of the battle again determined by one of Caesar's subordinate
officers. This time it was Labienus, sending the 10th to Caesar's aid, just
as young Crassus had ordered up the third line against Ariovistus and his
Germans. In the wake of the battle, three surviving Nervian nobles sent
to Caesar seeking peace terms, which Caesar agreed to.

Another Belgic tribe, the Atuatuci, was on its way to join Boduognatus when they heard of the defeat at the Sambre. They quickly turned
around and retreated to their stronghold. Caesar, taking seven of his eight
legions, marched on the Atuatuci, at the same time dispatching young
Publius Crassus with the 7th Legion to prevent tribes on the Atlantic
seaboard from intervening. Proving dependable yet again, Crassus would
force seven Gallic tribes in the west of France into submitting to Rome.

After Caesar lay siege to the Atuatucis' stronghold, the Belgae soon
surrendered. But Caesar had no generous peace terms for them. Sacking
their stronghold, he sold 53,000 of their people into slavery. Roman settlers from the south would take over Atuatuci territory. At last, Caesar's
legions could withdraw for a well-earned rest over the winter before em-
barking on a fresh campaign in the spring of 56 BC.

B ack in Rome, political events had come to a head that summer.
On August 5, Marcus Cicero returned to Italy. Stepping ashore
in Brindisi from a cargo ship from Greece, he was greeted by his loving
daughter Tulia and a large adoring crowd, the public having received advance notice of his return. Once he arrived back in Rome, Cicero again
took his place in the Senate, to the resounding approval of the House.

All of Cicero's properties, at Tusculum and Formiae and on the Palatine Hill, were returned to him, with Clodius receiving no compensation

for the Palatine property, which he had purchased. Because Clodius had built a temple on the Palatine site, he had made it uninhabitable, quite deliberately. So Cicero the expert lawyer and compelling speaker took his case to the College of Pontiffs, convincing its members that the consecration of the site should be rendered invalid. Once that consecration was annulled, Cicero would have the temple torn down. He then rebuilt his house, the former mansion of Crassus, stone by stone, brick by brick. Despite being in the heart of the city, this spacious house, Cicero was to say, was just as quiet and relaxing as his favorite country villas, apparently being surrounded by gardens.

Once Cicero resumed sitting in the Senate, having regained his place as one of Pompey's most intimate friends, he began to repay Pompey for his rehabilitation by proposing a new official appointment for his patron. Since the previous year, Italy had been suffering from a shortage of grain. Rationing to bakers and heads of families had been introduced, with foreigners in the capital banned from receiving supplies. Normally, grain acquisition and distribution was supervised by one of the four elected aediles, but in times of emergency a more senior Prefect of Provisions was elected to eliminate shortages. On Cicero's motion, Pompey was elected to the post of Prefect of Provisions, effective immediately, his appointment to last for a period of five years.

Clodius led opposition to Pompey's appointment, claiming it was a power grab on Pompey's part. Certainly, Pompey's powers as Prefect of Provisions were broad, extending to grain farmers, grain fleets, grain-exporting and -importing ports, port warehouses and land transport of grain from the ports to Rome, government granaries at Rome, and grain markets at Rome and elsewhere.

To stir up discontent, Clodius sent his Equite gang rampaging around the city. And behind Pompey's back Crassus, his own supposed ally, encouraged Clodius to be disruptive, out of jealousy of Pompey's potentially increased power. Pompey even confided to Cicero that he mistrusted Crassus so much that he even suspected the man was plotting his assassination. As a result, Pompey sent to his rural clients in Picenum and instructed them to send him fit young men to serve as his bodyguards.

Pompey's man Milo countered Clodius by creating his own gang of youths and sending it out to combat the Clodians, with street fighting between the two gangs becoming common. But the grain problem had become so acute that there was overwhelming public support for Pompey's appointment. Based on his past performance, it was believed that if anyone could fix the grain problem, he could, and the measure was approved by commoners and senators alike.

In his new role, Pompey went to work immediately, sending agents to Rome's three main grain-growing areas, the province of Africa and the islands of Sicily and Sardinia, to investigate the shortfall in supplies. It turned out there was no shortage of grain at the supply end. Apparently, it was being siphoned off by corrupt traders and officials between the farm gate and the plate.

Always the master organizer, and alert for opportunities to eliminate corruption, Pompey delayed the distribution of the new supplies while he had a census taken at the capital. This was because large numbers of slaves had been given their freedom over the previous twelve months. When a slave owner submitted his order for grain, he listed the number of slaves he had to feed. With the government in possession of the latest figures, slave owners would not be able to cheat by giving outdated figures and then selling excess grain on the black market.

Caesar, meanwhile, sent a colorful dispatch to the Senate, describing his sweeping Gallic campaigns that spring and summer and his raft of victories against the odds. Believing from his dispatch that Caesar had conquered all of Gaul, the Senate voted fifteen days of public thanksgiving, something which, Caesar himself was to proudly point out, had never before been decreed at any time in Roman history. But the Gauls were as yet far from conquered, as several of Caesar's generals were about to find out.

Caesar himself withdrew to his distant province of Illyria on the Adriatic to spend the winter and show himself to his subjects there. As he departed Gaul, Caesar sent Galba with the 12th Legion and part of his cavalry to open up a new route through the Alps from "the Province," as Romans then called Transalpine Gaul. Much later, this route would become known as Great St. Bernard Pass. Galba and his men occupied two villages in the pass's alpine valleys, intending to winter there. But the Celtic residents feared that the Romans intended annexing their territory, and attacked in force from the snowbound hills.

Later, Caesar was to say that Galba told him 30,000 Celts had fallen on his lone legion, another number that may suffer from Caesarian exaggeration. The men of the 12th Legion were surrounded and trapped behind the palisades of their largest camp, and began losing heart after the enemy rained missiles down on them for six hours straight. Chief centurion Baculus and one of the 12th's military tribunes, Volusenus, a young man of plebeian background who would ably serve Caesar for a decade as a tribune and prefect, came to Galba and proposed a plan to surprise the enemy. Galba, notoriously cautious and possessed of no innovative ideas of his own, saw that the only other option was their own annihilation, agreed, and preparations were quickly made.

On the word from Galba, men of the 12th charged unexpectedly out all four camp gates at the same time. Cutting down many, they sent other surprised Celts fleeing. The following day, Galba burned his camp and led the 12th on a retreat from the mountains. Having failed to complete their mission for Caesar, they would spend the remaining winter months encamped safely in friendly Allobroges territory in Transalpine Gaul.

To make this failure more palatable, Galba would claim that he and his men had killed 10,000 of the enemy. Conveniently, this was precisely the number required for qualification for a Triumph. Caesar would not publicly blame Galba for his failure in the Alps, and didn't oppose his promotion to praetor within several years, but the pair would later fall out, initially through a financial disagreement. It would also be strongly rumored that Caesar subsequently had an affair with Galba's wife. This humiliation, along with Suetonius's claim that Galba would be enraged by the fact that Caesar would repeatedly overlook him for the consulship in coming years, would combine to tip Galba into the camp of Caesar's assassins, twelve years after the battle in the Alps.

For the winter of 57–56 BC, another of Caesar's young generals, the capable Crassus, had been sent back to the seacoast by his commander, again leading the 7th Legion. His orders were to winter there to keep the tribes of western France pacified. To achieve this, Crassus had forced all tribes of the region to provide him with hostages—children of the elders.

At Rome, the new consuls for 56 BC were, in theory, supporters of the triumvirs. As a young man down on his luck, Gnaeus Cornelius Lentulus Marcellinus had been taken under Pompey's wing. Marcellinus had no speaking skills, so Pompey had him tutored in rhetoric. Marcellinus had no military experience, so Pompey had made him one of his legion commanders in the East in 67 BC. More recently, Pompey had supported the impoverished Marcellinus's appointment as governor of Syria for a year. Marcellinus, once a skinny man, had enjoyed his time in Antioch, returning to Rome from Syria wealthy and so overweight that he was bursting out of his clothes.

The year's second consul, Lucius Marcius Philippus, had family connections to Caesar. Philippus had become the stepfather of young Octavian following the death of the boy's father in 59 BC, marrying his mother, Atia. Ever since his marriage to Atia, Philippus had shown no interest in Octavian, and the six-year-old boy was now being raised by his grandmother, Caesar's sister Julia.

Despite these connections, Marcellinus was now speaking vehemently in opposition to both Caesar and Pompey, and in favor of Clodius. And Philippus was backing him. Foreseeing a difficult year ahead, Caesar, in Illyricum, made a pragmatic decision. To withstand the assaults of Marcellinus, Philippus, Cato, Clodius, *et al.*, his alliance with Pompey and Crassus would have to again be made solid.

Firstly, Caesar extended an invitation for almost the entire Senate to meet him at Luca in Cisalpine Gaul. Secretly, he invited Crassus to meet him at the Adriatic port of Ravenna, in Cisalpine Gaul, in advance of the arrival of the senators, as he himself traveled from Illyricum to Luca. Once in Luca, Caesar would have another secret meeting, with Pompey.

One of the principal irritants to both Caesar and Crassus was Pompey's friend Cicero. Despite giving his word not to do so, Cicero had reverted to his old ways, speaking against men and measures favored by both Caesar and Crassus—on principle. This made him popular with commoners, which encouraged him to continue. For all Cicero's philosophic wisdom and grand eloquence, he could be naïve, had a short fuse, had a habit of cutting off his nose to spite his face, and bore grudges with an intensity that burned deep. He despised Clodius, but he hated Clodius's backer Crassus even more, and that hatred made him forget his promise to Pompey.

In a court case that spring, in front of Pompey, who was a witness in the case, Cicero attacked the reputation of Publius Vatinius, a former Tribune of the Plebs, a client of Caesar. But when Cicero said nothing about Caesar himself, he was accused of being dazzled by Caesar's military successes in Gaul. Against this suggestion that he had reined in his opposition to Caesar, which he indeed had done as part of his deal with Pompey, Cicero could not help himself, speaking disparagingly of Caesar as he strove to show his independence. Then, on April 5, Cicero tabled a motion in the Senate regarding distribution of land in Campania, a proposal that was diametrically opposed to the interests of all three triumvirs. The consuls undertook to bring the matter to a vote on May 15.

When Cicero tabled his proposal, Pompey was in the process of leaving town, initially to secretly meet with Caesar at Luca. From Luca he would travel to Sardinia, and then to Sicily and Africa, in his capacity as Prefect of Provisions. He intended personally superintending the shipment of tons of grain that his agents had caused to be delivered into portside grain warehouses. As Pompey left Rome, he said nothing to Cicero, who was blissfully unaware for the moment that his patron was boiling with indignation and anger over his recent speeches, which were in contradiction of the terms of the deal responsible for his rehabilitation.

Crassus, in their secret meeting at Ravenna, would have informed Caesar that he would only play ball if Cicero could be reined in, which Caesar undertook to bring about. With that proviso, Crassus and Caesar agreed in detail what they wanted out of a renewed alliance with Pompey. Once Caesar arrived in Luca, he was joined by Pompey, who made it clear that he was livid with Cicero. The pair apparently agreed to give Cicero one more chance, which fact both would communicate to Cicero in no uncertain terms. Caesar shared with Pompey the terms that he and Crassus had agreed on at Ravenna for a renewed three-way alliance; and with Pompey adding his requirements to the mix, the pair ironed out the agreement for the five-year extension of the alliance between the triumvirs, shaking hands on it.

As a first step, it was agreed that Pompey and Crassus would stand for election that summer as consuls for 55 BC. Then, once they were in the job the following year, they would shepherd gubernatorial appointments for them all through the Senate. Crassus, who was known to be jealous of the military glory attained by both his colleagues, sought and was promised the governorship of Syria for five years, with four legions to add to the current garrison—enough troops for him to invade and pillage Parthia, a project suggested to him by Caesar.

As for Caesar, under the Luca deal his government of Cisalpine and Transalpine Gaul and Illyricum would be extended for another five years, taking his appointment to 49 BC. Because, by law, a former consul could not again sit as consul for another ten years, this neatly fitted his future plans. Knowing that enemies at Rome such as Cato would pursue the old charges against him once he was a private citizen and back in Rome, Caesar intended running for, and winning, the consulship of 48 BC.

The trio agreed that Pompey's share of the pie would be appointment as governor of Africa and both Spanish provinces, also for five years, with the power to also add four additional legions to his command. Because he could not be in three places at once, Pompey would be permitted to appoint deputies to act on his behalf in his provinces. All three members of the alliance promised to each keep themselves and their supporters in line going forward, starting with Cicero.

Following the meeting with Caesar, Pompey sailed for Sardinia from an east coast port. Days later, two hundred senators—half the Senate—flooded up from Rome and over the provincial border to Luca. So many proconsuls and praetors were present that one hundred and twenty lictors were seen outside Caesar's door toting the fasces of their masters. All senators were sent away with promises and gifts of money from Caesar. None was yet aware that Caesar, Pompey, and Crassus had restored, strengthened, and extended their triple alliance.

Meanwhile, Pompey had arrived on Sardinia, to find Cicero's brother Quintus also on the island. Taking Quintus aside, Pompey said, "Unless you remonstrate seriously with your brother, you must pay up what you guaranteed me on his behalf."[69]

Pompey went on to explain that he had reinstated Cicero with Caesar's full consent, and if Cicero could not support Caesar's cause and claims, he must at the very least cease to attack them. Shaken by this meeting, which intimated his financial ruin, Quintus Cicero hurried to Rome. When he saw his elder brother and passed on what Pompey had said, Marcus Cicero realized that he had erred, badly, and must show his gratitude to those who had helped him regain his position—Pompey and Caesar—and keep faith with Quintus's pledge to Pompey. In Cicero's own words, he pulled himself together.[70]

By the time another of Pompey's clients, Lucius Vibullius Rufus, arrived at Cicero's door with a direct instruction from Pompey to do nothing more in the Campanian matter until Pompey's return to Rome, Cicero was backtracking, fast—for he had received a letter from Caesar. While Cicero did not reveal the letter's precise contents, we know that Caesar used the carrot-and-stick approach. On the plus side, Cicero's brother Quintus would be given a generalship with Caesar's army in Gaul the following year. On the minus side, it's clear that Caesar informed Cicero that those who had remade the latter's life and career could destroy them just as quickly—and permanently this time. Cicero not only dropped the Campanian land matter, but on Caesar's explicit instruction he gave a speech lauding Vatinius, the former Tribune of the Plebs he had previously lambasted.

Weeks later, Pompey was in an African port, probably Utica, preparing to return home to Italy with a vast fleet of loaded grain ships. Just as he prepared to sail, a storm blew up, and the ships' captains refused to up anchor. Pompey, going aboard one of the ships, ordered the anchor raised. He reminded the captain that the people of Rome were starving, and they were his first concern.

"There is a necessity to sail, but no necessity to live!" he added, in a loud voice so that neighboring captains would hear.[71]

Shamed into setting sail, the captains of every ship raised their anchor, and the fleet got under way. Bypassing the storm, the fleet had an uneventful journey to Puteoli on Italy's west coast, the main grain-receiving port for Rome. There, the cargo was unloaded and distributed under Pompey's watchful eye. The census having been completed over the winter, grain was again in such supply at Rome that the populace had their fill and foreigners were once more permitted to acquire it. Plutarch writes that the grain was now disbursed like water from a spring, into all quarters in Rome and beyond. As a result, Pompey's popularity among commoners grew to new heights.

When Pompey and Crassus both returned to Rome, they said nothing to their supporters about what had been agreed on with Caesar at what has become known as the Luca Conference. But, seeing the pair on friendly terms once again, and with Pompey being more frequently seen in public in Rome than in the past, some of their opponents began to suspect that something was in the works. The more astute began to suspect that Pompey and Crassus were planning a run for the consulship. In the Senate, the consul Marcellinus and Pompey client Domitius Ahenobarbus wondered aloud whether the pair intended running in the next consular elections.

"Perhaps I will run, perhaps I won't," Pompey responded to one questioner in the street. When pressed on whether he would again seek the votes of the people, he added, cryptically, "I would ask it of the honest citizens, but not of the dishonest."

Crassus was more circumspect with his answer. "I will do what is judged most agreeable to the interest of the commonwealth."[72]

When the verbal attacks on Pompey in the Senate by consul Marcellinus became more vicious, Pompey unleashed a public response to his former client that was uncharacteristically barbed. "Marcellinus is certainly the most unfair of men," he said, "to show me no gratitude for having made an orator out of a mute, and converted him from a hungry starveling into a man so well fed that he cannot contain himself."[73]

Marcellinus and Philippus now pulled back their criticism of Pompey, and in May they pushed through a new measure that permitted Caesar to appoint ten generals to his army that year, and authorized the Treasury at Rome to take responsibility for the funding of the four legions that Caesar had previously raised on his own authority. This would save Caesar millions of sesterces a year. Some would have wondered whether the pair had been bribed by Caesar.

In western Gaul, with the arrival of the spring of 56 BC, Publius Crassus sent officers from his camp to acquire grain for his army from the surrounding tribes. When two Roman envoys of Equite rank arrived at the coastal capital of the largest tribe of the region, the Veneti, a seafaring people who traded with Britain, the Veneti made prisoners of them. The Veneti then sent messengers to seven neighboring tribes, to persuade them to likewise capture the Roman envoys sent to them by Crassus, and to combine to aggressively resist the Romans. As the Veneti prepared for war, they sent to Britain seeking reinforcements from allied British tribes.

When Crassus forwarded urgent reports to Caesar of the capture of his officers and the aggressive attitude of the Veneti and their neighbors, Caesar determined that come the spring, he would have to attack them. But, knowing that the Veneti would avoid land battles and rely on their ships, he set his sights on a naval campaign. First of all, he sent instructions to the Gallic tribes in the recently conquered areas to send ships to Crassus at the Loire River, instructing Crassus to build a fleet of additional warships on the banks of the Loire.

Caesar also sent orders to the Mediterranean coast of Transalpine Gaul for local officials to secure freedmen with maritime experience to serve as paid rowers and sailors on the new fleet. Planning to join Crassus in the spring for the operation, he appointed his favorite, Decimus Brutus, to the position Prefect of the Fleet, and sent him to take charge of shipbuilding and crew training.

In the spring, Caesar returned to Gaul. Sending Labienus into Treveri territory with most of his cavalry, to keep watch on the Belgae and prevent Germans from crossing the Rhine to join the Veneti and their confederates, Caesar sent two infantry forces under Crassus and Sabinus to suppress the Veneti's neighbors. He himself led four legions to join Brutus for the naval operation against the Veneti.

Finding his fleet not yet ready, Caesar impatiently launched attacks on Venetian coastal strongholds. But although he overran several of these, the Veneti always escaped by sea. This way, the tribe was able to avoid major battles for most of the summer. But then, one morning in late summer, Caesar's warships finally reached him, enabling him to take the war to the water.

The navies of the two sides were very different. Gallic ships were squat and heavy. Made from oak, they possessed flat bottoms and high sides, prows, and sterns; were powered by leather sails; and used anchors on sturdy iron chains. Roman anchors were attached to ropes. Most of the Roman ships were Liburnians, long, low, and sleek, with V-shaped hulls, powered by two canvas sails and a single bank of oars on each side. With their flat-bottomed boats, the Veneti were able to operate in much shallower waters and to weather storms at sea better than the Romans, but the Roman craft were faster and more agile.

When the Roman fleet appeared, two hundred and twenty Gallic ships came out of harbor and drew up facing it, as, on shore, Caesar and his legions lined up along the sea cliffs to witness the battle. Hostilities began at 10:00 AM, with Roman rowers propelling their ships toward the enemy sailing ships. At first, the Roman fleet was without a plan. Caesar was to write: "Neither its commander Brutus nor the military tribunes or centurions in charge of the individual ships could decide what to do or what tactics to adopt." When Roman ships tried ramming their opponents, they bounced off thick oak hulls. Even with wooden battle towers erected from which Roman soldiers launched javelins, the Gallic ships had the height advantage.[74]

But the Romans alone were equipped with grappling hooks attached to ropes, and, almost by accident, these were to prove the Romans' secret weapon. In the melee of congested ships, some Roman crews threw these grappling hooks to secure and destroy Gallic rigging and yards, hauling them away. Others used the grappling hooks to drag the Gallic ships alongside. Before long, two to three Roman ships were alongside lone Venetian ships, and Roman troops were clambering up the high sides. "After that," Caesar writes, "it was a soldier's battle, in which the Romans easily proved superior."[75]

Once several Gallic ships were captured, the remainder broke off and attempted to sail away, only for the wind to drop, becalming them and making them easy prey for Roman boarding parties as their ships rowed onto the scene. In a battle that lasted until sunset, those Gallic craft not captured in this manner ran themselves aground. In a single day, the Venetian fleet was destroyed.

The Veneti tribe, and all their allied coastal tribal neighbors that had conspired with them, surrendered. Because, by making prisoners of Crassus's envoys, they had violated the ancient international convention that gave immunity to ambassadors, Caesar had all members of the governing council of each tribe executed, and sold all their people into slavery.

Meanwhile, Caesar's subordinate Sabinus had arrived with the 12,000 men of two legions in the territory of the Venelli tribe in the northwest of modern Normandy. There, using a man who pretended to be a deserter, he lured the tribe into attacking his hilltop camp. Sabinus's troops killed or captured almost every attacker, after which all tribesmen in the region capitulated.

But farther south, in Aquitania, Publius Crassus had struck trouble. Advancing with 7,000 men from the complete 7th Legion and two cohorts from another of Caesar's legions, probably one of the newer, less-experienced ones, Crassus had been attacked on the march by the Sotiates tribe. After repulsing the attack, Crassus besieged the Sociates' stronghold at the confluence of the Gueyze and Gelise Rivers in southwest Aquitania. Expert copper miners, the Sotiates attempted to tunnel their way under his lines, but were caught. The disillusioned Sotiates surrendered.

Crassus next marched south, into the territory of the Vocates and Tarusates, which bordered northern Spain. These tribes had already sent for help from the Aquitani to their north and the Cantabri tribe of northern coastal Spain—Spaniards who had soldiered for Sertorius two decades earlier in his losing war against Pompey and Metellus. As an estimated 50,000 enemies assembled in a large fortified camp, Crassus, whose force was well outnumbered, called a council of war with his officers. All voted to attack the enemy camp without delay.

So Crassus sent the 7th Legion against the camp. As the assault raged, his cavalry scouts revealed that enemy defenses in the camp's rear were weak. Crassus sent his two reserve cohorts around the back, via a circuitous route, and, storming into the camp from the rear, these cohorts combined with the 7th Legion's frontal assault to overwhelm the defenders. Tribesmen fled over the camp walls and ran for their lives, chased across the plain by Roman cavalry.

Publius Crassus was to estimate that only one in four of the enemy fighters lived to see another day. As news of his victory spread, eleven Aquitanian tribes surrendered to Crassus, with only a few distant tribes holding back and hoping that winter would arrive to save them before the Romans arrived.

In the East, events were conspiring to obstruct the path back to the Egyptian throne for Ptolemy XII, Pompey's houseguest at Rome of the past year. For one thing, with Senate approval, Aulus Gabinius was preparing to launch a Roman invasion of Parthia the following year.

Gabinius's troops had already seen action in the Middle East, when, led by his cavalry prefect Mark Antony, his forces put down a 57 BC uprising in Judea led by Aristobulus, younger brother of Hyrcanus, the High Priest at Jerusalem installed by Pompey. Following Pompey's 61 BC Triumph, Aristobulus and his son Alexander had been imprisoned at Rome, but they later escaped back to Judea. This was quite possibly achieved with the aid of Clodius, who, we know, impudently freed another Pompeian prisoner, the Armenian prince Tigranes.

At the Judean fortress of Machaerus, Antony was the first to scale the rebel works. Then, in a pitched battle against a much larger force, Antony routed the opposition, killing most of the rebels and capturing Aristobulus and Alexander. Aristobulus was again sent to Rome in chains.

Hearing of Gabinius's plans to invade Parthia, Auchelaus, eldest son of Mithradates the Great's late general of the same name, came to Antioch offering his services. Seven years earlier, Pompey had installed him as High Priest of Comana in Cappadocia, but Auchelaus wanted more. Seeking Senate approval to give Auchelaus a role in his planned Parthian campaign, Gabinius had written to Rome, only to become suspicious when he learned that Auchelaus was in contact with the current Egyptian leadership, which was opposed to Rome. As Gabinius awaited an answer from Rome, he had Auchelaus reside with Antony in Antioch, under house arrest. Both were smart, athletic young men who enjoyed the good life, and the pair quickly became friends.

The response from Rome in the summer of 56 BC was disappointing for Auchelaus—the Senate would not approve of his accompanying Gabinius on campaign. But Auchelaus had a plan B. With Antony vouching for him, he was able to persuade Gabinius to release him. But once free, instead of heading home to Cappadocia, Auchelaus went south, to Egypt. Word soon reached Rome that Auchelaus was in Alexandria wooing Berenice IV, now sole regent of Egypt after the death in 57 BC of Cleopatra VI. By September, Auchelaus and Berenice would be married, with Auchelaus commanding the Egyptian army. Now, Ptolemy XII would face a formidable adversary in any attempt to wrest back his throne.

Other factors were also thwarting Pompey's plan to reinstate Ptolemy on the Egyptian throne with official Roman help. As a result of April's Luca Conference, Pompey was committed to shepherding through Crassus's five-year appointment as governor of Syria commencing in 54 BC, once he and Crassus were elected to the consulship for 55 BC. But that election now received an unexpected delay. The consuls Marcellinus and Philippus took the extraordinary step of postponing the next consular election until the following year. With both consuls vehemently opposed to Pompey, sentiment in the Senate to physically support his friend King Ptolemy's return to power evaporated.

So, by early autumn, and certainly before the sailing season ended in October, Ptolemy and the teenaged Cleopatra would sail from Italy, bound for Antioch. There, on Pompey's confidential recommendation, they would put a case to Gabinius for leading men from his Syrian garrison to Egypt to reinstate Ptolemy—without the approval of the Senate at Rome.

There can be little doubt that this plan was conceived by Pompey and executed in concert with Crassus and Caesar. For, as Ptolemy headed back to the East, he went with a secret loan of 70 million sesterces to finance the reestablishment of his reign. Years later, after the deaths of Crassus and Pompey, Caesar would claim to be the sole remaining creditor in relation to this loan. But it is highly likely that all three triumvirs had contributed to it—70 million sesterces was a lot for Caesar to find alone, and his fellow triumvirs were considerably richer. Besides, the potential outcomes suited all three—Pompey was keeping his word to Ptolemy and returning Egypt to the Roman orbit, and Gabinius was being sidetracked from his intended Parthian invasion, clearing the way for Crassus to invade Parthia as urged by Caesar.

To secure these funds, Ptolemy promised to seal a peace treaty with Rome once he was back on his throne, agreeing in writing that on his death he would be jointly succeeded by his children Cleopatra and Ptolemy XIII. Ptolemy further agreed that, in the event of any dispute between that pair once they took the Egyptian throne, the consuls of Rome would be the sole arbiters. The Roman copy of this agreement was to disappear, but Caesar would later locate Ptolemy's copy in the library at Alexandria.

We know that Pompey's eldest son Gnaeus, who was aged around nineteen at this point, would soon be serving in Gabinius's army as a military tribune and would end up in Egypt. No classical source reveals how or when Gnaeus Pompey joined Gabinius, but it is highly likely that he traveled out from Rome to Syria with Ptolemy and Cleopatra, sent as their escort by his father.

Weeks before the election season officially began in the late summer, Pompey and Crassus commenced their joint electioneering for consul at the capital. A number of other potential candidates had indicated that they intended running, but the one opponent most likely to win a large share of the vote was Domitius Ahenobarbus, whose wife Porcia was the sister of Cato the Younger and sister-in-law of Lucius Lucullus. Cato and Ahenobarbus were close, and Cato would throw his backing behind Ahenobarbus's campaign.

———————

E ven though the summer of 56 BC was ending, Caesar, in Gaul, was not finished with his military campaigning. Two coastal tribes in today's Pas de Calais region had not sought to surrender to him, so he now marched into the territory of the Moroni to subdue them and their neighbors the Menapii. When the Moroni withdrew into a forest, Caesar and his legions followed.

As the Romans began constructing a camp, tribesmen emerged from the trees and attacked. The Moroni were driven off, but as the legionaries gave chase over difficult ground they took casualties and were forced to retreat. Heavy rain began to lash the Roman campsite, and as conditions worsened Caesar withdrew his force south to the territory of the recently subdued tribes, where it was intended that they would spend the winter of 56–55 BC. He himself would once more winter at Luca in Cisalpine

Gaul, from where he would await news of the January 55 BC outcome of the postponed consular election at Rome, which was crucial to his future plans.

XVI.

AS POMPEY & CRASSUS RULE,
CAESAR INVADES BRITAIN

At Rome in late January, 55 BC, the postponed consular election finally took place. In the face of the two famous candidates in lockstep, all but one other candidate had withdrawn. Domitius Ahenobarbus alone stood against the pair. His backer Cato the Younger knew that Pompey and/or Crassus would win at least one of the two posts, if not both, but he was determined to put up a fight. "The contest is not now for office," he publicly and melodramatically declared, "but for liberty against tyrants and usurpers!"[76]

To help Pompey and Crassus win the election, Caesar had a trick up his sleeve, sending off-duty legionaries to Rome to vote for his fellow triumvirs, led there by Caesar's subordinate and Crassus's son Publius, making the journey all the way over the Alps and down through northern Italy. This was made possible by the fact that, on payment of a fee to his senior centurion, one Roman legionary in four was entitled to take a furlough from his winter camp each year. To buy their votes, Caesar would have paid the furlough fees of numerous men this year.

Adding to the intimidating effect, the Roman legionary was entitled to wear a sheathed sword while on furlough. Petronius Arbiter, in his first-century *Satyricon*, tells of a plain-clothes legionary on furlough being challenged by a city official for wearing his sword. The man haughtily shrugs off the inquiry by naming his legion and the centurion commanding his cohort.

At Rome, these legionaries from Gaul would have camped on the Field of Mars, and when they crossed the pomerium into the city to cast votes in their voting tribes—Caesar's Subura voting tribe was always the first to vote—they would have gone armed. With the additional votes of these Caesarian legionaries—who, as Roman citizens, were fully entitled to vote if they were at Rome—Pompey and Crassus were both elected in a landslide.

Business at Rome always began at dawn and ended at sunset, and just before sunrise on the morning that Pompey and Crassus were to be officially pronounced the successful consular candidates, now-former consul Ahenobarbus arrived at the Forum accompanied by Cato and a throng of supporters, intent on heckling and disrupting the announcement. They were preceded by a slave, Ahenobarbus's torchbearer; and as they entered the Forum, a waiting mob of armed supporters of Pompey and Crassus, quite possibly furloughed soldiers of Caesar, fell on them.

The torchbearer was killed, other men were wounded, and Ahenobarbus was hustled away by his attendants to a house beside the Forum. Cato, initially standing his ground as he attempted to defend his brother-in-law, was wounded in the arm and was the last to retreat to the house, which was quickly surrounded by the armed attackers. Pompey and Crassus were then officially proclaimed consuls from the Rostra, to the cheers of their massed supporters.

Pompey and Crassus would then have withdrawn to jointly conduct the customary sacrifices and auguries on the Capitoline to inaugurate the new year, weeks behind the customary date because of the delaying tactic of Ahenobarbus and Philippus. With good omens, the pair returned to the Forum and instructed the armed men to eject Cato and Ahenobarbus from where they were holed up. Several of the attendants of the two senators were killed in the ensuing struggle.

Once Cato, Ahenobarbus, and their surviving companions were removed from the Forum, another ceremony took place. As required by law, from the Rostra and watched by Pompey, Crassus, who would briefly sit as president of the Senate for the remainder of January before handing the duty over to Pompey for the February sittings, announced the intended gubernatorial appointments for 54 BC of Pompey and himself, and of Caesar.

The furloughed legionaries who had voted for the pair would have remained at Rome until late winter, when they could march back to Gaul over the Alps to rejoin their units once the snows had melted. In the meantime, the presence of Caesar's armed soldiers just outside the city would have ensured that opponents of the new consuls would remain quiet until after the troops' departure.

Publius Crassus returned to Gaul with the legionaries, to rejoin Caesar for the new military campaigning season and regale him with details of the events surrounding the election. Now that Crassus Senior's appointment as governor of Syria from 54 BC was guaranteed to happen, Publius would have been aware that his father wanted him to serve as his second-in-command in Syria and take part in the invasion of Parthia. Publius would soldier with Caesar in Gaul through this year and until the spring of 54 BC, after which he would set off to join his father in Syria, taking along two wings of crack cavalry donated to his father's force by Caesar.

At the same time, Publius's younger brother, another Marcus, who turned thirty around this time, would go to Gaul that same spring of 54 BC to serve as Caesar's new quaestor, replacing Caesar's current quaestor, Lucius Roscius, who would be promoted by Caesar to the command of the 13th Legion. It was a tradeoff in which Caesar swapped one able young Crassus for another.

Gaius Trebonius, a Tribune of the Plebs, would present the necessary bill to make the following year's gubernatorial appointments of Pompey, Crassus, and Caesar official. Trebonius, a quaestor five years earlier, came from a family of Equites who had never held office or sat in the Senate; so as he pursued a senatorial career, he was considered a "new man." As Trebonius's reward for presenting this enabling legislation, Caesar would make him one of his generals for 54 BC, replacing Publius Crassus.

When Trebonius presented the enabling bill, Cato predictably stepped up to oppose it, and in front of a vast crowd of supporters he commenced a filibustering speech. In response, Trebonius ordered Cato's arrest and removal to the city prison. As Cato was hustled from the Rostra, the crowd refused to part. In the face of this, Trebonius ordered Cato to be set free.

Eventually, Trebonius's law, the *Lex Trebonia*, was passed, enabling Caesar, Pompey, and Crassus to plan their movements for 54 BC with certainty. Through the spring and summer of 55 BC, Crassus would not be able to keep himself from boasting to friends and clients about what he was going to do once he was in the East. The Senate was not requiring him to invade Parthia, which at this time posed no threat to Rome's interests. It was Caesar who had put him up to it, probably as a favor to Pompey, getting him out from under Pompey's feet. Once the gubernatorial posts had been decreed, Caesar wrote from Gaul, stroking Crassus's ego by commending his resolution to embark on such a grand enterprise.

Crassus declared that he was going to conquer Parthia, and then, like Alexander the Great, push all the way to India and even dip his toes in the Indian Ocean. Plutarch would ridicule these boasts, saying these were vain and childish words and most out of character for the sixty-year-old Crassus.

———————

Already, events in the East were reshaping what lay ahead for Crassus. Ptolemy XII had persuaded Gabinius to invade Egypt by sweetening the deal with a bribe of 24 million sesterces from the triumvirs' secret 70-million-sesterce loan. At first, Gabinius was not interested in the enterprise. Most of the senior officers on his staff were against it, but several did argue in favor, among them Mark Antony, who was enticed by the military adventure involved. Another of the voices in favor was likely to have been that of young Gnaeus Pompey, acting on his father's behalf.

In the end, knowing he had just one more year left in the job in Syria before Marcus Crassus would arrive to take over from him, Gabinius decided to make hay while the sun shone. According to the Jewish historian Josephus, who rated him a courageous and honorable man, Gabinius had embarked on his planned Parthian invasion and had already crossed the Euphrates with his legions when he changed his mind and accepted Ptolemy's bribe.[77]

In January, 55 BC, while Gabinius brought the legions back across the Euphrates, he sent Mark Antony on ahead to Egypt with Ptolemy and Roman cavalry. Antony's orders were to secure the passes into Egypt, which he would do with the help of Jewish partisans organized by Antipater of Idumea, father of the future Herod the Great. Antipater also provided grain and other supplies to the Roman army as Gabinius subsequently passed through Idumea on his march south along the Mediterranean coast. Behind him in Syria, Gabinius left a garrison of mostly auxiliary troops.

Mark Antony not only quickly secured the Egyptian passes, but he also went on to storm the coastal stronghold of Pelusium, the first Egyptian city beyond the passes. As was his habit, the bold, brave Antony was the first Roman soldier over the enemy battlements, and he quickly forced the Egyptian defenders to surrender. In later years, Antony would show a cold-blooded streak, but, to his credit, when King Ptolemy entered captured Pelusium and vengefully wanted every Egyptian prisoner executed, Antony would not allow it.

Once Gabinius joined Antony, skirmishes with Egyptian forces followed, before a major battle took place outside Alexandria. The Egyptian army was led by Antony's new friend Auchelaus, and he fought bravely and well. But it was not enough. Auchelaus fell, with his men, as the Egyptians were routed by the smaller but more professional Roman army. On the battlefield following the battle, Antony searched among the Egyptian dead until he found the body of his friend Auchelaus. He subsequently buried the body at Alexandria with royal honors.

The war in Egypt was over by the end of February. As the last Egyptian resistance crumbled and Alexandria surrendered, Gabinius entered the city, imprisoned Berenice, and returned Ptolemy XII to his throne. Gabinius quickly departed Alexandria to march for Palestine, where Jewish rebels were again causing problems. Following Gabinius's exit from Egypt, Ptolemy executed his betraying daughter Berenice.

Gabinius left Ptolemy a 2,000-man bodyguard, formed into a unit that became known as the Gabinii, or the Gabinians, made up of one thousand auxiliary cavalry and one thousand legionaries from Gabinius's legions. These legionaries were most likely men on the verge of retirement after twelve years of service. One of the Gabinians' centurions, Salvius, had served with Pompey against the Cilician pirates twelve years earlier. These Gabinians, paid well by King Ptolemy to protect him, settled down in Alexandria, taking Egyptian wives, fathering children, and adopting Egyptian ways while retaining Roman ranks, formations, and fighting methods. Their commander was a Roman military tribune.

Young Gnaeus Pompey was to command the Gabinians for several years before he was recalled from Egypt by his father in 49 BC. During that period, Gnaeus appears to have formed a relationship with Cleopatra, who was five years his junior. Whether that developed into a physical relationship, we don't know. But as Cleopatra's next two romantic partners—Caesar and, later, Mark Antony—were Roman strongmen who protected her, it is highly likely that she and Gnaeus became close.

Gnaeus was considered arrogant by Cicero, and certainly the young man used his father's cognomen Magnus as if he too deserved the mantle of greatness. Nonetheless, he proved steadfastly loyal to those to whom he was attached. Several years later, as soon as Gnaeus left Egypt, Cleopatra's brother Ptolemy XIII would attempt to eliminate Cleopatra, forcing her to flee into southern Palestine. When Gnaeus learned of this, he would urge his father to restore Cleopatra to her throne.

As war raged in Egypt in the early months of 55 BC, Julius Caesar had a new enemy to confront, with German movement across the

Rhine on Gaul's northern border. Near the mouth of the Rhine, tens of thousands of Germans were flooding across the river in a mass migration from beyond the Rhine by the Usipetes and Tencteri tribes. They were farmers, and no match for their more numerous and aggressive neighbors the Suebi as they expanded into their territory.

For three years, these two tribes had been moving toward the Rhine in stages, harassed by the Suebi all the way. On arriving on the Rhine's far bank, they forced the local residents of the smaller Menapi tribe to flee to the Gallic bank. The two tribes then marched away for three days, making the Menapii feel secure, before force-marching back to the river and, in the night, using Menapian boats, crossing to massacre the Menapii, seizing all their property.

All this was reported to Caesar in Cisalpine Gaul, from his own sources and from highly alarmed Gallic chieftains who feared that the Germans would next invade their territory. Gauging that the two German tribes had no plans to expand farther into Gaul, Caesar didn't rush back to Gaul. After completing his court duties in Cisalpine and Transalpine Gaul, in the spring he returned and calmly arranged the year's corn supply for his legions and called together the leaders of Gallic tribes now under Roman sway. Assuring the Gallic leaders that he had everything under control, he called on them to provide cavalry for a campaign he intended leading against the Usipetes and Tencteri that spring.

Once he had selected his cavalry, now five thousand strong with the addition of further Gallic contributions, including from Aquitanian tribes, Caesar marched his army toward the Usipetes and Tencteri. As the Romans approached, the two tribes sent envoys to Caesar, telling him they had only entered Gaul and taken the lands of others because their land had been taken from them, and warning him that they were afraid of no one except the Suebi.

Caesar must have smiled. Apparently no one had told these two tribes that he had previously sent the Suebi fleeing out of Gaul. He replied that the Usipetes and Tencteri might settle with the Ubii, a German tribe that lived on the eastern bank of the Rhine opposite what was to become the city of Cologne. As it happened, Ubian envoys were currently with Caesar, having come to ask for Roman help against Suebi attack, and combining the three German tribes against the Suebi made eminent sense.

Usipetes and Tencteri envoys asked Caesar to stay put for three days to allow their leadership to decide their response; but suspecting this a ploy to gain time for the return of the tribes' cavalry, which was away foraging, Caesar refused and continued advancing. The following day, their envoys again asked for three days—this time to confer with the Ubii—and Caesar agreed to limit the following day's march to four miles, after which he expected the German leaders to meet him.

But as Caesar's five thousand cavalry continued moving ahead of the Roman infantry, the eight hundred German cavalry who had remained with their tribes suddenly charged. Caught off guard and losing seventy-four troopers, his "scatter-brained" Gallic cavalry, in Caesar's own words, galloped in disorder back to the approaching Roman infantry to gain their protection.[78]

The following morning, chiefs and elders of the two tribes came to Caesar, seeking forgiveness for their cavalry's rash attack. Caesar made prisoners of them all, using the excuse of the previous day's unprovoked attack, and in contravention of the protocols surrounding ambassadors—the very same dishonorable crime with which Caesar had accused the Veneti the year before. When this became known in the Senate at Rome, Cato the Younger was so disgusted that he moved that the Senate disown Caesar and hand him over to the Germans for punishment. Of course, with Pompey or Crassus in the Senate's curule chair, Cato's motion was dismissed as petty politics and went nowhere.

Caesar then marched his army eight miles to the enemy camp, which contained, according to Caesar's fluid numbers, 430,000 German men, women, and children, which sounds improbable—the camp would have been roughly half the size of the city of Rome! Nonetheless, catching the leaderless Germans by surprise, the legions burst into the camp. Some warriors offered resistance at their wagons, others fled in all directions with their family members. Many were massacred on the plain. Some were chased by Roman cavalry all the way to the Rhine, where many drowned while trying to escape. Caesar's troops, meanwhile, suffered not a single fatality. Following the destruction of the German column and the looting of their camp, Caesar set the captured German leaders free.

On learning that the German cavalry away foraging had linked up with the Sugambri Germans east of the Rhine, Caesar sent a message to the Sugambri demanding that they hand them over to him, to be punished for making war in Gaul. The Sugambri refused to do this, declaring that the Rhine was the limit of Roman authority. Taking this as a challenge, Caesar called in Balbus, his prefect of engineers, and gave him a task—build him a bridge across the Rhine.

The Ubii had offered Caesar a fleet of small boats for use crossing the Rhine, but he wanted to make a statement. And Balbus made that statement by building a wooden bridge on piles driven into the fast-flowing river. Caesar would take sole credit for the bridge's design and construction, which were "in accordance with the laws of physics," in his words.[79]

Ten days after the first trees were felled to produce lumber, Roman troops were crossing the completed bridge and entering Germany. Ahead of Caesar, the Sugambri and their Tencteri and Usipetes allies fled to the forests. After spending eighteen days east of the Rhine destroying deserted German villages, farm buildings, and crops, and on hearing that other German tribes were massing to go to war with him, Caesar withdrew his troops to Gaul, destroying the bridge behind him.

While Caesar was that summer conducting what he called the German War at and near the Rhine, in the Middle East Gabinius had departed Egypt to return to Judea and Syria and deal with new threats on his doorstep. During his absence, brigands had ranged throughout Syria, robbing and pillaging almost with impunity as the small Roman garrison struggled to maintain law and order. Meanwhile, Alexander, son of Aristobulus, had escaped custody and raised a new rebellion in Judea and

Galilee against his uncle Hyrcanus II, the ruler installed at Jerusalem by Pompey.

Near Mount Gabor in Lower Galilee, Gabinius and his army met and destroyed Alexander's force. Gabinius would claim ten thousand enemy dead—enough for a Triumph back at Rome. Once Gabinius returned to Antioch, he dispatched troops to deal with the brigand menace. By year's end, order would be restored in Syria, just in time for Gabinius to hand over command to his replacement Crassus.

That summer, too, at Rome, Pompey was presiding consul as the August elections of the aediles for 54 BC took place and violent rioting again broke out. Several men at Pompey's side were killed, and Pompey's clothes were spattered with blood. Pompey sent servants home to the Carinae to fetch clean garments; but when Pompey's young wife Julia saw his bloodstained gown, she thought the worst and, in shock, collapsed into unconsciousness. It was only with difficulty that she was revived. It turned out that Julia was pregnant, and she now went into labor, suffering a miscarriage. While the child died, Julia would recover.

Pompey seems to have been unaware of Julia's pregnancy prior to this, and it is likely that she was only in the first trimester, the time when a pregnant woman is most likely to suffer fainting. What Pompey's family physician would have been unaware of was the fact that this fainting spell was actually cardiac arrest—and a sign of potential future problems with pregnancy. Plutarch says that even Pompey's adversaries, especially those who were critical of his links with Caesar, sympathized with Pompey and his devoted wife over the loss of their child.

Perhaps to take his mind, and that of his wife, off this, and certainly to strengthen his popularity with the public, Pompey decided to stage a spectacular event at his new theater. The theater would not be fully completed for another three years, with its formal opening taking place in 52 BC, but enough of the banked seating in the open-air auditorium had been raised for Pompey to announce that he would stage performances there as he dedicated the Temple of Venus that formed the building's centerpiece. The dedicatory performance date is unknown, but it may have been around Pompey's birthday in late September. Some years after this, Caesar would inaugurate an annual Festival of Venus on September 26.

Pompey called a famous tragic actor out of retirement to perform in a play during the dedicatory event, and also put on a gladiatorial show in which the gladiators went against wild animals, and elephants from the Laurentum elephant farm established by Pompey were involved— perhaps the gladiators threw missiles at the beasts from wooden "castles" fastened to the elephants' backs, as was the case with North African war elephants used by enemies of Rome.

I n the late summer, while Pompey was preparing his theater spectacular at Rome, Caesar, in Gaul, embarked on another audacious operation, the invasion of the island of Britannia, today's Britain. Much as he'd bridged the Rhine just to show that he could do it, Caesar's British operation of 55 BC was intended to show off Roman military might. It was also designed to dazzle the Roman public with Caesar's accomplishments while taking the luster from Pompey's theater dedication. In Plutarch's words, Caesar had "a love of honor and a passion for distinction."[80]

Even while his Gallic ambassador King Commius of the Atrebates was on British shores discussing peace with tribal leaders, and selecting his favorite 10th Legion and the well-performed 7th Legion, Caesar sailed at dawn from today's Boulogne in the Pas de Calais with eighty ships. A further eighteen ships carrying a cavalry detachment were due to sail from farther up the Gallic coast.

The main fleet crossed the English Channel and passed up the coast of Cantium, as the Romans called today's Kent, dropping anchor off a beach near South Foreland around 9 AM. But Caesar was unhappy with this landing site, chosen by his advance man Gaius Volusenus, formerly a military tribune with the 12th Legion under Galba, who had surveyed the coast in a single ship. Caesar was also waiting for his cavalry, whose flotilla had missed the outgoing tide and was awaiting the next tide. In the afternoon, Caesar convened a conference of his senior officers aboard his ship, and, watched by waiting British warriors from the cliffs, they agreed to relocate up the coast.

In the late afternoon, the postponed landing went ahead between present-day Deal and Walmer Castle, without the cavalry, and with armed Britons massed on the beach to oppose them. When the ships slid into shore, Caesar's legionaries hesitated to jump into the water. It took the eagle-bearer of the 10th, roughly the equivalent of a sergeant-major today, to splash over the side and lead the way.

"Jump in, boys!" the eagle-bearer called from the water, holding the sacred silver-eagle standard of the 10th aloft. "Unless you want to surrender our eagle to the enemy! I, for one, intend doing my duty by my homeland and by my general!"[81]

Jumping over the sides of their ships, men of the 10th and 7th charged up the beach as more legionaries rowed ashore in small boats. They easily drove the opposing British warriors off the beach, and Caesar established a walled camp a little inland. British tribes then returned Caesar's captured envoy Commius and sought peace. But when, four days later, the cavalry's flotilla arrived, it was driven away by a storm which also swamped or damaged all the ships of Caesar's main fleet, stranding the invaders.

Seeing this, Britons quietly massed in a forest overnight and prepared to attack. With most of the 10th Legion engaged refloating and repairing ships, the 7th Legion, out harvesting wheat in a field, was surrounded and cut off by a large British force that included chariots, cavalry, and infantry. Caesar hurried to the scene with the two guard cohorts of the 10th and linked up with the 7th. When they saw six more cohorts of the 10th approaching, the Britons withdrew. But after several days of torrential rain confined the Romans to their camp, the reinforced Britons again went on the attack, only for the solid lines of Roman infantry to repulse them. Again the Britons sought peace, and Caesar demanded hostages to ensure that they kept to their word.

All but twelve of Caesar's ships were now seaworthy, so, packing all his men aboard them, and after spending only some twenty days on British soil, the Roman general made a hasty withdrawal back across the Channel to Gaul. Two of his ships separated from the fleet en route, and when their troops landed in the territory of the Gallic Morini tribe, which had yet to submit to Caesar, they came under attack. Caesar's cavalry was finally able to contribute to the operation by going to the rescue of these men.

As the 10th and 7th went into winter camp, Caesar crossed the Alps to winter in Cisalpine Gaul and Illyricum. He would paint the British operation as a success; but, like his crossing of the Rhine, it had been a mere sideshow and had achieved no lasting benefit for Rome. And Caesar knew it: he was already planning a much larger and more profitable British incursion for the following year.

B ack in Rome, Crassus heard glowing reports of how Caesar had become the first Roman commander to land in Britain, the largest island known to the Romans, and strained at the leash to grab his own piece of military glory. Instead of waiting for the spring to travel out to Syria to take up his command there, once the Senate had sat with Crassus as president for the last time that November, and with his consular duties thus discharged and Pompey to serve as Senate president through December, Crassus prepared to immediately depart Rome.

By this time, at Caesar's urging Crassus had fully reconciled with Pompey, who was showing him every courtesy in public and in private. Pompey in turn was able to persuade Crassus and Cicero to reconcile. This had come after the pair had recently exchanged barbed words in public, with Cicero again flaring up and letting fly with intemperate language that was contrary to his agreement with Pompey, and which he again soon regretted. Cicero's excuse was Crassus's "grossly injurious acts" toward him in the past, which he claimed had led to a pent-up rancor toward Crassus that was a surprise to himself when it emerged![82]

To nip this renewed conflict in the bud and ensure that Cicero would not work against the interests of his fellow triumvir once Crassus was in the East, Pompey took Crassus aside; and within days, to Cicero's amazement, Crassus was delivering a speech in praise of Cicero. Pompey then impressed on Cicero the need for a truce between the pair, and on Pompey's sage advice Crassus wrote to Cicero asking him to name a date when they could dine together as friends. Crassus subsequently let it be known that once he left Rome to travel overland via the Appian Way to Brindisi, where he would join a fleet bound for the East, he would dine with Cicero en route. That dinner would take place at the country retreat of Cicero's then son-in-law Furius Crassipes.

Despite having terminated hostilities with Cicero, Crassus still had numerous enemies, especially those who were cynical of his appointment to the lucrative governorship of Syria. On the day that Crassus departed the city for Brindisi, he knew that Gaius Ateius Capito, a Tribune of the Plebs who was an enemy of both Crassus and Cicero and a vocal opponent of Crassus's well-publicized plan to invade Parthia, would attempt to stop him from leaving. So Crassus asked Pompey to accompany him as he passed out of Rome, knowing, says Plutarch, that Pompey "had a great name among the common people." Pompey, basking in the glory of his recent theater dedication, agreed to his colleague's request and walked with Crassus, smiling his gentle smile to all the members of the public who lined their way.[83]

Sure enough, Ateius appeared in their path from the Forum and tried to prevent Crassus from departing. When Crassus attempted to walk around him, Ateius ordered his arrest. The other seven tribunes were also present, almost certainly at consul Pompey's instigation, and they stepped in to prevent Crassus's arrest. So, Ateius ran to the city's Capena Gate, where he set up a brazier, began to burn incense, and called down all manner of curses upon Crassus from the heavens above.

Ignoring this performance, Pompey and Crassus exchanged friendly farewells, and then Crassus walked past Ateius and exited the gate.

Followed by his entourage, he departed into the suburbs for his dinner appointment with Cicero and his appointment with destiny in the East. Pompey would never see Crassus alive again.

XVII.

WITH TWO DEATHS, EVERYTHING CHANGES

The next two years, 54 and 53 BC, proved momentous for Caesar, Pompey, and Crassus, and for their partnership. In Gaul over the winter of 55–54 BC, Caesar's troops and the tribes now allied to Rome made preparations for Caesar's large-scale second invasion of Britain. This time, after settling unrest in the city of Trier in the spring, Caesar would take five legions and 2,000 cavalry to Britain, using twenty-eight warships and more than seven hundred transports, a fleet much larger than the Spanish Armada that would sail these waters in 1588.

That summer, leaving Labienus in Gaul with the 11th, 13th, and 14th legions, Caesar crossed the Dover Strait with the 7th, 8th, 9th, 10th, and 12th, landing on a beach between Deal and Sandwich. The British tribes, daunted by the size of the Roman fleet, withdrew inland, allowing the unopposed landing of Roman infantry and cavalry. Caesar then made camp where a golf course today fringes the coast.

From Britons captured by patrols, Caesar learned that tribes of southern Britain were massing at the Stour River; and at midnight, leaving the 12th Legion and 300 cavalry to guard the camp, he marched his four Spanish legions and 1,700 cavalry twelve miles through the night. At daybreak, the Roman army surprised the Britons beside the Stour, not far from present-day Canterbury. Using chariots, the Britons attacked.

There were good reasons the Romans didn't use war chariots as the Britons did. As impressive as the light British chariots appeared, speeding over the plain, they were vulnerable to Roman cavalry, whose horses were larger, faster, and more nimble than the chariots' pairs of harnessed ponies, and also vulnerable to missiles aimed at the horses—the standard legion defense against chariot attack. Caesar's cavalry easily drove off the chariots, after which the British infantry retreated to a stockade in a wood. Caesar gave the 7th Legion the job of taking this stockade, which, in *testudo* or tortoise formation with locked shields, they achieved with mechanical efficiency.

The weather gods once again proved to be Caesar's enemy. A storm blew up and wrecked forty of his ships and damaged many more. Returning to his coastal camp, Caesar assigned his men to ship-repair duties, and sent word to Labienus to have replacement vessels quickly built in Gaul. Ten days later, Caesar resumed his offensive. Returning to the Stour with his four Spanish legions, he found the Britons back in position and reinforced by King Cassivellaunus and his powerful Catuvellauni tribe from north of the Thames River; the Tamesa, as Celtic Britons called the waterway.

During a number of skirmishes here, one of Caesar's new generals, Gaius Trebonius, who had served the triumvirs well in Rome as a Tribune of the Plebs, proved a calm and steady legion commander as British attacks were repeatedly repulsed by the well-disciplined legions. Caesar was able to cross the Thames. As the legions continued to advance north, six tribes sent envoys to Caesar seeking peace terms.

Near the site of the later city of St. Albans, the legions overran Cassivellaunus's stronghold, fighting off a chariot force numbered at 4,000 by Caesar. Meanwhile, back at the Roman camp on the Kent coast, the 12th Legion beat off an attack by four tribes. King Cassivellaunus now surrendered, and, providing hostages, agreed to become a Roman ally and pay an annual tax to Rome.

With the autumn approaching, Caesar withdrew to the coast, and in two sailings he ferried all his troops, hostages, and prisoners back to Gaul. Once again, although he had gone farther and stayed longer in Britain than he had the previous year, Caesar left no permanent Roman presence by establishing a settlement or legion base there. Apart from the alliances forged with several tribes, most of which would fall apart over time, it was as if the Romans had never been in Britain.

It would be another ninety-seven years before invading legionaries again set foot on the island. Only one plus came out of Caesar's British expeditions: Plutarch says that some earlier Greek and Roman historians had doubted that this island of Britannia even existed, considering it as mythical as Atlantis and the unicorn. Caesar had at least put Britain on the map.

The Roman general now divided his force, distributing his legions at different sites throughout northern and central Gaul for the winter, as Caesar based himself in Transalpine Gaul. But dividing his army was to prove a fatal mistake. Caesar's generals Sabinus and Cotta, with the 14th Legion and five cohorts from another legion, built a camp at Atuatica on the Geer River. The Belgian city of Tongres would later grow on the spot. The aggressive local Eburone tribe under their chieftain Ambiorix saw their opportunity to strike a blow against the outnumbered Romans, and, allying with Germans from across the Rhine, they surrounded the fortified Roman camp in their tens of thousands.

Sabinus, the senior Roman commander, feared being starved into submission, and went against the advice of his deputy Cotta and most other senior officers by negotiating a Roman withdrawal with Ambiorix. But after the Romans had departed the camp and were on the march, Ambiorix broke his word to allow them safe passage. Two miles from the camp, the tribesmen ambushed the legionaries as they passed through a forest. Forced into an *orbis*, the circular legion formation of last resort, Sabinus, Cotta, and most of their men died fighting. Several hundred legionaries fought their way back to the Atuatica camp, where, surrounded and cut off, all took their own lives. Only a handful of Romans managed to escape and tell of the disaster in which some eight thousand Roman soldiers had perished with Sabinus and Cotta.

Meanwhile, a legion camped at the Sambre River farther south in Gaul also came under attack. The commander here was Quintus Cicero, younger brother of Marcus Cicero. Quintus Cicero was made of tougher stuff than Quintus Sabinus, and he and his men held off enemy attacks on their camp for more than seven days. Cicero was eventually able to smuggle out a message to Caesar, eighty miles away, who marched rapidly to Cicero's aid with just a single legion and 2,000 cavalry.

Caesar's men hurriedly built a marching camp, which the Gauls rushed to surround. But one of the fort's earthen walls was false, and on Caesar's order it was collapsed and his troops came charging out, surprising and routing the tribesmen. With his assailants dispersed, Caesar was able to relieve young Cicero and his legionaries, one in ten of whom had been wounded. Gallic resistance was snuffed out for the time being; but news of the loss of Sabinus, Cotta, numerous young military tribunes from leading families, and thousands of Roman legionaries was received with shock at Rome, and Caesar's reputation as an all-conquering general took a hit.

To make up for his manpower losses, without Senate approval Caesar immediately ordered the levying of three new legions in his three provinces over the winter—a totally new enlistment of the annihilated 14th Legion, and the new 15th and 16th Legions. The deaths of Sabinus and Cotta and their soldiers were not the only losses that Caesar suffered this year. While in Britain, he had received word that, back in Rome, his mother Aurelia had passed away on July 29, just ten days after Caesar's forty-sixth birthday.

Aged in her mid-sixties and dying from natural causes, Aurelia was highly respected at Rome for her intelligence, her discretion, and the way she protected her son and advanced his career during the dangerous days of Sulla's proscriptions. Unless she visited her son at Luca, it's likely that the last time Aurelia saw her only son was when he had left Rome for his Gallic command four years earlier.

Caesar's losses kept mounting, with the death around this same time of his daughter and only legitimate child, Julia, who was Pompey's devoted wife. Recovering from her miscarriage of the previous year, Julia had again become pregnant to Pompey. While this pregnancy was more advanced than the last, Julia's heart was not strong enough to cope, and she died while giving birth.

This child of Julia and Pompey, the grandson of Caesar, was a boy by most accounts, with only the much-later historian Cassius Dio stating that it was a girl. The baby survived only a short while before also dying. Pompey was inconsolable at his double loss, despite a wave of public sympathy. Caesar wasted no time in attempting to cement a fresh marital bond between Pompey and himself, by proposing that Pompey marry his grandniece Octavia, sister of Octavian. Octavia was already married, to the senator Gaius Marcellus, and to enable marriage to Pompey she would have to divorce Marcellus. Pompey quickly scotched this idea, but the proposal made Marcellus the implacable enemy of Caesar.

This same year, Pompey suffered a major political reverse. In the spring, Aulus Gabinius had returned from Syria, only to be charged, by enemies of his patron Pompey, with three crimes when he appeared in the Senate to give an account of his Syrian governorship. This attack was driven by the tax-farming Equites with contracts covering the province of Syria, who had lost large amounts to the brigands who robbed their agents of their collections while Gabinius was in Egypt with the bulk of his armed forces. Knowing that Gabinius had made millions from his Egyptian expedition, the tax farmers wanted retribution, and their patrons in the Senate set out to destroy Gabinius on their behalf.

The least of the three charges, that Gabinius had committed illegal acts while running for his consulship, was dropped. The much more serious charge of high treason was subject to capital punishment if he was found guilty. This charge related to the fact that he had led troops from his province without Senate permission. Gabinius had indeed done this, at the triumvirs' instigation; yet, in the face of the facts, he was found not guilty. It would be rumored that the judges were bribed, no doubt by Pompey, who did everything he could to help his loyal client.

The third charge was that Gabinius had committed extortion while governor of Syria, with particular regard to the large bribe he had accepted from Ptolemy XII. Despite the fact that the triumvirs had funded the bribe money, that Pompey had Cicero conduct his defense, and that Pompey and witnesses from Alexandria testified in his favor, Gabinius was convicted on this count of extortion. Gabinius's property was confiscated and he was sent into exile beyond Italy's shores. Pompey almost certainly provided him with money to survive in exile, but he would be unable to have his client's conviction overturned the way he had done in Cicero's case.

Meanwhile, in the East, the third triumvir, Marcus Crassus, was heading for a fall. Impatient to exercise his proconsular powers in the East and rack up booty and glory, he had sailed from Brindisi at the worst time of the year, during the late autumn, long after all cargo vessels had tied up until after winter storms had passed, with the official Mediterranean sailing season not reopening until the following March. With the seasonal winds against him, several of his ships were wrecked in storms, but Crassus stubbornly sailed on.

Sailing with Crassus as his quaestor was the tall, spare, thirty-one-year-old Gaius Cassius Longinus. The brother-in-law of Marcus Brutus, the illegitimate son of Caesar, Cassius came from a noble family. It was said that he had exhibited a dislike of tyrants since a young age, becoming embroiled in a fight at school with Sulla's son Faustus, who, like Cassius, served as a quaestor in 54 BC.

Crassus descended on the city of Hierapolis, in the southwest of today's Anatolia, location of a famous Temple of Cybele and home to fifty thousand Jews, and proceeded to loot the undefended temple of its hoard of golden offerings. Linking up with the four legions stationed in Syria, Crassus put a bridge across the Euphrates at the town of Zeugma in Commagene, then marched his army into Mesopotamia, Parthian territory. A number of Parthian towns surrendered without resistance. But when the people of Zenodotia, near the modern Raqqa, massacred a hundred of his troops, Crassus stormed the town, looted it, destroyed it brick by brick, and sold its inhabitants into slavery.

For this minor military victory, Crassus had his troops hail him Imperator, to match Pompey and Caesar. Leaving seven thousand infantry and a thousand cavalry to garrison these towns, Crassus took the majority of his troops back across the Euphrates to winter in Syria. Back in the governor's palace at Antioch, he spent his time weighing the gold from Hierapolis and sending out letters to regional allies demanding troops, or money in lieu thereof. In the East, the name of Crassus now became despised and ridiculed, says Plutarch.[84]

In Parthia in 57 BC, King Phraates's sons Mithradates IV and Orodes II had murdered their father and taken joint control—only, like Romulus and Remus of Rome and Eteocles and Polynices of Greece's Thebes, to fall out. Mithradates had fled to Syria, from where, in 55 BC, he'd launched an offensive against his brother with logistical support from the Roman governor Gabinius. At Seleucia on the Tigris River, not far from present-day Baghdad in Iraq, Mithradates had been besieged by Orodes's general Surena. As Crassus wintered in Antioch, that siege was ongoing, tying up two Parthian armies.

Crassus was confident that the siege of Seleucia would still be continuing the following spring, when he would cross the Euphrates, march to Seleucia, defeat Surena's besieging force, and then complete the siege, eliminating both Parthian armies in one fell swoop. Or so he thought. But as he waited for the new year, his strategic advantage dissolved. Mithradates and his troops came out from behind the brick walls of Seleucia, fought Surena's men on the battlefield, and lost. Mithradates was captured, and executed, after which Surena crowned Orodes II sole king of Parthia.

In the autumn, Crassus's son Publius had joined him with his thousand cavalry from Gaul. As the spring of 53 BC began, the pair traveled south of Antioch to Heliopolis, "City of the Sun." Later Baalbek in today's Lebanon, it was then in the Roman province of Syria and housed several major temples, including the world's largest Temple of Jupiter. Heliopolis was also home to a smaller, round Temple of Venus, to which Marcus and Publius paid a visit to make offerings in the hope of securing good omens for their upcoming campaign. As the pair was coming down the temple steps, Publius stumbled and fell, tripping his father, who fell over him. This, superstitious Romans later claimed, was an omen of what would befall father and son that summer.

At Zeugma, Crassus assembled his 50,000-man army—seven legions, backed by almost four thousand cavalry and a similar number of lightly armed auxiliary troops supplied by vassal states. Crassus was also joined by King Artavazdes II of Armenia, who, on the death of Tigranes the Great, and with the approval of the Roman Senate, had succeeded his elderly father two years earlier. Artavazdes urged Crassus to enter Parthia via Armenia, offering to add ten thousand cavalry and thirty thousand infantry to his army as he passed through his kingdom.

This roundabout route through mountainous territory made for difficult marching, but also made it difficult for the fluid operations of Parthian cavalry, the strength of the Parthian army. Giving the king his cold thanks, the arrogant Crassus informed him that he knew best how to wage war. So Artavazdes wished him good luck and departed, detaching his 6,000-man personal cavalry bodyguard to serve Crassus—most of whom Crassus would leave in Syria.

In the meantime, King Orodes of Parthia had divided his forces in two. One army, headed by his general Arsaces, he sent into Armenia that spring to deal with Artavazdes's army, which was swiftly overwhelmed. Artavazdes was forced into an alliance with the Parthians, and to cement that alliance he agreed to marry his sister to Orodes's son Pacorus. In this swift, deft move behind Crassus's back, Rome had lost a vassal state that Pompey had brought under her control.

Roman soldiers garrisoned east of the Euphrates arrived to tell Crassus that a second Parthian army, under Surena, had surrounded and cut off Crassus's Roman garrisons. Parthian envoys shortly after came to Crassus. The chief Parthian envoy, Vagises, passed on a message from Orodes: If the Roman army massing at the Euphrates had been sent by the Senate of Rome to wage war with Orodes, he would give it war, beginning with the wiping out of Crassus's garrisons east of the river. But should Crassus's motive be private profit, Orodes would take pity on him because of his old age and send his garrisons back to him. Crassus replied that he would give his answer to Orodes at Seleucia.

Laughing, Vagises held up his palm. "Hair will grow here before you see Seleucia!" he declared.[85]

After Crassus led his army across a bridge of boats into Parthia, his quaestor Cassius urged him to march beside the Euphrates so he could be supplied by boat, and this was the course he initially adopted. But an Arab chieftain named Ariamnes came to Crassus. Ariamnes had meritoriously served Pompey during the Mithradatic War; but, unbeknownst to Crassus, he was now in the pay of the Parthians.

Ariamnes persuaded Crassus to leave the river and take the direct route to Seleucia, across the Mesopotamian desert; so, against the advice of his son and quaestor, as the summer began the Roman general led his army into the desert. At the same time, a message arrived from Artavazdes in Armenia, saying he had been detained by the Parthians and could not send any more troops to help him. Still, the stubborn Crassus struck out across the desert.

As the marching Romans approached the Balikh River, a tributary of the Euphrates, Parthian troops were spotted ahead. Led by Surena, this highly mobile, fully mounted Parthian force was made up of a thousand cataphract heavy cavalry and nine thousand fast, nimble horse-archers. Auxiliaries sent to deal with this threat were driven back to the main Roman column. Even though his guide Ariamnes had disappeared from the camp overnight, Crassus still had no idea that he was marching into a trap. Forming a huge marching square, he continued toward Seleucia with son Publius commanding one wing, Cassius the other, and Crassus himself in the center.

Surena's cataphracts kept the Roman cavalry busy while the horse-archers rained arrows on the Roman infantry. If Roman cavalry gave chase, they fell victim to the famous "Parthian shot," or "parting shot." Parthian horse-archers were adept at accurately firing back over their steed's rump as they rode away. They also fired from beyond the range of Roman javelins, and never seemed to run out of ammunition—Surena had brought along a camel column loaded with arrows to resupply his archers.

Crassus, seeing his force increasingly take casualties, sent son Publius out to deal with the Parthians, leading 4,800 legionaries, 500 archers, and 1,300 cavalry. Publius's force was soon surrounded, so he established a defensive position on a low rise, where he was quickly surrounded again. As his men were felled all around him, Publius saw that all was lost, and he and his officers fell on their swords rather than be captured.

When Crassus saw his son's severed head being paraded on the end of a spear, he broke down. So boastful at Rome of becoming another Alexander the Great, the man who had dealt the slave army of Spartacus a crushing blow and come to consider himself a general worthy of a Triumph had no answer to the relentless Parthian missile attacks. No Pompey, no Caesar, in a shocked daze he ceased to direct operations.

Cassius, his quaestor, kept the Roman army together. Maintaining their square formation but continually taking casualties, the Romans shuffled toward the town of Carrhae. The rain of Parthian arrows only ceased with nightfall. That night, three hundred Roman cavalry broke away. They would succeed in escaping to Syria. These men were quite possibly Armenians, members of King Artavazdes's bodyguard, deserting Crassus's proverbial sinking ship.

The following day, the Parthians launched fresh arrow attacks. As the Roman square disintegrated, with many infantrymen fleeing for the Euphrates, Cassius also escaped, taking five hundred cavalry with him. Crassus, lost and disoriented, was left with junior officers and the rump of his infantry. Parthian envoys arrived to invite Crassus to the Euphrates to sign a treaty, which he agreed to. As he mounted a Parthian horse, one of his officers refused to let him go. At this, the Parthians drew their swords. Crassus and many with him were massacred.

Twenty thousand Roman troops were killed in the protracted Battle of Carrhae. Another ten thousand were taken prisoner, to be taken back to Parthia to become slaves. According to one legend, these captured Roman legionaries were sold on to other masters farther and farther east, ending up in China, where they settled and fought for a Chinese warlord. To many Romans, to lose scores of sacred Roman standards to the

Parthians at Carrhae was as humiliating as the loss in men. Decades later, Tiberius, stepson of the emperor Augustus, would negotiate the return of those standards from the Parthians.

As for Crassus, his decapitated head was sent by Surena to his king. Orodes was at that time enjoying the wedding celebrations of his son Pacorus and the sister of Artavazdes. The wedding guests were watching a Greek play, and, to the amusement of all present, Crassus's head was used as a prop in the play. According to one story, molten gold was also poured into the mouth of the greedy Roman general.

Orodes subsequently sent his son Pacorus at the head of a Parthian army to invade Syria, believing the Roman province undefended. But Cassius the quaestor, regrouping some twenty thousand Roman survivors in Syria, met and fought the Parthians, driving Pacorus back across the Euphrates.

News of Crassus's massive defeat was met with horror at Rome. Carrhae was the largest Roman defeat since the Carthaginian general Hannibal overwhelmed the Romans at Cannae in southern Italy in 216 BC. News that Cassius had defeated Pacorus calmed the situation, but calls for Pompey to take sole charge to stabilize Rome's government in this time of crisis grew louder. As for Pompey's alliance with Caesar, with the death of Julia and now that of Crassus, that partnership seemed to have run its course, which would have pleased the critics of both men.

And then, this same summer, Romans were rattled by the news that their other star general, Caesar, was in trouble in Gaul. There, a massive revolt of the subjected Gallic tribes had broken out, taking Caesar by surprise. To help him put down this revolt as it spread across Gaul, Caesar would look for help, from none other than Pompey.

XVIII.

THE REVOLTING GAULS PRESSURE CAESAR

Festering in late 53 BC and spreading like an epidemic in 52 BC, revolt erupted in Gaul as many tribes took up arms to revolt against subjection by Julius Caesar. The first Roman losses came early in the winter of 53–52 BC, when the Cornute tribe rose up and massacred Roman troops billeted in their mountaintop capital, Gergovia, today's Orleans in the north of central France. Inspired by this when he learned of it in January, 52 BC was Vercingetorix, a young noble of the Averni tribe in the Auvergne Mountains in south central France. Aged around thirty, the son of the late chief of the Averni, Vercingetorix began agitating for his people to also rise against the Roman occupiers of Gaul. This terrified his uncle and other leaders of his tribe, and Vercingetorix was thrown out of Gergovia.

Vercingetorix persisted with his rebellious rhetoric in the villages of the area, exciting his fellow Gauls. Soon he was able to return to Gergovia at the head of an armed force and eject his uncle and other negative elders of the tribe, taking charge of the Averni. Vercingetorix then sent emissaries to tribes from the Seine to the Bay of Biscay, urging a massive unified revolt. Tribes humiliated by Julius Caesar just a few years earlier grabbed at this opportunity to unite in resistance. Electing Vercingetorix their commander-in-chief, numerous tribes mobilized for war.

Once Caesar learned of this, he hurried from his winter quarters in Cisalpine Gaul. Leaving his favorite Decimus Brutus in command in southern Gaul, Caesar summoned his ten legions from their winter camps. At the head of several legions, Caesar stormed the rebel Gallic towns of Orleans and Montargis, then confronted Vercingetorix's cavalry when it approached. Following cavalry skirmishes, Caesar's army marched toward Avaricum, modern Bourges sixty miles southeast of Orleans. Vercingetorix and most of his troops camped eighteen miles from Bourges, and under their noses Caesar stormed the city. Only eight hundred of the forty thousand occupants of Bourges survived the Roman assault.

Caesar now divided his army. Sending his longtime deputy Labienus north with four legions to deal with rebellious tribes in the area of modern Paris, Caesar himself marched south with six legions to take Vercingetorix's undefended capital. When Vercingetorix realized the Roman general's intent, he too marched for Gergovia, with all speed. Vercingetorix won the race, so Caesar set up two camps nearby, connecting them via a trench line.

Ten thousand men of the Aeduan tribe were marching to Gergovia, supposedly to support Caesar. But learning through spies that the Aeduans had changed sides and were intending to attack him, Caesar marched four legions to meet them, covering twenty-four miles in a day. On seeing the legions approach, the Aeduans surrendered. Caesar added them to his force and, giving his men just three hours to rest, turned back for Gergovia.

Meanwhile, Vercingetorix had been besieging the two legions left to hold Caesar's camps. Arriving back at dawn, Caesar sent the 13th Legion hurrying away on a feint, accompanied by his mule drivers riding their own mules and pretending to be cavalry. This ruse drew off many of Vercingetorix's men and gave Caesar the opportunity to attack and overrun three enemy camps outside Gergovia. But now the men of his reliable 10th Legion became overconfident and launched an attack on the walls of Gergovia itself, ignoring the "Recall" when Caesar had it trumpeted.

Led by the 8th, other legions joined the 10th under the walls of Gergovia, and were soon struggling against superior enemy numbers as the Gauls drawn off by the ruse flooded back. When Caesar sent the Aeduans to support his legionaries, many Romans thought this a Gallic attack from the rear, panicked, and began to give ground to Vercinge-torix's men. Personally rallying the 10th Legion, Caesar made a stand on a slope. Other legions joined him, and eventually, after desperate fighting, the Gauls withdrew to Gergovia.

But Caesar had lost eight hundred legionaries, including forty-six centurions. If the Averni were to be believed, Caesar even lost his own sword in the struggle. A century and a half later, the writer Plutarch would be shown the sword hanging in a temple in Gergovia, by then a very Romanized city. After Caesar's men cremated their dead and tended their wounded, he realized that his position was untenable and withdrew his army from the mountain. It was the first major military reverse of his career.

While this had been going on, Labienus had defeated a Gallic force that attacked his legions on marshy ground at Grenelle south of the Seine, now part of modern-day Paris. Despite his victory, Labienus perceived the dangers of being cut off in the north, and soon marched his legions to rejoin Caesar in the south.

With both Roman armies retreating, eighty thousand armed and elated Gauls flocked to Vercingetorix's standard. To help command his army, Vercingetorix appointed three fellow generals, including an Averni relative, apparently a cousin. He then chose to concentrate his forces at another mountaintop city, Alesia, modern-day Alise Saint Reine, on the plateau of Mount Auxois, thirty miles north of today's Dijon. On learning this, Caesar, determined to quickly reverse his fortunes before his men's morale suffered, marched for Alesia as soon as Labienus and his legions linked up with him.

By this time, Caesar had a new quaestor marching with him, Mark Antony. Although Antony was related to Caesar on his mother's side, in a Roman political world in which even brothers could take opposing sides, blood relations were never a guarantee of which faction you embraced, or embraced you. Antony had been given his first opportunity to shine as a soldier by Pompey's client Labienus, and he could have been expected to have enjoyed Pompey's patronage. But Caesar had recently found his way to Antony's heart, via his purse, paying off his substantial debts. Antony would prove a fanatically loyal lieutenant, even after Caesar's death.

That September, on arriving below Alesia, Caesar had his ten legions dig a ten-mile double-sided entrenchment line around the rebel city, dotting the line with twenty-three forts, with several camps established behind the trenches. A museum onsite today recreates part of that impressive trench line. Learning of Vercingetorix's plight, tribes allied to him assembled a massive relief force and marched on Alesia. Caesar wrote that this force numbered 330,000 men—probably another of Caesar's self-serving exaggerations. It's nonetheless likely that the relief force contained at least 100,000 men. Among the rebel Gallic commanders was King Commius, formerly Caesar's envoy in Britain.

Initially, the Gallic relief force threw itself at Caesar's outer defense line, without effect. Then, coordinating with Vercingetorix inside Alesia, the relief force sent sixty thousand men against Caesar's outer wall while Vercingetorix sent a similar number of men from Alesia against the inner wall. Labienus now told Caesar that the time was right to launch a counterattack, and on his advice Caesar was one of several Roman commanders who burst out from their lines with select parties of infantry and cavalry and attacked the rear of the Gallic relief force.

The result was panic in Gallic ranks, and the relief force was devastated. Thousands of Gauls were slain. Tens of thousands threw down their weapons and surrendered. Before long, in Alesia, surrounded, out of food and water, Vercingetorix's men lost the will to fight and called on him to give up. Laying down their arms, they filed from the city and surrendered themselves to the waiting Romans. Caesar was to say that he gave every one of his legionaries a Gallic slave from among the prisoners of Alesia. He released another twenty thousand captives, in return for the submission of their tribes.

Vercingetorix himself rode down from the city and surrendered to Caesar personally. Caesar rated himself a merciful man, but six years after this he had Vercingetorix garroted to death at Rome after he had been led in chains through the streets in Caesar's Gallic Triumph. Although the execution of an enemy commander as the culmination of a Triumph was an age-old tradition, it was something that Pompey was not known to ever have done.

At Rome during 53 BC, unrest caused by Crassus's defeat in Parthia and street-fighting between opposing mobs meant that the consular elections for 52 BC could not be undertaken. With no consuls to inaugurate the year on January 1, 52 BC, the Senate appointed a number of its members who had served as consul or praetor to act as *interreges* until new consuls could be safely elected. The *interrex* acted as consul for just five days before passing power on to another *interrex*. If, once all the appointed *interreges* had served their allotted five days, still no consul had been elected, the cycle would begin over again with the first *interrex*.

On January 18, 52 BC, one of the latest *interreges* was in office when a violent event took place that shook the people and government of Rome. This violence erupted after the old enemies Clodius and Milo happened to pass each other sixteen miles outside Rome on the Appian Way. Men at the tail ends of both parties began to scuffle, and their comrades joined in. Clodius's party included thirty armed slaves, but Milo was escorted by armed gladiators, and they soon had the upper hand. In the fighting, Clodius was wounded by a gladiator named Birria and took refuge in a wayside inn as his men fled. Milo sent his gladiators to finish off his enemy, and Clodius was dragged from the inn and killed. A passing senator subsequently discovered Clodius's body and had it returned to Rome.

Clodius's wife Fulvia, defying the law, encouraged her late husband's supporters to cremate his body on a massive funeral pyre beside the Curia Hostilia, as the Senate House was called. Inevitably, and probably not coincidentally, this fire spread to the Senate House, which was razed to the ground. The Curia would not be rebuilt for some years, and in this crisis the Senate immediately convened in a temple to discuss a way to return stability to Rome's government.

The senators were soon in agreement that a strong man must be appointed to return order and calm. There was just one man for the job. Knowing that it had previously been suggested that Pompey be made Dictator, and had rejected the idea, it was now proposed that he be appointed sole consul for the year. Even Cato backed the idea. When this was conveyed to Pompey at his Carinae house, he took the job. To restore order, he levied troops in the city to augment the Praetorian Guard complement, and let it be known that he favored the arrest of Milo for murder, followed by a swift trial.

Milo returned to the city and attempted to build public support, and on January 22 he climbed the hill to Pompey's house and asked for an interview with Pompey, but the new consul refused to see him. Pompey, having decided that Milo's trial would calm stormy waters, had him charged and set a trial date for February. It would be said that Pompey handpicked the fifty-one jurors, but the presiding magistrate was Cato's brother-in-law Lucius Domitius Ahenobarbus, one of Pompey's leading critics. And, to represent the accused, Pompey called on Marcus Cicero, the finest defense lawyer in Rome.

Pompey allocated five days for the hearing. The first day descended into chaos as Clodius's supporters in the gallery shouted down witnesses. So for the second day Pompey sent in armed troops to keep the gallery quiet, allowing the sitting over the next four days to proceed with decorum. On the last day, Cicero delivered his lengthy prepared speech in which he beseeched the jury to exonerate Milo. Some later said that, affected by Clodian hecklers, Cicero failed to complete his address. Others would disagree, stating that his presentation was complete but lacked its usual verve. Cicero would subsequently publish his argument.

The jury found Milo guilty, thirty-eight votes to thirteen, and judge Ahenobarbus sentenced him to confiscation of assets and exile from Italy. Milo would serve that exile in Transalpine Gaul, in Massilia. In 48 BC, he would take up arms against Caesar and lose his life. As for Clodius's wife Fulvia, she would go on to marry again, first to Curio the Younger, close friend of both Mark Antony and Clodius, and then, after Curio's death, Mark Antony himself. Claudia, Fulvia's daughter with Clodius, would become Octavian's first wife.

With the Milo trial completed, Pompey proceeded to govern Rome as sole consul with a light touch. To honor his alliance with Caesar, he guided through a new bill supported by all ten Tribunes of the Plebs that gave Caesar the right to stand for consul from outside Italy.

Some of the other legislation passed under Pompey positively thrilled the likes of Cato. One new bill required consuls to not take up provincial governorships until five years after they served as consul, as opposed to the current system where consuls took governorships immediately following their consular year. During Pompey's consulship, too, a new law was brought in increasing the penalties for bribery during election campaigns. This would certainly not have pleased Caesar. It was as if Pompey chose to give a little to both allies and enemies.

Most importantly, Pompey restored law and order to Rome, enabling the annual elections to take place at their usual time. The consuls elected that summer for the following year were Claudius Marcellus, who was not well disposed toward Caesar, and Servius Sulpicius Rufus, the friend of Cicero and supporter of Pompey whose son was serving as a legate of Caesar in Gaul.

For Pompey personally, it was a year of joy. To begin with, he remarried. Around the middle of this year, he was approached with a marriage proposition by Quintus Caecilius Metellus Scipio Nasica. This Scipio, a man of praetor rank who was eleven years Pompey's junior, had a widow on his hands: his twenty-one-year-old daughter Cornelia Metella had been married to the ill-starred Publius Crassus, who had been killed in Parthia with his father, and Scipio proposed that Cornelia become Pompey's new wife.

Possibly seeing this as a way of maintaining the links of the triumvirate, at least in spirit, by wedding his late ally Crassus's daughter-in-law, Pompey agreed to the match. The strict dictates of Roman society meant that Pompey might have never seen Scipio's daughter before, and he certainly would not have spoken with her previously. He was her elder by thirty-two years, and she was younger than his elder children. He was no longer the lithe, fit young general he had once been—as busts sculpted of him at the time reveal, he had developed a paunch and a double chin. Yet he had not lost the charm, grace, and kindly nature that Plutarch said made him so attractive to women. Pompey quickly fell in love with his fiancée, and she with him. Cornelia was a beauty, of good character, well-read, interested in geometry and philosophy, and a gifted lyre player. Proving her husband's intellectual peer, Cornelia would also have a good relationship with her stepchildren and prove intensely loyal to Pompey.

The couple soon married, probably that summer, and to cement the familial alliance of the Pompey family and Scipio's Metellus family, Pompey appointed his new father-in-law his co-consul for the remainder of the year, commencing September 1, with Scipio chairing the Senate for two of the next four months. This same year, Pompey officially opened his new theater on the Field of Mars with free theatrical performances that wowed the Roman population. It is possible that, as previously, Pompey staged the event on his birthday, September 29, attending the opening to receive the plaudits of the crowd for both his building and his bride.

That September, too, Caesar was overcoming Vercingetorix and his Gallic rebels in Gaul. Following his victory at Alesia, there was great relief at Rome when a report was received from Caesar stating "The whole of Gaul was now conquered." Caesar's legions were on their way to winter quarters, and all seemed back on an even keel as far as Romans were concerned, with Pompey and Caesar between them having righted the ship of state.[86]

Caesar himself seems to have believed that Gaul was truly conquered and the Gauls cowed, for he once more split his legions one and two at a time across numerous winter camps throughout central and northern Gaul. Yet, despite the Roman victory at Alesia, the Gallic revolt was far from over. Not all the Gallic rebel leaders had fallen or been captured at Alesia. Men such as Commius had escaped and were talking up resistance among tribes who gave them sanctuary. As Caesar was to learn in December, tribes farther afield would continue to resist, with rebellion flaring across Gaul, first here and then there, like spot fires in wildfire season.

The Roman general's spies told him what was in the minds of Gallic leaders, as he himself would write: "The Gauls all realized that they could not resist the Romans even with the largest possible army, if it was to be concentrated in the one place, but thought that if a number of tribes made simultaneous attacks in different places, the Romans would not have enough men or resources to meet them all in time."[87]

Not only would the Gauls' new war policy stretch the existing Roman forces in Gaul; but as Caesar also wrote in his account of the Gallic Revolt, his troops were exhausted following the grueling battles of 52 BC and in need of rest. The Gauls, meanwhile, would be using fresh recruits. Caesar needed reinforcements, fast. And they had to be hardened, experienced Roman troops, not green recruits who would need to be nursed through their first battle. The very men he needed lay just across the Pyrenees from Gaul. But they were Pompey's men, in Pompey's legions, for Pompey still governed the two Spanish provinces from Rome, via the agency of his deputies Afranius and Varro.

Early that winter, Caesar wrote urgently to Pompey at Rome, seeking the loan of at least two of his best legions from Spain. Without hesitation, Pompey agreed to help Caesar, dispatching orders for his best unit, his renowned 1st Legion, to depart its base at Cordoba in Farther Spain, with the seasoned Spanish legionaries of his 6th Legion to also set off for Gaul, from their base in Nearer Spain. Both units were under orders to march over the mountains into southern Gaul and put themselves at Julius Caesar's disposal. Far from having been terminated by the deaths of Julia and Crassus, the alliance between Pompey and Caesar seemed to be holding firm.

On December 29, having summoned these Pompeian reinforcements, Caesar, receiving reports that the Bituriges of Bourges were ready to rise, left his Besançon headquarters under the command of quaestor Mark Antony and hurried north with a cavalry escort. He had stationed the 13th Legion in Bituriges territory for the winter, and he called them to arms. Whether the Bituriges were about to revolt as reported is disputable, for Caesar found their men tilling their fields when he arrived. He nonetheless led the 13th Legion on a sweep through Bituriges territory, killing, pillaging, and burning, after which the tribe's leaders quickly sued for peace, providing Caesar with hostages.

Returning to Besançon in February after a forty-day absence, Caesar found that Pompey's 6th Legion had arrived in Transalpine Gaul from Nearer Spain. Mark Antony had sent it to join the understrength 14th Legion at the Saône River, a tributary of the Rhône in eastern Gaul, to collect corn from the locals for the upcoming campaigning season. Caesar began conducting court sittings in Besançon, but just eighteen days later he received messages from his new allies the Bituriges that they were being attacked by their neighbors the Carnutes. Without waiting for confirmation, Caesar summoned both the 6th and the 14th Legions, then marched north with them, plus Gallic cavalry and German auxiliaries, arriving unexpectedly in Carnute territory.

With the Carnutes fleeing in all directions, Caesar quartered his men at the tribe's capital, today's Orleans, for the remainder of the severe winter, as his cavalry and auxiliaries looted surrounding districts. Hearing that Roman allies the Remi were now under threat from the Belgic Bellovaci, in Caesar's opinion the best fighters in Gaul, whom he'd subdued six years earlier, calling out another four legions from their winter camps he marched on the Bellovaci homeland in today's Picardy. Learning from captives that the Bellovaci were led by their chieftain Correus and the Atrebates's indefatigable renegade king Commius, who had concentrated their people in a wood surrounded by marshland, where they were joined by members of five other tribes, he went on the offensive.

Surprised by enemy numbers, the Roman general built a heavily fortified marching camp and sent for a further three legions. For days, the Gauls remained in their own camp, sending out select men to harass Caesar's foraging parties and cutting off and destroying a Remi cavalry unit. Learning that Gaius Trebonius was approaching with three additional legions, the rebels sent their dependents away before creating an ingenious wall of flames, behind which they withdrew their warriors to a new position ten miles away.

From prisoners, Caesar learned that his opposite numbers planned to lead him into an ambush, so he played along, all the time with his troops primed to act. With a bloody counterattack, the Romans surprised and turned the tables on their enemies. Caesar estimated that half the rebels were killed, along with their leader Correus. Once again, Commius succeeded in getting away. Crossing the Rhine, he found sanctuary with German tribes. Surviving a trap set by Titus Labienus, Commius would ultimately end up living among the tribes of southern Britain, declaring that he never wanted to see another Roman in his life. The surviving Bellovaci surrendered, entering into a peace treaty with Caesar.

As the improved weather of the spring of 51 BC arrived, Caesar sent legion detachments throughout Gaul to punish every hint of rebellion. Two legions went with Labienus to the Moselle homeland of the restless Treveri, where he soon defeated Treveran forces and their German allies. Meanwhile, Gaius Fabius and Gaius Caninius Rebilus put down revitalized resistance in the lands of the Pictones south of the Loire River in central Gaul, then hastily intercepted and routed a rebel force marching on Transalpine Gaul.

By the midsummer of 51 BC, in southwest Gaul another rebel force made up of Cadurci and Senones tribesmen occupied an Iron-Age hill fort called Uxellodunum, just to the north of the Dordogne River in today's Lot department. With two legions, Caninius Rebilus surrounded the hill. He was soon able to destroy most of the rebels in the open when they attempted to bring in supplies at night. His colleague Fabius took over the siege of Uxellodunum, and Caesar arrived soon after with his cavalry. Taking charge, Caesar used his troops to cut off the stream that flowed by the enemy fort.

The rebels, believing the sudden loss of their water supply the work of their gods, lost heart and surrendered. One of the two Gallic commanders committed suicide. The other escaped, only to be handed over to Caesar by friendly Gauls. Caesar, exhausted by having to dive first one way and then another to snuff out resistance, decided to send a signal to all of Gaul. Accepting the surrender of two thousand rebels, he chopped off both their hands and then let the men go, to fend for themselves for the rest of their lives as best they could. Eighteen hundred years later, France's Emperor Napoleon, while an admirer of Caesar, would brand this act "cruel" and "quite atrocious."[88]

With all quiet once more in Gaul, Caesar ordered his legions into winter quarters and journeyed to Transalpine Gaul to conduct the assizes. This time, the Gallic Revolt truly was at an end. By Plutarch's estimation, over the past eight years Caesar had killed a million Gauls, sold another million into slavery, and brought eight hundred Gallic cities and towns firmly under Roman control. The annual taxes being imposed on the Gauls would from this time forward add 40 million sesterces a year to the coffers of the Treasury at Rome, and auxiliary Gallic cavalry provided to Rome as part of the peace treaties that the tribes of Gaul signed with Caesar would make them among the most numerous in the Roman army. But, unlike Pompey in the East, Caesar would not create new Roman provinces in Gaul. That would come after his time.

The consuls for 50 BC elected in the summer of 51 BC were Lucius Cornelius Lentulus and Gaius Marcellus. Lentulus had led the prosecution of Clodius Pulcher over the Bona Dea scandal involving Caesar's then-wife, and was never a friend of either Clodius or Caesar. His colleague Marcellus, a close friend of Cicero, despised Caesar, for this was the Marcellus who Caesar had attempted to deprive of his wife, Octavia, by proposing that she divorce him and marry Pompey after the death of Julia. Not only would the new consuls be his enemies, but Caesar was convinced that their election was rigged. He had supported another candidate at that election—Servius Galba, his subordinate in Gaul, who left his service and returned to Rome in the winter of 51–50 BC. According to Caesar, and in a claim that has a very modern ring to it, Galba was more popular and received more votes than Lentulus or Marcellus, yet lost.

Despite Galba's electoral defeat, Caesar had other means of maintaining political influence at Rome. In the elections of 51 BC, one of the ten Tribunes of the Plebs elected for service in 51–50 BC was the younger Gaius Curio, boyhood friend of Mark Antony. For years, Curio and his father had been bitter opponents of Clodius, and Curio had never demonstrated any support for Caesar. In fact, he was viewed very much as a friend of Cato and an opponent of Caesar. Yet, as he was to demonstrate once he was a tribune, Curio had become a secret agent of Caesar's, and it would be said that Caesar had paid him a massive bribe to come over to his side.

Caesar would also control newly elected consul for 50 BC Lucius Aemilius Paullus, paying him a bribe of 36 million sesterces. At the same time, Caesar bribed several magistrates to sit on their hands. These would have included the praetor responsible for prosecuting financial crimes such as bribery of officials, with which Caesar had already been charged. Another would have been the praetor responsible for prosecuting crimes by provincial governors, with Caesar's conscription of the men of the 15th and 16th Legions being without Senate approval and therefore illegal.

With the Tribunes of the Plebs wielding so much power in the legislature, including the power of veto, Caesar took a new army quaestor onto his staff for 50 BC and sent Mark Antony back to Rome to stand in the summer elections for the next tribunate. Antony, well liked by commoners for his prowess with the sword, the wine cup, and the ladies, would be duly elected a Tribune of the Plebs for 49 BC. He would also be elected augur—a part-time religious role which, while prestigious, had no political power. Replacing Curio as Caesar's principal mouthpiece in the Senate, Antony would take up his post of Tribune of the Plebs on December 10, 50 BC, for, in one of the quirks surrounding the election of officials of the Roman Republic, Tribunes of the Plebs served from December 10 in one year until December 9 the following year.

Another of the new Tribunes of the Plebs elected for 49 BC along with Antony would be Quintus Cassius Longinus. A brother or cousin of the Marcus Cassius who had served as Crassus's quaestor in Parthia, this Cassius had himself served as a military quaestor in 54 BC, a year ahead of his relative. Quintus Cassius had served under one of Pompey's generals in Farther Spain, either Varro or Petreius, indicating that he was a client of Pompey. It would therefore have been assumed that Cassius was a Pompey man when he was elected; but, as he was to show once he took up his post as a Tribune of the Plebs, Cassius had changed his colors to become a Caesar man. Within a year, Cassius would prove to be an immensely greedy and rapacious young man, losing his life in his quest for gold. And this, along with his actions as tribune, leave little doubt that he was another whose loyalty had been purchased by Caesar.

———————

O nce a new consul took the curule chair in January, 50 BC, in a move that annoyed Caesar even more than Galba's electoral defeat, Caesar and Pompey were required by the Senate to each donate a legion for service in a new Senate-approved campaign against the Parthians being prepared by the current governor of Syria, Marcus Bibulus—Caesar's fellow aedile in 65 BC and his alienated fellow consul six years later.

Caesar and Pompey both complied with the order. Caesar delegated his 15th Legion, one of his newer and less-experienced units, to the Parthian campaign, dispatching it from its winter base in Gaul to march to Italy and embark from Brindisi for the East as the Senate required. Pompey ordered his elite 1st Legion to Italy to join the 15th for the transfer to Syria.

Despite having borrowed the 1st Legion from Pompey for his operations in Gaul, Caesar had never used it for active service during the Gallic Revolt, apparently leaving it in reserve in Transalpine Gaul. The revolt was over; Caesar said so himself; so he had no further use for Pompey's legion. Just the same, Caesar railed over Pompey's recall of it for use in Parthia. The 1st was now his legion, Caesar said, its current enlistment lately recruited in his province of Cisalpine Gaul—some time before he became governor, it has to be said. Caesar implied that Pompey had deliberately taken the legion away from him to reduce his military strength.

What happened next really sparked Caesar's fury. Instead of sending the 1st and the 15th to the East, once the units arrived in Italy proper, the consul Marcellus ordered the two legions to encamp together outside the city of Capua, just to the south of Rome, amid the twenty thousand former soldiers of Pompey who had been settled in the area on the initiative of Pompey but promulgated by Caesar when he was consul. And who was now residing in Capua? Pompey. Caesar was convinced that this was all Pompey's doing, a move designed to wound him. Yet never at any stage in his writings would Caesar reveal why Pompey was in Capua at that time.

In fact, Pompey was gravely ill. The nature of his illness was never revealed, but it laid him low for months, and the indications are that he never fully recovered. He seems to have initially been bedridden at his Alban villa. But Capua's warm, dry summer climate may have had something to do with his choice of it as a place of respite. This sort of climate was recommended by physicians for sufferers of tuberculosis, called *tabes* by the Romans. If that was indeed what Pompey was suffering from, he would have been advised by his doctor to leave before the winter, which could be very damp in Capua and unhealthy for tuberculosis sufferers. Just the same, tuberculosis tends to show itself when sufferers are quite young, and there is no evidence that Pompey had suffered from the disease earlier in life. The precise nature of his serious ailment is likely to forever remain a mystery.

Riled by the removal of two legions from his command, Caesar, unaccompanied by armed troops, crossed his southernmost provincial border into northern and central Italy, making surprise visits to towns and military colonies where he gave speeches and was welcomed by adoring crowds. All the talk was of the Gallic Triumph that he was expected to ask the Senate to award him once his gubernatorial terms expired in a year's time. But, as he had demonstrated previously, Caesar was prepared to wait for his Triumph. As far as he was concerned, power, and consequently self-preservation, came before glory.

His Italian tour was like a modern election campaign to motivate voters. And that was precisely what Caesar was doing, drumming support for his deputy Labienus, whom he intended backing in the next consular election, and for himself in the consular election of the following year. Before any of his enemies in Rome knew he was in Italy and a praetor could seek his arrest on the outstanding charges, or an antagonistic Tribune of the Plebs could levy new charges for his blatantly illegal enlistment of legions in Cisalpine Gaul, Caesar slipped back across the border. Swiftly traversing Cisalpine Gaul and the Alps, he returned to the bosom of his army in Gaul.

The slowly recovering Pompey, possibly hearing that Caesar had said unpleasant things about him on his flying visit to Italy, sent a trusted client to collect his 6th Legion from Caesar's army in Gaul and return it to its Senate-assigned station in Nearer Spain. This client was Appius Claudius Pulcher, who had been a consul in 54 BC. Appius was the elder brother of Clodius Pulcher, but as a close friend of Cicero he had never supported his sibling's disruptive, destructive politics or his vendetta against Cicero. Appius had become a high-ranking client of Pompey when his daughter married Pompey's eldest son Gnaeus.

In withdrawing the 6th Legion from Caesar's command, Pompey would have reasoned that, again, with the revolt in Gaul put down, Caesar had no need of it. For the very same reason, there were those who would have questioned why Caesar had not already sent the legion back to Pompey's command of his own volition.

Be that as it may, with this latest reduction of his military capacity Caesar was hopping mad. But cunning soon overrode his temper. Appius, the general leading the legion back to Spain, would subsequently report to Pompey that, as the 6th marched out of Gaul, Caesar had come to it and personally presented every single man in the unit with a gift of around one thousand sesterces—more than their annual salary of 900 sesterces—hoping, he said, that they would remember him kindly. It was an investment, of more than 5 million sesterces, in Caesar's future military plans.

Once Appius had relocated the 6th Legion to Nearer Spain, he returned to Italy and conferred with Pompey at Capua. He informed his patron that the mood he had gauged among Caesar's troops in Gaul was one of weariness with Caesar and affection for Pompey. Appius was of the opinion that if Caesar should lead his legions across the frontier into Italy, his men would throw their allegiance behind Pompey. Appius, it would turn out, was either a fool or had been fooled. But Pompey, unwell and hoping this affair would just go away, chose to believe him.

Apparently to take the heat out of their presence so close to Rome, and to himself, Pompey had Appius lead the 1st and 15th Legions away from the capital, marching them southeast into the Apulia region, today's Puglia, where they made camp for the winter as Appius returned to Rome to resume duties as one of the current censors. As the winter approached and politics heated up, Pompey, still physically weak and sickly pale, returned to Rome and his house in the Carinae to closely monitor Caesar's latest political and military maneuvers.

As that summer had come to an end, the thirty-one-year-old aedile and former Tribune of the Plebs Marcus Caelius Rufus had written to his patron and friend Marcus Cicero, who was then serving a short term as governor of Cilicia: "I see quarrels ahead in which strength and steel will be the arbiters. Fate is preparing a mighty and fascinating show." How right he was.[89]

XIX.

THIS MEANS WAR

Pompey, at Rome at the beginning of December, 50 BC, could not believe that his longtime ally Caesar would be so unwise and so unpatriotic as to go to war against his own country. At his city house, Pompey was visited by numerous senators who sought his counsel on what should be done to appease or oppose Caesar.

In Gaul, Caesar commanded nine legions, the 7th through the 14th, and the 16th. He would soon also commission a new legion in Cisalpine Gaul. This was the unit composed of freedmen to whom Caesar would grant citizenship. It would take the name the Alaudae (Crested Larks) Legion. Some years later this unit would be combined with the 5th Legion to become the 5th Alaudae Legion.

The Senate had eight legions it could immediately call on, the two encamped in Puglia and six under Pompey's lieutenants in the two Spains—the 2nd through the 6th plus the Valeria, an old legion originating in central Italy. When it was learned that Caesar was raising a tenth legion in Cisalpine Gaul, the Senate would authorize the raising of a new republican legion in Farther Spain. Because all the Spanish legion numbers were allocated, this would be called the Indigena or Native Legion. Although Caesar had sent his Gallic cavalry back to their tribes for the winter, he was known to have 4,400 German auxiliary cavalry in several winter camps in Gaul and Cisalpine Gaul.

Many senators were worried by the fact that Caesar's troops were nearer to Italy than most of the legions that the Senate could call on. When the hundreds of senators who sought Pompey's advice asked where the troops would come from to prevent Caesar from marching on Rome, Pompey replied, "Whenever I stamp with my foot in any part of Italy, there will rise up forces enough in an instant, both horse and foot." He was referring to his retired soldiers now living throughout Italy.[90]

Likewise, Cicero, still absent from Rome in Cilicia on government business, was convinced from his letters that Pompey had everything under control. "Should Caesar take leave of his senses," Cicero wrote to his friend Titus Atticus, "Pompey is quite contemptuous of anything he can do, and confident in his own and the Republic's forces."[91]

In contrast, writing more than a century later, Plutarch, while more inclined toward Caesar than to Pompey, was nonetheless in no doubt that Caesar had long planned to take power at Rome by force if he had to, and that he'd used Gaul as the "exercise ground" for his troops in preparation for an invasion of Italy.[92]

For this winter, Caesar had come across Cisalpine Gaul to the Italian east-coast port city of Ravenna, just above the Po River border between his province and Italy proper. Contrary to his previous practice, he had brought a number of troops with him for the winter break. Camped with him at Ravenna were his regular bodyguard contingent of 300 German mercenary cavalrymen, the most elite, dedicated, and reliable of his Batavian, Ubi, and Treveran riders. Accompanying them was the 13th Legion, which was down in strength because of casualties in the Gallic campaigns to a little above five thousand men.

As for the rest of his forces, Caesar had moved almost all units closer to Italy. Only several legions remained in occupied Gaul for the winter. The 8th and 12th Legions had crossed the Alps and were encamped separately in Cisalpine Gaul, only a few days' march from Ravenna and from Caesar. His reliable general Fabius was at Narbo Martius (Narbonne) in Transalpine Gaul with three legions including the 10th, as well as 400 cavalry detached from Labienus's command, strategically placed to intercept any of Pompey's legions that might attempt to reach Italy overland from Spain. Titus Labienus was on the Rhine close to Treveri territory with 3,700 Germanic cavalry.

Caesar's plan had been to run for consul, and he no doubt intended that once in the curule chair he would shepherd legislation through that legalized all those things that currently left him open to conviction, loss of property, and banishment. But if he could not achieve what he wanted by fair means, he was fully prepared to do so by foul.

When talk arose in Rome in March, 50 BC, of removing Caesar's Gallic command from him once it expired the following year, Tribune of the Plebs Gaius Curio made his support for Caesar clear when he proposed that if Caesar was required to surrender his command in Gaul, then Pompey must be required to also give up his Spanish command. This idea proved extremely popular with commoners, but it was voted down in the Senate. So, for much of the remainder of his term in office, Curio vetoed any further discussion of Caesar's current provincial command. In the summer, there was talk of Caesar being granted an extension of his command, but this found little support, and nothing was brought to a vote.

Come December, with just nine days left in office, Curio faced a Senate motion from Pompey's client Appius, father-in-law of Pompey's son, that Curio be ejected from the House. At Curio's urging, this was voted down by a majority of senators. Soon, in the Comitium, the public meeting space next to the Senate building, Mark Antony was reading aloud letters from Caesar that seemed to drip with compromise. In the House, Cicero's client Marcus Caelius Rufus, who was now an aedile, surprised all by speaking in favor of allowing Caesar to retain his command. Caelius had changed sides, almost certainly joining the long list of corrupt officials who accepted bribes from Caesar.

Curio now asked the Senate whether Caesar alone should step down and surrender his forces. A majority of senators withdrew from the chamber—in Senate votes, those who gave their assent to a motion remained present, while those who opposed it withdrew from the House to allow the counting of those who assented. So, the motion was defeated. Curio then moved that both Caesar and Pompey step down from their commands. This was approved, 370 votes for, 22 votes against. Presiding consul Marcellus applied his veto to prevent it becoming law, but this didn't stop Curio from going out to the people and crowing that only twenty-two senators supported Pompey.

In the House, as more senators rose to speak on other matters, presiding consul Marcellus angrily jumped up, declaring, "I will not listen to speeches when I see ten legions already crossing the Alps on the march toward Rome. On my own authority, I will send someone to oppose them in defense of the country!"[93]

Adjourning the sitting and acquiring a sword, Marcellus led a large party of senators—including consul-elect Lucius Cornelius Lentulus Crus—across the Forum, heading for Pompey's house. Pompey was at that moment coming in their direction, and the two parties met in the middle.

"I hereby give you orders, Pompey," Marcellus loudly announced, "to defend your country, to employ the troops you now command, and to levy more." Ceremoniously, he handed the sword to Pompey, who accepted it. Consul-elect Lentulus also gave a martial speech. But, according to Plutarch, a sense of mourning now prevailed in the city, as indicated by the fact that in the next few days some senators even went about in mourning black.[94]

Pompey issued orders for the levying of troops throughout Italy, and draftees answered the call. But, dreading the thought of another civil war, many were slow to do so, and some failed to present themselves to their local recruitment officers. Despite this, the indications are that thirty to forty thousand Italian men were conscripted for the Republic under Pompey's orders. This was well short of the numbers the consuls were expecting—130,000—but, together with the existing legions, the Republic counted more men under arms than Caesar.

With his tribunate ending on December 9, Curio appeared on the Rostra and complained bitterly about consul Marcellus, and about Pompey, who he blamed for the concerted opposition to Caesar. Departing Rome, he rode northeast to Ravenna, where he conferred with Caesar. He then hurried back to Rome. Regularly changing horses en route, he covered 270 miles in three days. Curio then took his seat in the Senate as an ordinary member of the House, priming Caesar's few allies with his master's instructions for tactics going forward.

On December 21, new Tribune of the Plebs Mark Antony overcame the objections of presiding consul Marcellus, who declared that Caesar was nothing more than a robber and deserved to be branded an Enemy of the State, to give a speech in the Senate in which he made scathing comments about Pompey and read aloud a severe letter from Caesar. In that letter, Caesar declared, in a not particularly veiled threat, that if he was not granted an extension of his gubernatorial command, he would bring succor to his homeland and himself.

Three days later, Cicero arrived back in Rome from his Cilician posting. The following day, he visited Pompey at home, and found him livid over Antony's speech. "How do you expect Caesar to behave if he gets control of the state, when his feckless nobody of a quaestor dares to say this sort of thing?" Pompey demanded.[95]

Cicero quickly became involved in negotiations between moderate senators and Caesar's friends, and was urged by his own friends to personally act as an intermediary between Pompey and Caesar to head off any armed conflict. Cicero declined to go to Caesar, and he would later express regret for having failed to do so. He proposed that Caesar should be given the governorship of Illyricum and two legions, from where he would be permitted to stand for consul. Pompey was not happy with this, and neither was the consul Lentulus.

Cato the Younger, who had lately become a solid supporter of Pompey without being bribed to do so, cried, from his Senate bench, "Pompey did nothing to be deceived again!" Apparently he was saying that he didn't trust Caesar to comply with this or any other deal.[96]

As it was to turn out, all who sought compromise were wasting their time. Caesar had already chosen his course of action. And in the wake of Antony's inflammatory speech, Pompey was no longer in the mood for compromise.

With the new consular year beginning seven days later on January 1, 49 BC, Marcellus was again consul, together with Lentulus. Neither man was a friend of Caesar, and both had short tempers. With Lentulus sitting as president of the Senate for the first month of the year, Pompey's father-in-law Scipio rose and suggested that if Caesar did not lay down all his arms by a set date, he should be declared an Enemy of the State. Because of Scipio's close connection with Pompey, it has always been assumed that Pompey was behind this provocative move, although there was no proof of it.

In response, Tribunes of the Plebs Antony and Caelius jointly proposed a last-minute compromise: that Caesar and Pompey both retain their provincial commands with just a single legion each. This was wholly impractical, and it was vehemently opposed by Cato during debate, but enthusiastically backed by Curio. When the time came to vote, Curio and Marcus Caelius were the only senators to withdraw.

The writing was on the wall—close to four hundred senators: all the members of the House including Pompey's longtime critics, except Caesar's two paid lackeys, had chosen not to buckle under to Caesar, and had chosen to throw their support behind the Republic's new commander-in-chief Pompey. Led by Cato, the House now proceeded to unanimously declare Caesar an Enemy of the State under a *senatus consultum ultimum*, or "final decree of the Senate."

Caesar's last four influential friends in Rome—Antony, Curio, Cassius, and Caelius—hastily hired a two-wheeled carriage and, dressed as rural slaves, fled the city. Heading northeast up the Flaminian Way, they went to join Caesar and inform him that his cause at Rome was lost. But Caesar had not waited to learn the outcome of his pleas to the Senate. Even before he heard that he had been declared an Enemy of the State, he made his move.

XX.

BATTLE OF THE GIANTS

On the evening of January 10, Caesar dined in his quarters at Ravenna. Those sharing his table included a general, a lawyer, the forty-one-year-old senator Aulus Hirtius, and several young Equites on Caesar's staff including cavalry prefect Gaius Asinius Pollio. Caesar's secretary Gaius Oppius was also there, along with Lucius Balbus, son of Balbus, Caesar's former Spanish prefect of engineers. Another diner was the thirty-six-year-old Gaius Sallustius, or Sallust as we know him. He'd recently fled to Caesar after being ejected from the Senate for immorality. He would prove a poor soldier but a capable writer.

A solitary man, Caesar accepted counsel but rarely sought it. And he had set his course many months before; perhaps years before. Opportunity is like virginity—once lost, it can never be regained. And according to Plutarch, Caesar was gifted with the faculty of seizing the right moment. Now Caesar had gauged that the right moment to go to war with his country had arrived. Following dinner, he climbed into a two-wheeled carriage and drove off, followed by Pollio at the head of Caesar's 300 German cavalrymen. In pitch darkness, the carriage's driver initially became lost, before finding his way to a bridge over the River Po.

Climbing from the vehicle, Caesar studied the passing waters of the Po. He knew that, once he crossed this river with his men, he would be breaking the law that barred provincial governors from leading armed troops across their provincial borders without Senate approval. On doing that, he would automatically be considered an Enemy of the State. As yet unaware that he already enjoyed that status as a result of the *senatus consultum ultimum*, in the early hours of the morning of January 11 he muttered a short statement, mounted his waiting horse, and, with Pollio riding at his side, led the cavalry across the bridge into Italy.

It has become legend that Caesar said "The die is cast" on this occasion ("die" being the singular of "dice"). The later Roman historian Appian claimed Caesar actually quoted a Greek saying popular at the time, "Let the die be cast." Either way, this was a massive roll of the die by Julius Caesar, invading his homeland.[97]

He had prepared the operation with care. Hours earlier, a small commando group of selected cavalrymen and legionaries from the 13th Legion had already crossed the river in the darkness, led by a young prefect. Wearing swords under disguising farmers' cloaks, they simply walked into the nearest major Italian coastal city, Arminium, today's Rimini. When the citizens of Rimini awoke the next day, they would find it under the control of Caesar's men. When Caesar subsequently arrived, he made his temporary headquarters in Rimini, where Antony, Curio, Cassius, and Caelius would soon join him from Rome. At dawn on January 11, the 13th Legion also crossed the river.

Caesar's audacious move took Pompey and all at Rome completely by surprise. Invading Italy with a single legion! It was madness. It was also genius, catching his opponents wholly unprepared while creating a wedge between senatorial forces in Spain and southern Italy. In the coming days, dividing his few troops between Antony and himself, Caesar progressively moved down through Picenum, Pompey's home territory, taking town after town against little or no opposition from the shocked locals. He was joined two days into the invasion by the 8th Legion, and shortly after that by the 12th.

Refugees fleeing to Rome from Picenum brought the news that Caesar had taken Rimini. Stunning Rome, Pompey ordered a mass evacuation from Italy to Greece, where he proposed to regroup all senatorial forces for a counteroffensive. Sending away their wives and children to country estates or distant islands, the consuls and almost every senator, including Cicero and Cato, and countless Equites departed Rome with their male relatives and staff. En masse, they flooded southeast to Brindisi, following Pompey—out of loyalty to and affection for Pompey, says Plutarch. At Brindisi, the 1st and 15th Legions and thousands of new recruits assembled.

After a short siege of Corfinium, the principal city of Picenum, Caesar accepted the surrender of the senatorial commander, Domitius Ahenobarbus, who, swearing to now stay out of the war, was allowed to go on his way. Caesar then took the eighteen thousand senatorial recruits in Corfinium into new legions he formed on the spot, then hurried to the capital.

Arriving at Rome and finding the more prosperous districts veritable ghost towns, Caesar went to the Treasury and demanded that it be opened. When a tribune named Metellus refused, declaring it illegal, Caesar lost his temper, snarling that he would do as he pleased, before threatening to put Metellus to death, adding, "And this, you know, young man, is more disagreeable to me to say than to do."[98]

Sending for workmen, Caesar broke open the doors to the Treasury and seized the contents. He had taken Rome without a fight, but he was sorely disappointed to find that tribune Metellus was representative of a broad lack of support. There were no cheering crowds, no Senate delegation seeking terms. He had expected the 15th Legion, a unit he'd personally raised and led for more than five years, to defect back to his command. But, remaining in southern Italy, it gave its loyalty to Pompey and the Senate.

Caesar would soon be devastated to learn that his staunchly reliable deputy of ten years, Titus Labienus, had abandoned him. Unwilling to go to war with his own country and considering Caesar a traitor, Labienus led the 3,700 German cavalry under his command from the Rhine to link up with Pompey and the Senate. Other men close to Caesar also abandoned him. His illegitimate son Brutus followed Pompey. Caesar's cousin Lucius Caesar decided not to support either side, remaining neutral. On the positive side of the ledger, Publius Sulla, Pompey's brother-in-law, took the rebel's side, probably for money.

Following Pompey to Brindisi with the three legions that had invaded Italy and two newly formed legions, Caesar blockaded Brindisi through February and into March. From the city walls, Pompey, the Senate, and their troops defied the invader as they waited for a senatorial war fleet to arrive. When it did, in early March, Pompey evacuated half his people by sea from Brindisi across the Adriatic to Dyrrhachium, today's Durres in Albania, then principal port of the Greek region of Epirus.

The fleet returned, and on the night of March 16–17 Pompey and the remainder of his men slipped away from Brindisi while using ruses to fool Caesar into believing they were still in the city. In this way Pompey masterfully shipped twenty-five thousand men away and across the Adriatic under Caesar's nose, regaining the confidence of senators who had accused him of blundering in abandoning Rome.

In sixty days, Caesar had made Italy his. But being without shipping, instead of following Pompey to Greece, he decided to first neutralize the senatorial forces in Spain while subordinates gathered cargo vessels. As Fabius led six legions into Spain, Decimus Brutus used the 11th Legion to besiege Massilia, which remained loyal to the Senate, and Curio and Pollio set off with two new legions for Sicily and Africa, to bring those areas under Caesar's control. As his recruiting officers forcefully levied enough recruits in Italy to give Caesar, along with captured Senate levies, a total of ten new legions, Caesar himself returned to Rome.

There, over April 1 and 2, he convened a meeting of a new, replacement Senate, its members appointed by him. To put backsides on Senate benches he recalled old men, added members of his staff, promoted men from Equite ranks, elevated provincials to the Senatorial Order, and even created senators out of centurions from his legions. This was Caesar's rubber-stamp Senate, which approved a rash of Caesarian appointments. Then, leaving Mark Antony in charge at Rome, Caesar dashed overland to Spain, completing the journey in twenty-seven days.

In Spain, he was again disappointed when the 6th Legion remained loyal to Pompey, despite the handsome bribe he'd previously paid its men. In a short, sharp campaign in Nearer Spain, Caesar initially suffered a

reverse at a river crossing while trying to outmaneuver Pompey's deputy Afranius. When this was reported at Rome, a crowd of commoners
gathered outside Afranius's house, raucously celebrating what they saw as
Caesar's defeat. But those celebrations proved premature.

Caesar subsequently outfoxed Afranius, cutting him off from supply and
forcing the surrender in present-day Catalonia of Afranius's five legions including the 6th. Caesar freed Afranius and his deputy Marcus Petreius when they
swore not to take any further part in the civil war. The two surrendered Pompeian legions originating in Cisalpine Gaul were marched to Transalpine Gaul
and discharged, and, on August 4, the Spaniards of the 4th, 5th, and 6th were
discharged on the spot in Spain and also sent home.

In Farther Spain, Pompey's commander Varro also surrendered to
Caesar, after the newer of his two legions, the Indigena, refused to obey
him. Varro was also pardoned by Caesar, who now controlled all of Spain.
As Caesar departed for Italy, he left Marcus Lepidus in charge in Nearer
Spain and Marcus Caelius in command of Farther Spain. The corrupt
Caelius proceeded to plunder his province, then flee with a ship full of
gold, only to go down in a storm with his ship and his gold.

Meanwhile, Massilia had also fallen to Caesar's forces. Subsequently,
sixteen warships sent by Pompey from Greece to help the defenders of
Massilia linked up with two warships from the city and pulled into Tarragona, capital of Nearer Spain. Afranius and Petreius were in Tarragona,
and believing that an oath given to a traitor did not count, they collected
3,500 men from the disbanded 4th and 6th Legions, loaded them onto
the warships, and set sail for Greece to join Pompey and continue the
fight against Caesar.

In another stunning setback for Caesar, in Africa, Curio and his two
legions were wiped out by the army of Senate ally King Juba. Curio's deputy Pollio managed to escape Africa and join Caesar, who, now ready to
go after Pompey, massed an army at Brindisi to invade Greece. To get
his best Spanish units to this point, Caesar and his deputy Mark Antony
had both decimated their own rebellious legions, including the 9th, by
executing one in ten of the mutineers.

"We have come almost to the end of our toils and dangers," Caesar assured his troops at a mass assembly outside Brindisi. After just one more battle, he promised them, they could go home. He told his officers that in Spain he had gone against an army without a general, and now he would go against a general without an army.[99]

On a cold, dark night in the late autumn of 49 BC, Caesar had gathered enough cargo vessels to ship fifteen thousand men from seven legions across the Otranto Strait to Epirus. Because the Spaniards of his veteran 7th, 8th, and 9th Legions continued to be mutinous, demanding their long-overdue discharge and promised bonuses, they were left behind at Brindisi with Mark Antony. On the fleet's return to Brindisi the next day in daylight, thirty ships were captured and burned by a senatorial fleet, which would continue to harry Brindisi. For months, Caesar sent almost daily messages to Antony, demanding that he bring the remaining legions to him, as Antony was kept in port by storms and the senatorial fleet. At one point, Caesar even contemplated taking a small boat back to Brindisi to hurry up his reinforcements.

That March, as Caesar broke winter camp and moved his first-wave troops up the coast toward Dyrrhachium, Pompey was setting off from Macedonia, where he, the Senate, and the army of the Republic had wintered. To be closer to his supply port, Pompey was also heading for Dyrrhachium. He had recovered from his illness sufficiently to train with his men, although only on horseback. Even so, he showed that he was still deadly accurate with a dart. His spirits, and those of his men, were up— two of Caesar's new Italian legions, the 24th and the 28th, had defected to Pompey when they became stranded on the Greek island of Corfu.

On learning that Antony had landed in Epirus with the eleven thousand men of Caesar's second wave, Pompey changed his line of march to intercept him. Caesar, coming to Antony's rescue, outmaneuvered Pompey and reached his deputy first. When Pompey made camp south of Dyrrhachium on high ground overlooking a cove, Caesar applied the same strategy he'd used against Vercingetorix at Alesia, surrounding the other side's base with a double line of entrenchments. Here, the inner encirclement was fifteen miles long; the outer, seventeen. To counter Caesar, Pompey built his own inner entrenchment line, launching attacks from this on select parts of the opposition lines. A stalemate developed, lasting months.

Then, in June, Pompey lured Caesar to Dyrrhachium with a fake offer from the townspeople, that of letting Caesar into the port city, whose gates had until then been closed against him. At dawn, when Caesar arrived with a cavalry escort at the town gate near the city's Temple of Artemis, he rode into an ambush. He only just escaped with his life. Simultaneously, Pompey launched an infantry attack on Mark Antony's sector in the encirclement, an attack that lasted four hours and left every surviving 8th Legion defender wounded, but which was ultimately unsuccessful in breaking through the trench lines.

In early July, two defectors from Caesar's army came to Pompey. Brothers, members of the Allobroges tribe in Transalpine Gaul and commanders of Caesar's Gallic cavalry, both had been made members of Caesar's Roman Senate the previous year. Caesar would later explain away their change of sides by saying he suspected the pair of embezzlement. The brothers told Pompey where Caesar's line was weakest, and, at dawn on July 7, Pompey launched an assault on that sector, which was manned by the 9th Legion.

Despite Antony bringing reinforcements, Pompey's troops succeeded in breaking out and occupying an abandoned Caesarian camp at the water's edge. Caesar personally led a counterattack on this camp, outnumbering the Pompeian defenders three to one, only for Pompey himself to appear at the head of five republican legions in his rear. The Pompeian troops in the waterside camp now charged, and, caught in a pincer, Caesar's men panicked, turned, and ran, trampling their own comrades. One of Caesar's fleeing standard-bearers even tried to stab Caesar when he stood in the way of the wild retreat. Caesar was forced to retreat, too.

But Pompey did not give chase. Caesar later belittled him for not following up on this victory and sweeping around behind the remainder of Caesar's army and destroying it, sarcastically remarking that the

Republic's forces could have had a complete victory if they had been led by a general who knew how to gain it. But even Caesar admitted that Pompey was probably wary of being lured into a trap, and had achieved his objective of breaking the siege line.

Caesar lost a thousand men that day. Many more were wounded. At a subsequent assembly he berated his men and demoted those who ran, declaring, "The setback we have sustained cannot be blamed on me."[100]

Finding his situation untenable, and in need of supplies, Caesar withdrew his forces, abandoning his Dyrrhachium position. First sending his baggage away just after sunset, he followed with the troops in the early-morning darkness. Pompey, also breaking camp, cautiously followed his adversary. As Caesar marched into Macedonia, Pompey's army kept on his tail for four days before turning away to link up in Thessaly with Pompey's father-in-law Scipio, who had marched two Roman legions from Syria to reinforce him. After the two armies of the Republic came together amid loud cheers, they jointly resumed the pursuit of Caesar. In early August they found him encamped on a plain near the town of Pharsalus, modern Farsala, harvesting grain.

Pompey, in his camp, was surrounded by hundreds of armchair generals, senators who, buoyed by the success at Dyrrhachium, urged him to bring Caesar to battle, pointing to their superior numbers and the high morale of their troops. Pompey's gut instinct was to avoid an all-out battle and grind Caesar down. Most of Caesar's troops were tough, experienced fighters, their force a cohesive one. The Senate's army had been thrown together, with most of its men lacking battle experience. At a council of war, Pompey counseled avoiding overconfidence and impatience; but eventually, with Caesar's former deputy Labienus assuring his colleagues that the omens were good after that day's religious sacrifices, Pompey was worn down. Against his better judgment, he agreed to offer Caesar battle.

On the hot, dry midsummer morning of August 9, Caesar's army was breaking camp when the republican army marched from its camp and formed up in three battle lines beside the Enipeus River.

"The wished-for day has come at last!" Caesar declared.[101]

Ordering his officers to take Pompey alive if they could—so that he could seal an end to the civil war face-to-face, with a republican surrender across the board—and stipulating that the life of any Roman citizen-soldier in the republican army who surrendered should be spared, Caesar made his dispositions, and "Battle Order" was trumpeted.

Caesar fielded an army of twenty-one thousand men in nine under-strength legions, plus one thousand cavalry. As his troops formed three battle lines, Mark Antony commanded on the left with the 7th, 8th, and 9th Legions. Domitius Calvinus commanded in the center, where the newer, least-experienced units were placed. Publius Sulla commanded on the right, put there in part because he was Pompey's brother-in-law. Caesar's pet 10th Legion occupied the vulnerable extreme right wing.

The senatorial army consisted of forty thousand men, with twelve understrength legions, auxiliaries including 3,600 archers and slingers, and seven thousand cavalry. Its left was commanded by Domitius Ahenobarbus, who, like Afranius, had broken a promise to Caesar not to continue fighting him. On the extreme left stood the experienced 1st and 15th and two legions raised by Pompey in Italy the previous year; Caesar, in his memoirs, unable to bring himself to admit that his 15th now marched for Pompey, called it the 3rd Legion.

The republican center, commanded by Pompey's father-in-law Scipio, contained the legions from Syria, the two Italian legions that had defected from Caesar on Corfu, and a unit that Caesar called the Gemina or twinned legion, comprising cohorts detached from two Italian legions recently stationed in Cilicia by Cicero when governor there. The right was commanded by Lentulus, the previous year's consul, with the combined Spanish cohorts of the 4th and 6th Legions on the extreme right, under their old standards—Caesar, in his commentary, would contemptuously refer to them as merely "the Spanish cohorts," because he had disbanded their legions in Spain.

Pompey, with little confidence in his infantry, was counting on his vast cavalry advantage to win the day for him. Commanded by Labienus, his seven thousand troopers included the Germans, riders provided by eastern Roman allies, and one thousand cavalry detached from the Gabinians, brought from Egypt by Pompey's son Gnaeus. To Gnaeus's frustration, his father now left him in the senatorial camp, along with Afranius, in whom Pompey had little faith as a field commander after his performance in Spain. With the river protecting his own right flank, Pompey intended launching a massive cavalry charge against Caesar's exposed right.

Foreseeing this, as the republican cavalry formed up, in what would prove a masterstroke Caesar not only placed his cavalry on his right, but he hurriedly detached one cohort from each legion of his third line— 2,000 to 3,000 legionaries—and put them out of sight in a fourth line behind the 10th Legion. The Caesarian army's watchword, or password, for the day was "Venus, Bringer of Victory." The republican army's watchword issued by Pompey was "Hercules, the unconquered." Both generals were invoking their families' mythological pasts.

The battle began with Labienus leading his cavalry in a charge, covered by a rain of missiles from archers and slingers. Caesar's cavalry also charged. Overwhelming Caesar's troopers, Labienus led his men around to the rear of the 10th Legion, only for Caesar's waiting fourth line to spring up and swarm in among the surprised cavalry, pushing javelins into troopers' faces. As Labienus strove in vain to regroup them, his cavalrymen panicked, turned, and galloped away. Once dispersed, they would never reform or return.

Caesar, positioned on his army's right, now ordered his first two lines to charge Pompey's infantry. In savage fighting, the experienced legionaries on the republican wings held their ground, but the soft center gave way as green recruits ran for the rear. Soon, Pompey's wings were under threat of encirclement. Entire cohorts stationed beside the Enipeus splashed in good order across the river to escape. Pompey, commanding from his right, was whisked back to his camp for safety.

On Caesar's right, Sulla chose not to pursue retreating Pompeian troops, instead returning to the Caesarian camp. This enabled eighteen thousand republican legionaries and numerous generals and senators to escape and reach Greece's west coast, where they would board ships for Africa. Several thousand senatorial soldiers were killed in the battle, while another ten thousand were surrounded, surrendering as the battle soon ended.

Pompey, in his tent, was in a daze. His dedicated staff officer Marcus Favonius put him on a horse, and, with just a handful of companions, Rome's most celebrated general escaped east. On the Aegean coast, Favonius commandeered a grain ship for Pompey to continue his flight.

Marcus Cicero, disillusioned, returned to Rome from Greece, where, pardoned by Caesar, he would sit out the rest of the war as a neutral. In Africa, the escaped republican forces would regroup under Scipio, Afranius, Petreius, Labienus, and Cato the Younger. If Pompey had known that, he might have also headed for Africa. But, after collecting wife Cornelia and youngest son Sextus from the Greek island of Lesbos, he sailed for Egypt, whose young rulers, since the death of their father Ptolemy XII in 51 BC, the sixteen-year-old Ptolemy XIII and his twenty-one-year-old sister Cleopatra, owed their throne to him. They had an army and money, and his plan was to cement a military alliance with them against Caesar.

Caesar himself wanted to pursue Pompey, but his entire army, led by the mutinous Spanish legions, who now decided they'd fought their last battle, refused to follow him. Sending his own troops back to Italy with Antony, but not discharging them, Caesar resorted to paying nine hundred men captured at Pharsalus, men of Pompey's 6th Legion, the same legion he'd attempted to bribe several years earlier, to march with him and his three hundred German cavalry bodyguards as he set off in Pompey's wake. Locating and pardoning his illegitimate son Brutus, who guessed that Pompey would head for Egypt, Caesar took Brutus's advice and also set his course for Egypt. The chase was on.

XXI.

BOTH ASSASSINATED

After arriving with a small flotilla of warships off the Egyptian coastal city of Pelusium, Pompey was greeted by the Egyptian general Achillas and two Roman officers from the Gabinians—the tribune Lucius Septimius and a centurion, Salvius, who had served under Pompey against the Cilician pirates. By this time, with Gnaeus Pompey's departure from Egypt, Ptolemy XIII had deposed Cleopatra, who was in hiding.

Sensing danger, Pompey's wife Cornelia pleaded with him not to go ashore with Achillas. But Pompey agreed to accompany the Egyptian in a small boat with just four companions including two centurion bodyguards from the legions in Cilicia, whose troops joined Pompey as he passed by Cilicia from Lesbos gathering warships and men.

As the boat ground onto the beach, Pompey and his bodyguards stood up. Behind them, Achillas, Septimius, and Salvius also rose up, and plunged their swords into all three. From the deck of their anchored warship, Pompey's horrified wife and son saw Pompey's murder take place, and Pompey, to spare them the sight of his death throes, pulled his cloak over his face. This treacherous murder would go down in Roman history as "an act that brought shame to Caesar himself [for initiating the civil war], and will forever be a reproach to heaven," according to the poet Lucan a century later, writing during the reign of the emperor Nero, last of the Caesar family dynasty.[102]

Four days later, Caesar landed from a flotilla of his own in Alexandria with his small force, and was presented with Pompey's severed head by the Egyptians. Caesar claimed he'd wanted to negotiate an end to the conflict with Pompey once he caught up with him, and in tears he refused to accept the gory trophy. He was soon embroiled in a land-and-sea war with the Egyptians and their Gabinian accomplices, who saw their opportunity to eliminate him while accompanied by so few troops. After many months of fighting, and with Ptolemy XIII drowning in the Nile, Caesar won the war with the help of his admiral Tiberius Claudius Nero and Jewish forces led by Antipater the Idumean, who had previously aided Pompey's general Gabinius.

After an affair with Cleopatra and fathering a son with her, Caesar set her on the Egyptian throne and returned to Rome, en route defeating King Pharnaces, who had rebelled following news of the death of Pompey, who had enthroned him. This was at the Battle of Zela in Pontus, following which Caesar sent his famous message "I came, I saw, I conquered." Back in Rome, Antony bought Pompey's Carinae mansion cheaply at auction, with nobody else willing to bid, while Caesar acquired Pompey's Alban villa, which he would rarely visit.

In late 47 BC, Caesar sailed from Sicily to Africa with an army based around his best Spanish legions. With more promises, he had kept these men under arms, and now he led them in a campaign that culminated in the April 6, 46 BC, Battle of Thapsus, where, with Caesar laid low by an epileptic fit, his legions defeated republican forces and the army of King Juba. Scipio, Afranius, Petreius, Faustus Sulla, and Juba died as a result. Cato committed suicide. Labienus escaped to Spain with Sextus Pompey and some republican troops, and there, with Sextus and Gnaeus Pompey, built a new army. Spaniards with fond memories of Pompey flocked to them, and several of Caesar's legions, including the 8th, defected to this last republican army.

Back in Rome, Caesar celebrated four Triumphs, for two victorious battles in Egypt and the victories in Pontus and Africa. To outdo Pompey, he employed forty elephants in his triumphal celebrations, each with a burning torch held in its trunk. But the Roman crowd, seeing pictures being carried in the Thapsus parade depicting the deaths of noble

Romans—Scipio, Afranius, Petreius, Faustus Sulla, and, notably, Cato—audibly groaned. Smarting at the reception, Caesar set off for Spain.

On March 17, 45 BC, Caesar culminated a grueling Spanish campaign against the republicans with the Battle of Munda. Leading his troops in an uphill charge, Caesar found his exhausted men faltering. But his famous luck held—with one last desperate call he restarted the charge, which brought final victory. Labienus, his former deputy, fell at Munda. Gnaeus Pompey escaped, only to be killed days later. Young Sextus Pompey successfully fled Spain by sea. The forces of the Republic of Rome had finally been vanquished. Caesar, the autocrat, had won.

Once Caesar was back in Rome, in February 44 BC his compliant Senate declared him Dictator for life, in effect a king. Sidelining the difficult Mark Antony, Caesar appointed Marcus Lepidus his Master of Horse, the Dictator's official deputy. Pardoning men who'd previously opposed him, and sending home his German bodyguards, Caesar, a soldier at heart, began planning an invasion of Parthia, to succeed where Crassus had failed. But then, less than a year after becoming the undisputed ruler of Rome, Caesar was assassinated, by his own Senate.

Sixty members of the Senate appointed by Caesar joined the plot, led by his illegitimate son Brutus and Brutus's brother-in-law Cassius, former quaestor of Crassus. The final planning meeting by plotters took place under the guise of the coming-of-age toga party of Cassius's son.

Various motives for Caesar's murder have been advanced by historians. Certainly, many Romans were offended by Caesar's miscalculated Triumph for his African victory, which celebrated the deaths of Roman citizens, who had friends and relatives at Rome. Some opponents accused Caesar of planning to make himself king. Others felt their ambitions restricted under Caesar, although most had fared well under his rule, with several assassins including Decimus Brutus given senior appointments by Caesar to be taken up in 44 BC, while his general Trebonius, a leading conspirator, had been Caesar's appointee as consul the previous year.

While personal grievances influenced some, the fact that the Republic was dead—democratic elections were a thing of the past, and Rome was governed at the whim and decree of Julius Caesar—was what, publicly, drove them all. Calling themselves the Liberators, they declared that they were liberating Rome from a tyrant.

So focused on removing Caesar were they, the conspirators assumed that with his death, democracy would automatically return, overlooking the fact that Caesar had provided the blueprint for autocratic rule that others such as Antony and Octavian could—and would—follow. To show that the Liberators' quarrel was only with Caesar, Brutus naïvely stipulated that only Caesar be killed—not his deputy Lepidus, the still-loyal Antony, or other hard-line Caesarians. It would prove a fatal mistake.

So, on March 15, the Ides of March, with Caesar due to depart Rome the following day for the East and his Parthian campaign, the Senate met in the vestibule of the Theater of Pompey. Caesar was warned not to attend, by his wife Calpurnia, who had dreamed that he would be murdered, and by the haruspex who conducted the morning's ill-omened official sacrifices—turned into a fortune-teller by Shakespeare. But Caesar was persuaded to attend by conspirator Decimus Brutus, the general who'd taken Massilia for him, a man Caesar treated and trusted like a son, and who escorted him to his death.

While Trebonius deliberately delayed Antony to prevent his intervention, the assassins struck, using their styluses, Roman penknives, to frenziedly stab Caesar twenty-three times. Caesar died in a pool of blood, at the foot of a life-size statue of Pompey.

Caesar's brother-in-law Lucius Cinna, son of his late patron Cinna, declared after Caesar's assassination that the world was a better place for his death, a sentiment echoed by Marcus Cicero. And Tiberius Nero, who'd helped Caesar win his war in Egypt, stated that Caesar's assassins should have received a reward from the State for their deed.

Caesar's killers included, apart from Brutus, Cassius, Decimus Brutus, and Trebonius, his boyhood friend Casca and his general Galba. All would also die violently within several years. The last surviving assassin, Cassius Parma, would be killed thirteen years after Caesar's death by Caesar's heir Octavian, following the 31 BC defeat of Antony and Cleopatra that made Octavian, to become known as the emperor Augustus, sole autocratic ruler of Rome.

In 42 BC, Octavian, Antony, and Marcus Lepidus, labeling themselves the new Triumvirate, declared Caesar a god, and Octavian later erected the Temple of Julius the God beside the Forum. The Christian Church demolished that temple in the fifteenth century. Only its foundations remain. A monument was created in Egypt for Pompey, where his ashes were deposited, and 170 years after his death the emperor Hadrian visited and reverently restored it. Pompey's monument was destroyed by Jewish rebels. Nothing remains.

The so-called Pompey's Pillar in Alexandria dates from three centuries after his death, and had no connection with him. And the ruins of a villa on the Appian Way outside Alba identified in more recent times as Pompey's Villa have no proven connection with him. It's likely that Pompey's actual villa at Alba, which became the property of the emperors, was incorporated into the vast Alban villa of the emperor Domitian, at today's Castel Gondolfo, late in the 1st century, which ultimately became the summer residence of the Popes.

Pompey died a day short of his fifty-seventh birthday. Caesar was fifty-five when he died. Pompey's career as a general and statesman lasted thirty-five years; Caesar's lasted seventeen. Pompey celebrated three Triumphs. To outdo him, Caesar celebrated four (one in controversial circumstances). Pompey was the youngest-ever general to Triumph, and the first Equite to do so. Pompey was uncomfortable mixing with the rank and file; Caesar made an art of it. Yet Caesar decimated his own troops, punishing them by executing one mutinous soldier in ten. Pompey never did so. Pompey's legions never defected to his enemies, while four of Caesar's legions did so at different times. Pompey was assassinated by foreigners, Caesar by his own people. The wives of both men tried, in vain, to talk them out of going to their deaths.

Pompey delivered 140 million sesterces a year in annual revenue to Rome from his eastern conquests. Caesar delivered 40 million a year from his conquest of Gaul. In his career prior to the civil war, Pompey conquered or freed three thousand cities, towns, and strongholds in Spain, the Near East, and the Middle East; Caesar conquered eight hundred in Gaul.

Pompey swept the seas clean of pirates, restored Rome's grain supply, and built Rome's largest theater at his own expense. Caesar initiated a new forum, basilica, and Senate house, but never lived to see them completed. He reduced Rome's traffic congestion and created the world's first newspaper. He created the Julian Calendar, which remained in use in Europe until replaced in the sixteenth century by the Gregorian Calendar of Pope Gregory XIII, which corrected Caesar's version.

Pompey was respected, even by his enemies, and revered by the common people. Caesar was popular with commoners for his military successes, but purchased the loyalty of senior men around him. Caesar wrote intelligent, cogent, and self-propagandizing memoirs. They became standard reference works, and remain so to this day. If Pompey did pen any memoirs, they were lost, or destroyed after his death to preserve Caesar's legacy.

Pompey was a democrat, Caesar a despot, for, when Pompey had total power as sole consul, he handed it back to the Senate and people of Rome, while Caesar, once he had total power, held on to it as Dictator for life. Pompey strove to preserve the Roman Republic; Caesar destroyed it. Pompey looked to the past, and wanted to retain it; Caesar looked to the future, and wanted to mold it.

On a personal level, neither man drank or ate to excess or lived ostentatious lifestyles. Caesar enjoyed an occasional gamble, went to the horse races, and liked blood sports, maintaining his own troupe of gladiators. Pompey enjoyed art, the theater, and gardening. Both men were attractive to women, although Caesar was frequently unfaithful to his wives. Pompey was faithful to his wives, although he ditched his first wife, the orphan Antistia, for a political marriage to Sulla's stepdaughter, for which he was widely criticized, both then and later. Neither man was overtly religious. Caesar was a man of his word, and remained faithful to those who remained faithful to him, although there is evidence that he worked to undermine Pompey during their alliance. To preserve that alliance, Pompey threw his friends and clients Cicero and Gabinius under a bus, so to speak, although he did make it up to Cicero.

Many historians have characterized Caesar as the leader of the Populares faction, fighting on behalf of the rights of the common man against the Optimates, the wealthy aristocrats, who made Pompey their champion. Caesar himself never used the terms Populares or Optimates in his writings or speeches, and never apart from once, a decade before the civil war he launched, claimed to be fighting on behalf of the common man. Caesar was interested in the rights of just one man, himself. As Lucan wrote, a strong man cannot be denied his due. But in forcibly taking what he believes is his, a strong man will frequently pay a high price; Caesar certainly did—assassinated less than a year after becoming the sole ruler of Rome. Could Caesar's rebellion have been avoided? Not while so many at Rome distrusted, feared, and opposed him. From the moment Caesar built an army in Gaul, he was always going to seize power by force.

From my own perspective, I think I would choose the witty, literate Caesar as an entertaining dinner companion over the restrained, dignified Pompey. If I had a battle to fight, I would employ tactical genius Caesar as my general. To conduct a war, I would use strategic genius Pompey, and then ask him to implement the post-war peace settlement. To run a democracy, I would also turn to Pompey—although I don't think he would want the job. I would never make Caesar my head of state if I wanted fair, stable, incorruptible government.

Of course, the month of July was named after Caesar. Pompey, on the other hand, has no month of the year named after him. Yet Pompey was one of a small number of leaders down through history given the title Great—in his case, at the age of just twenty-three. Caesar was awarded no such appellation. But Caesar alone was declared a god. Pompey would have scoffed at the prospect of deification—for himself, or for any other mere mortal. And, had the idea been suggested to Caesar while he lived, I suspect that he too would have laughed.

NOTES

INTRODUCTION

1.   Schwarzkopf, *It Doesn't Take a Hero.*

I. A BOLT OF LIGHTNING CHANGES EVERYTHING

2.   The exact date of this event is unknown. However, several things tell us that this was in the late summer, probably in September. Thunderstorms were common at Rome during the summer. We are told that Pompey the Great was twenty at the time—he would turn twenty-one on September 29. And the events that would unfold in the weeks following this thunderstorm are known to have taken place in late 87 BC.

3.   Technically, with his last name a nickname, Gneius Pompeius Strabo should be called Pompeius in modern histories of Rome, just as he was by ancient writers. But because Strabo's son, another Gnaeus Pompeius, made the family name of Pompeius far more famous, later historians came to use the name Strabo to differentiate father from son.

4.   According to the later Roman historian Appian (*Roman History*), other members of the Roman aristocracy apart from Strabo were also struck by lightning in this storm. Several modern historians claim that Strabo succumbed to the same illness afflicting his troops, suggesting that it was dysentery. This is possible, but no ancient source refers to "the bloody flux," as dysentery was then known. But swamps in and near Rome meant that malaria was so common at this time that within several years, Julius Caesar himself would contract it. All accounts agree that Strabo's death was sudden and unexpected, which makes the lightning story credible. Plutarch and Appian were firm in their

conviction that it was the lightning strike that killed Strabo. Velleius Paterculus, writing nine decades after the event, doesn't indicate what caused Strabo's death, saying only that he died at this time.

5. Velleius Paterculus, *Compendium of Roman History.*

6. Pompey's rank in his father's army isn't given by ancient sources, but we are told he shared a two-man tent, a clear indication, along with his age, of his tribune status. Common soldiers then shared ten-man tents, and centurions had tents to themselves—Pompey, as an Equite, could never serve as a centurion, a conscripted plebeian.

II. CAESAR'S UNCLE TAKES POWER, POMPEY ON TRIAL

7. Plutarch, *Parallel Lives*, "Marius."

III. CAESAR THE PRIEST, POMPEY THE BOY GENERAL

8. This was likely to have been Lucius Cossutius Sabula, who made his fortune minting money at Rome.

9. Plutarch, "Sulla."

10. Vegetius, *Military Institutions of the Romans.*

11. Plutarch called the river the Arsis. Some later historians identified this as the Aesis, but that was on Picenum's *northern* boundary.

12. Plutarch, "Pompey."

IV. CAESAR IN JEOPARDY, POMPEY BECOMES GREAT

13. Suetonius, *The Twelve Caesars.*

14. Plutarch, "Pompey."

15. Ibid.

16. Ibid.

17. Ibid.

18. Ibid.

19. Ibid.

V. CAESAR HIDES, POMPEY TRIUMPHS

20. Suetonius.

21.   Ibid.

22.   Plutarch, "Pompey."

23.   Ibid.

24.   Ibid.

25.   Ibid.

26.   Ibid.

27.   Ibid.

VI.   AFTER SULLA, POMPEY & CAESAR ON OPPOSING SIDES

28.   Plutarch, "Pompey."

29.   Plutarch, "Sulla."

30.   Suetonius claims that, from Rhodes, Caesar raised a force of auxiliaries and drove Mithradates's deputy from Asia. But Mithradates was not then at war with Rome. Plutarch doesn't mention the episode. The only time it could have occurred was during the 73–63 BC third war against Mithradates, but Caesar wasn't in the East during this period.

31.   Seneca, *Dialogues and Letters*, "On the Shortness of Life."

32.   Appian, *The Civil Wars*.

33.   Plutarch, "Sertorius."

34.   Some historians place Gnaeus's birth in 75 BC. Unless Pompey was not the father, that would have been impossible. Pompey wouldn't return from Spain until 71 BC, and Mucia remained at Rome while he was away. We know Gnaeus was born before Pompey's daughter Pompeia, so the boy must have been born in 77 BC and the girl likely in 76 BC.

VII. CRASSUS THE PROPERTY DEVELOPER & CICERO THE LAWYER

35.   Scothard, *Crassus: The First Tycoon*.

36.   Plutarch, "Caesar."

VIII. SNEAKY SERTORIUS VERSUS PERSISTENT POMPEY

37.   Plutarch, "Sertorius."

38.   Frontinus, *Stratagems*.

39.   Plutarch, "Sertorius."

40.   Ibid.

IX. PESKY SPARTACUS TERMINATED BY CRASSUS AND POMPEY

41.   That these were Praetorian Guard troops is highly likely but unrecorded. The nearest reference to Praetorians being employed by the praetors in this era comes a decade later, in January, 62 BC, when Sallust, then a teenager, tells us that the praetor Marcus Petreius led a Praetorian Guard cohort in the defeat of Catilina and Manlius north of Rome that terminated the Catiline Conspiracy.

42.   Plutarch, "Crassus."

43.   Plutarch, "Pompey."

X. AS CAESAR WEEPS, POMPEY CONQUERS THE EAST

44.   Suetonius.

45.   Ibid.

46.   Suetonius; and Plutarch, "Caesar."

47.   Plutarch, "Pompey."

48.   Ibid.

49.   Cassius Dio, *Roman History.*

XI. CICERO RULES, CAESAR'S STAR RISES

50.   Suetonius.

51.   Plutarch, "Caesar."

52.   There were thirty-five voting districts in Rome. Votes from the Subura district, where Caesar lived, were traditionally the first counted.

53.   Sallust, "The Conspiracy of Catiline."

54.   Plutarch, "Caesar."

XII. POMPEY'S TRIUMPHANT RETURN,
CAESAR IMPERATOR IN SPAIN

55.   Dio.

56.   Lucan, *The Civil War (Pharsalia).*

57.   Plutarch, "Caesar."

XIII. CAESAR, POMPEY & CRASSUS RULE ROME

58. Plutarch, "Caesar."

59. Plutarch, "Pompey."

60. Plutarch, "Caesar."

61. Ibid.

62. Plutarch, "Crassus."

63. Plutarch, "Pompey."

64. Ibid.

XIV. CAESAR BEGINS TO CONQUER GAUL, POMPEY REHABILITATES CICERO

65. Caesar, *Gallic War.*

66. Ibid.

67. Plutarch, "Caesar."

XV. CAESAR SUBDUES GAUL & AGAIN EMBRACES POMPEY

68. Caesar, *Gallic War.*

69. Letter to Lentulus, 54 BC, Cicero, *The Letters to His Friends.*

70. Ibid.

71. Plutarch, "Pompey."

72. Ibid.

73. Ibid.

74. Caesar, *Gallic War.*

75. Ibid.

XVI. AS POMPEY & CRASSUS RULE, CAESAR INVADES BRITAIN

76. Plutarch, "Cato."

77. Josephus, *Jewish Antiquities*, and *The Jewish War.*

78. Caesar, *Gallic War.*

79. Ibid.

80. Plutarch, "Caesar."

81. Caesar, *Gallic War.*

82. Cicero, letter to Lentulus, 54 BC.

83.   Plutarch, "Crassus."

XVII. WITH TWO DEATHS, EVERYTHING CHANGES

84.   Plutarch, "Crassus."

85.   Ibid.

XVIII. THE REVOLTING GAULS PRESSURE CAESAR

86.   Caesar, *Gallic War.*

87.   Ibid.

88.   Napoleon, *Chronicles of Caesar's Wars.*

89.   Cicero, *Letters.*

XIX. THIS MEANS WAR

90.   Plutarch, "Pompey."

91.   Cicero, *Letters.*

92.   Plutarch, "Caesar."

93.   Plutarch, "Pompey."

94.   Ibid.

95.   Plutarch, "Cicero."

96.   Plutarch, "Pompey."

XX. BATTLE OF THE GIANTS

97.   Appian.

98.   Plutarch, "Caesar."

99.   Caesar, *The Civil War*; Plutarch, "Caesar."

100.   Caesar, *The Civil War.*

101.   Appian.

XXI. BOTH ASSASSINATED

102.   Lucan.

BIBLIOGRAPHY

BOOKS

Appian, *Roman History*, trans. H. White (Cambridge, MA: Loeb Classical Library, Harvard University Press, 2000).

Caesar, G. J., *The Civil War: Together with the Alexandrian War, the African War, and the Spanish War by Other Hands*, trans. J. A. Gardner (London: Penguin, 1967).

———, *The Conquest of Gaul*, trans. S. A. Handford (London: Penguin, 1982).

Carcopino, J., *Daily Life in Ancient Rome* (London: Pelican, 1956).

Cassius Dio, *Roman History*, trans. E. Cary (Cambridge, MA: Loeb Classical Library, Harvard University Press, 2004).

Cicero, *The Letters to His Friends*, trans. W. Glynn Williams (Cambridge, MA: Harvard University Press, 1965).

Dando-Collins, S., *Caesar's Legion: The Epic Saga of Julius Caesar's Elite Tenth Legion and the Armies of Rome* (Hoboken, NJ: John Wiley & Sons, 2002).

———, *Cleopatra's Kidnappers: How Caesar's Sixth Legion Gave Egypt to Rome and Rome to Caesar* (Hoboken, NJ: John Wiley & Sons, 2007).

———, *Legions of Rome: The Definitive History of Every Imperial Roman Legion* (London: Quercus, 2010).

———, *Mark Antony's Heroes: How the Third Gallica Legion Saved an Apostle and Created an Emperor* (Hoboken, NJ: John Wiley & Sons, 2007).

———, *Nero's Killing Machine: The True Story of Rome's Remarkable Fourteenth Legion* (Hoboken, NJ: John Wiley & Sons, 2005).

———, *The Ides: Caesar's Murder and the War for Rome* (Hoboken, NJ: John Wiley & Sons, 2010).

———, *Rebels Against Rome* (Nashville, TN: Turner, 2023.)

Frontinus, *The Stratagems*, trans. C. E. Bennett (Cambridge, MA: Loeb Classical Library, Harvard University Press, 2003).

Gibbon, E., *The Decline and Fall of the Roman Empire* (Chicago: Encyclopaedia Britannica, 1989).

Goldsworthy, A., *Caesar: Life of a Colossus* (New Haven, CT, Yale University, 2006.)

Grant, M., *Cleopatra* (Harmondsworth, UK: Penguin, 1972).

———, *Gladiators* (Harmondsworth, UK: Penguin, 1967).

———, *Roman History from Coins* (New York: Barnes & Noble, 1995).

———, *Julius Caesar* (Harmondsworth, UK, Penguin, 1969).

Hill, G. F., *Historical Roman Coins: From the Earliest Times to the Reign of Augustus* (London: Constable, 1909).

Josephus, *The New Complete Works of Josephus*, trans. W. Whiston (Grand Rapids, MI: Kregel, 1999).

Keppie, L., *The Making of the Roman Army: From Republic to Empire* (Totowa, NJ: Barnes & Noble, 1994).

Matyszak, P., *Sertorius and the Struggle for Spain* (Barnsley, UK: Pen & Sword, 2013).

Napoleon, *Chronicles of Caesar's Wars* (A. Barzani, transl.) (Washington, DC: Barzani, 2018). Based on *Precis des Guerres der Caesar par Napoleon*, Paris, 1836.

Petronius Arbiter, G., *The Satyricon* (W. Heseltine, transl.) (London: Loeb, 1913).

Pliny, *The Letters of the Younger Pliny* (B. Radice, transl.) (London: Penguin, 1969).

Plutarch, *The Lives of the Noble Grecians and Romans* (the Dryden translation) (Chicago: Encyclopaedia Britannica, 1952).

Sallust, *The Histories* (H. Maffett, transl.) (Farmington Hills, MI: Gale Ecco, 2010).

Scothard, P., *Crassus: The First Tycoon* (New Haven, CT: Yale University Press, 2022).

Schwarzkopf, General H. N., *It Doesn't Take a Hero* (New York: Bantam, 1992).

Seneca, *Dialogues and Letters*, (C. D. N. Costa, transl.) (London: Penguin, 2005).

Shakespeare, W., *The Complete Works of Shakespeare* (Secaucus, NJ: The Wellfleet Press, 1987).

Strauss, B., *Ten Caesars: Roman Emperors from Augustus to Constantine* (New York: Simon & Schuster, 2019).

———, *The Spartacus War* (New York: Simon & Schuster, 2009).

Suetonius, *The Twelve Caesars* (London: Penguin, 1989).

Tacitus, P. C., *The Annals* and *The Histories* (A. J. Church, transl.) (Chicago: Encyclopaedia Britannica, 1952).

Vegetius, *The Military Institutions of the Romans* (J. Clark, transl.) (Harrisburg, PA: Military Service Publishing, 1944).

Velleius Paterculus, *Compendium of Roman History* (F. W. Shipley, transl.) (Cambridge, MA: Loeb Classical Library, Harvard University Press, 2002).

Wightman, E. M., *Roman Trier and the Treveri* (New York: Praeger, 1970).

Wiseman, E. J., *Roman Spain* (New York: Bell, 1956).

WEBSITES

www.poetryintranslation.com: "Lucan, *The Civil War (Pharsalia)*."

INDEX

Achillas, 249

Acta Diurna, 138–39

Adolescent Butcher. See Pompey the Great

Aemilia, stepdaughter of Sulla, 33, 85, 256

Afella, Quintus Lucretius, 30–32, 44–45, 61

Afranius, Lucius, 58, 92, 245, 250

Africa, 170, 174, 176, 241

Africanus, Scipio, 38, 44

agrarian bill of Pompey, enacting, 137

Ahenobarbus, Gnaeus Domitius, 35–37

Ahenobarbus, Lucius Domitius, 144, 185-187, 218

Aisne River, 165

Alban Hills, 95, 122, 144

Alba Longa, 12-13, 227, 233, 250, 253

Alesia (Alise Saint Reine), 215–17

Alexander, son of Aristobulus, 127,181, 193-4

Alexander the Great, 7, 83, 210

Ambiorix, 203

Antipater of Idumea, 33, 189, 250, 256

Antistia, wife of Pompey, 14, 30, 33, 256

Antistius, judge, father-in-law of Pompey, 13-14, 30

Antonius, Marcus. *See* Antony, Mark

Antony, Mark, 15, 143
  and Caesar legislation, 138–40
  Gabinius and, 158–59
  invading Egypt, 188–90
  as new quaestor, 215–16, 225, 235, 240, 242, 251

Apennines, 29–30, 76–77, 112

Appian, 56

Appian Way, 119, 198

Appius, Claudius Pulcher, 228-29, 233

Aquitani, tribe, 179–80, 191

Arbiter, Petronius, 185

Ariobarzanes, 98

Ariovistus, 154–57, 168

Aristobulus, 99-100, 127, 181, 193

Artavazdes II, 208-09, 211

Asia, 21, 39-42, 49, 53, 69, 90, 101, 250

Asiaticus, Lucius Cornelius Scipio, 25

assassination, of Pompey and Caesar, 249–53

Atrebates, tribe, 166, 195, 222

Atia, niece of Caesar, 98, 172

Atticus, Titus, 232

Auchelaus, 181, 189

Augustodunum (Autun), 152

Augustus, emperor of Rome, 152, 211, 253

Aurelia, mother of Caesar, 18, 34, 40, 83, 106, 114-115, 204

Baculus, legion centurion, 167, 171

Balbus, Lucius Cornelius, 150, 193, 237

Balikh River, 209

Bardyiae, 13

Battle of Alesia, 213–17

Battle of Carrhae, 206–11

Battle of Dyrrhachium, 241–44

Battle of Mount Tifata, 29

Battle of Munda, 251

Battle of the Colline Gate, 3–9, 61, 73

Battle of the Janiculum, 11, 12

Berenice IV, regent of Egypt, 162, 181, 190

Bibulus, Marcus, 104, 137, 226

Bithynia, 39-40, 69-70, 90, 98

Bituriges of Bourges, 221–22

Board of Three (Triumvirate). See Caesar, Julius; Crassus, Marcus Licinius; Pompey the Great

Boduognatus, king, 167

Bona Dea Festival, scandal, 114–16, 142, 224

Bonaparte, Napoleon, 1, 224, 264, 266

Bosporan Kingdom, 96–98

Brindisi (Brundisium), 23-25, 76, 88, 102, 119, 121, 168, 198, 216, 239-242

Britain

    Caesar's first invasion of, 195–97

    Caesar's second invasion of, 201–4

Brundisium. *See Brindisi*
Brutus, Decimus, 149, 178, 213, 240, 251–53
Brutus, Marcus Junius, 18, 24, 54, 107, 140, 142, 163, 206

Caepio, Gnaeus Servilius, 92, 132
Caesar, Julius, 1–2, 78
    assassination of, 249–53
    assessment of, 255–57
    Battle of Alesia, 213–17
    becoming Enemy of the State, 231–36
    and Catiline Conspiracy, 107–14
    conquering Cisalpine Gaul, 147–58
    dealing with pirates who captured him, 51–53
    and death of Strabo, 3–9
    donating legion to Senate, 226–29
    embracing Pompey, 165–84
    end of Gallic Revolt, 219–24
    following death of Sulla, 49–59
    German War, 190–93
    heir of, 98–99
    imperator in Spain, 119–29
    invading Britain, 195–97
    losses of, 201–11
    love life of, 17–20
    Luca Conference, 172–77
    maintaining political influence, 224–26
    marrying Pompeia, 87
    mourning aunt of, 81–84
    in Mytiline operation, 42
    name, origin and use, 17
    as part of First Triumvirate (Board of Three), 131–46
    as Pontifex Maximus, 105–7
    priesthood of, 17–20
    progressing career of, 61–64
    rising star of, 103–17
    subduing Gaul, 165–84
    support for Pompey, 86, 91
    terminating marriage with wife Cornelia, 114–17
    time in jeopardy, 29–38
    uncle of (Marius), 11–16
    and Veneti tribe, 177–80

Caesoninus, Lucius Calpurnius Piso, 140-41, 143

Calpurnia, wife of Caesar, 140–41

Cantabri, tribe, 180

Capito, Gaius Ateius, 198

Capua, Italy, 71, 76, 129, 137, 226–29

Carbo, Papirus, 5, 29–32

Carrhae, Parthia, Roman defeat near, 210-11

Carrinas, Gaius, 24, 31

Cassivellaunus, king, 202

Catilina, Lucius Sergius, 107–14

Catiline Conspiracy, 107–14

Cato the Younger, 110–11, 126, 192, 247

Cato, Marcus, 18, 92, 120–21, 131

Catulus, Quintus, 50-3, 55-6, 90–91, 102, 105-06, 110, 112, 149

Celer, Metellus, 125

Celts, 24, 72, 151, 153, 171

Censorinus, Gaius, 13, 30–31

Cethegus, Gaius Cornelius, 109–10

Cicero, Marcus Tullius, 63, 91, 133, 141–42, 247

    and Catiline Conspiracy, 107–14

    and Milo trial, 217–19

    reconciliation with, 197–99

    rehabilitating, 158–64

    resuming sitting in Senate, 168–69

Cicero, Quintus, brother of above, 160, 175, 203–4

Cilician pirates, 52-53, 84-91

Cinna, Lucius Cornelius, 53, 55, 57–58, 89

    death of, 21–22

    and death of Strabo, 4–9

    reentering Rome, 12–16

Cisalpine Gaul, 23, 29, 134, 145, 147–64, 241

    legion increases in, 147–48

    meeting in Luca, 172–77

Civic Crown, award for bravery, 42

civil war, Caesar

    Battle of Dyrrhachium, 241–44

    blockading Brindisi, 240

    capturing Italy, 238–41

    confronting Pompey, 244–47

    exclaiming "The die is cast," 238

    outfoxing Afranius, 240–1

Rubicon river, crossing, 237–38

seizing Treasury contents, 239

setbacks in Greece, 240–41

siege of Corfinium, 239

Claudia, daughter of Clodius and Fulvia, wife Octavian, 219

Cleopatra VI of Egypt, 162, 181

Cleopatra VII of Egypt, 1, 140, 162-64, 182-83. 190, 247, 249-250, 253

Clodius (Claudius) Pulcher, Publius, 114-16, 133, 140-46, 149, 158-59, 161-62, 168-70, 172-73, 181, 217-19, 224-25, 228

Cloelius, Titus, 24

College of Tribunes, 144

Colline Gate, civil war at, 30–31. *See also* Battle of the Colline Gate

Comitium, Rome, 136, 253

Commius, 195–97, 216, 220, 222–23

Considius, Publius, 148, 152

Cordoba (Corduba), Farther Spain, 122–25

Corfinium, Picenum, 138, 239

Cornelia, wife of Caesar, 18–20, 33, 52, 57, 63, 83, 219–20, 247, 249

Cornelia Metella, wife Pompey, 247, 249, 252

Cornelius, Gaius, 58, 85, 109

Cornelius, Gnaeus, 172–77

Cossutia, fiancée of Caesar, 19

Cossyra, 34

Cotta, Gaius Aurelius, 40

Cotta, Lucius Aurunculeius, 149–50

Cotta, Marcus, 69

courtesans, 15

Crassus, Marcus Licinius, 23–24, 31–32, 40, 81, 84, 89, 102, 110, 116, 187

Battle of Carrhae, 206–11

First Triumvirate, and, 131–46

first tycoon, 61–64

losses of, 201–11

Luca Conference, 172–77

reconciling with Pompey, 197–99

Spartacus, defeating, 71–73

Crassus, Publius, son of above, 168, 177–80, 179, 187, 188, 210

Creticus, Metellus, 90

Crus, Lucius Cornelius Lentulus
234

Curia Hostilia, 217

Curio, Gaius Scribonius, the Elder, 103, 111, 140, 149, 218, 228, 233-34, 236, 240

Curio, Gaius Scribonius, the Younger, 111, 140, 218, 224-25,241
Curius, Quintus, 108
cursus honorum, 45, 56
Cyprus, 142, 163

Daily Acts. See *Acta Diurna*
Damascus, Syria, 98–100
Damasippus, Marcus Junius Brutus, 24, 31, 32
Deiotarus of Galatia, 101
Delos, 88
Dictator of Rome, 1, 39, 41, 43, 51, 103, 218, 251, 256
Dio, Cassius, 20, 101, 104, 119
Dodecanese, 52
Dora, courtesan, 15
Doubs River, 154

Eastern Mediterranean, 88
Egypt, 105, 142, 161–63, 181–83 193, 205, 246–47, 249–53
    plotting war in, 188–90
    war in, 188–90
8th Legion, 123, 147, 167, 201, 214, 232, 242, 243
Elbe River, 154
elephants, 37–38, 42–46, 195, 250
11th Legion, 148, 167, 201
Enemy of the State, becoming, 231–36. *See also* Caesar, Julius
English Channel, 195–97
Equestrian Order, 19, 45, 78
Esquiline Hill, 61
Eteocles of Thebes, 207
Euphrates River, 95

Fabius, Gaius, 223
Farther Spain, 65, 67, 83, 147, 225, 231
fasces, 81
Field of Mars, 3, 46, 119–20, 143, 186
15th Legion, 204, 226, 239
5th Legion, 123
fire fighting at Rome, 62–63
1st Legion, 23, 37, 58, 221, 226
First Battle of Zela, 90
First Mithradatic War, 21. *See also,* Lucullus, Lucius

14th Legion, 159, 167, 201, 204, 222, 231

4th Legion, 245

Frontinus, Sextus Julius, 66

Fulvia, wife of Clodius, 217-19

Gabinians (Gabinii), Egyptian military unit, 191, 246, 249

Gabinius, Aulus, 85–88, 92, 99, 141-43, 158–59, 180-82, 188-90, 193–95, 205–7, 250, 256

    invading Egypt, 188–90

    Gabinius, Sisenna, son of above, 158

Galba, Servius, 149, 170–71, 195, 224-26, 252

Gallaeci, tribe, 124

Gallic Revolt

    Battle of Alesia, 213–17

    end of, 219–24

Gallic Triumph of Caesar, 216–17, 227

Gelise River, 180

Geminius, 15, 54–55

Glabrio, Manius Acilius, 33-4, 85, 90, 94-5, 250-51, 261

Gnaeus, son of Pompey. *See* Pompeius, Gnaeus

Gnipho, Marcus Antonius, 19

Gueyze River, 180

Hannibal, 33, 38, 211

    allying with, 31

Heliopolis, 207

Helvetian Republic, 150

Helvetii, Caesar's campaign against, 150–54

Hercules, 122, 139, 246

Hiarbus, 37

Hiempsai I, 37

Hierapolis, 206

Hirtuleius, Lucius, 68

Hybrida, Antonius, 109

Hypsicratia, mistress of Mithradates the Great, 96

Ides of March. *See* Caesar, Julius: assassination of

Illyricum, 172–74, 197, 235

interrex, 217

Isauricus, Publius Servilius Vatia, 45. 47, 49, 105

Jerusalem, besieged and captured by Pompey, 99-102

Jordan River, 100

Josephus, 89

Juba, king, 241, 250

Julia, aunt of Caesar, 6, 18, 82

Julia, daughter of Caesar, wife of Pompey, 52, 56, 63, 83, 106, 132, 138, 145-46, 162, 194, 204-5, 211, 221, 224

Julia, sister of Caesar, 18, 172

Labienus, Titus, 148, 168, 223, 232, 239

Laelius, Decimus, 58

Latin shorthand, invention of, 135

Lentulus, Lucius Cornelius, 110, 224

Lepidus, Marcus, 50, 79, 108, 241, 251–53

Lesser Armenia, 95

Lex Trebonia, 188

Licinia the Vestal Virgin, 40, 62

Livy, 151

Loire River, 151, 177

Longinus, Gaius Cassius, 206

Longinus, Quintus Cassius, 225–26

Luca (Lucca), Cisalpine Gaul. 147. 172-77

Luca Conference, 172–77, 182

Lucan, poet, 120, 249, 257, 262, 264

Lucullan Feast, 95

Lucullus, Lucius, Licinius, 23, 69-72, 75, 77, 81, 84, 90, 92-95, 115, 120-22, 133, 135, 137, 139, 141, 183

Lucullus, Marcus, brother of above, 23, 75-76

Lusitani, tribe, 124

Macedonia, 244

Machaerus, 181

Magna, Pompeia, 58

Magnus, Gnaeus Pompeius, 58

Magnus, Pompeius. *See* Pompey the Great

Manlius, Gaius, 107–14

Marcellinus, Lentulus, 172–77

Marcellus, Claudius, 219

Marcellus, Gaius, 205, 224, 227, 233-35

Marcius, Ancus, 82

Marians, 17, 29–31, 33, 35, 46, 53–55, 59, 62, 112

    Battle of the Colline Gate, and, 9

Pompey defeating their forces, 21–26
Marius, Gaius, consul and general, leader of Marian faction
    and death of Strabo, 4–9
    and Pompey trial, 11–16
Marius, Gaius, Jr., death of, 29–32
Martia Legion, 94
Memmius, Gaius, 34, 68, 94, 144
Merula, Lucius Cornelius, 4
Metellus, Caecilius, Pius, 5, 89
Metellus, Quintus Caecilius, 66, 89
    awarding Triumph to, 77–79
    role in winning Sertorian War, 73–77
    strategic victory for, 68–70
Milo, Annius, trial of, 217–19
Milo, Titus Annius, 160-61, 170, 217-19
Mithradates IV, 207
Mithradates VI Eupator (Mithradates the Great), 4, 16, 19, 21, 26, 40, 44, 69–71, 75, 77,
        84, 90, 92, 98, 101, 109, 120–21, 126-27, 129, 181
    statue of in Pompeian Triumph, 126
    surviving children of, 127, 181
Molo, Apollonius, 52-3, 64
Mommsen, Theodor, 20
Moselle River, 167
Mount Gabor, 194
Mussolini, Benito, 1
Mytiline, Lesbos, 42, 128

Narbo Martius (Narbonne), 58–59, 232
Nasica, Quintus Caecilius Metellus Scipio, 219–20 205, 219, 252-53
Nearer Spain, 65, 67, 221, 228–29, 241
Nicomedes IV, king, 40, 69
9th Legion, 123, 147, 201, 242
Norbanus, Gaius, 29, 31

Octavia, sister of Octavian, 205, 224
Octavian, (Gaius Octavius Jr.), 99, 172,
Octavius, Gaius, 99
Octavius, Gnaeus, 4, 7, 12–13, 15, 32
Octavius, Lucius, 89
Oppian Hill, 108
Optimates, faction, 19–20

orbis, 203
Orodes II, 207-08
Otranto Strait, 242

Paetus, Publius Autronius, 104
Palatine Hill, 62, 99, 141, 168
Parma, Cassius, 252–53
Parthian shot, 209
Paterculus, Velleius, 7, 115, 260
Paullus, Lucius Aemilius, 153, 225
Pedius, Quintus, 149, 159
Perpenna, Marcus, Vento, 34, 58, 67, 74,
Petreius, Marcus, 58, 109, 113, 225, 241, 247, 250–51
Pharmacusa, 52
Pharnaces II, 97–98, 101, 250
Philippus, Lucius Marcius, 56-57, 172–77, 182, 186
Phraates III, 93, 207
Picenum, region, 6, 8, 15, 21–25, 30, 37, 39, 58, 109, 138, 148, 169, 238–39
pirates. *See* Cilician pirates
Piso, Gaius Cornelius, 85, 104
Pius, Gnaeus Caecilius Metellus, 5, 89
Plutarch, 34, 120, 124, 132–33, 195, 203, 215
Po River, 145
pomerium, 3
Polynices of Thebes, 207
Pompeia, daughter of Cinna, wife of Caesar, 87, 114, 140
Pompeia, daughter of Pompey, 58, 77, 84, 92, 114-15, 121, 132, 261
Pompeius, Gnaeus Magnus (Pompey the Great) 1–2
    Alban villa, construction of, 122
    appointed Roman commander-in-chief, 90–92
    assassination of, 249–53
    assessment of, 255–57
    award of first Triumph, 77–79
    building army of, 20–27
    campaigning against Cilician pirates, 84–91
    Cicero, rehabilitation of, 158–64
    code of ethics of, 15–16
    conquering East, 84–98
    Crassus, reconciling with, 197–99
    defending Rome against Caesar, 231–36
    donating legion to Senate, 226–29

Dyrrhachium, Battle of 241–44

elephants in Italy, and, 42–46

embraced by Romans, 165–84

father Strabo, death of, 3–9

First Triumvirate, and, 131–46

following death of Sulla, 49–59

gaining proconsular powers, 54–57

Jerusalem, siege of, 99–102

legislation passed under, 219–20

losses of, 201–11

Luca Conference, 172–77

Milo trial, and, 217–19

missing family life, 92

planning for campaign in East, 92–93

Prefect of Provisions, 168–70

Roman Spain, reorganization of, 73–75

Sertorius, campaigns against, 65–68, 73-77

Sicily campaign, 29–38

Spanish operations, 53–59

Spartacus, and, 71–73

strengthening popularity, 193–95

Third Mithradatic War, winning, 93–98

toga party of, 7–8

trial of, 11–16

Triumphs of, 42–47, 125–29

Triumphant to Italy return of, 119–29

Pompeius, Gnaeus, eldest son of Pompey, 58, 83-4, 88, 92, 121, 129, 188–90, 228, 246, 249-51, 261

Pompeius, Sextus, youngest son of Pompey, 92, 242, 250-51

Pompey the Great. *See* Pompeius, Gnaeus, Magnus

Pompey's Pillar, 253

Pontifex Maximus, 30, 41, 46, 105–6, 110, 114, 116

Popular Assembly, 39, 59, 77, 86, 91, 112, 115–16

Populares, faction, 19–20

praetor peregrinus, 163

Praetorian Guard, 72, 109, 113, 161, 218

Prefect of Provisions, 168–70, 173

Ptolemy XII of Egypt 105, 142, 161–63, 180–83, 188–90, 205

Ptolemy XIII of Egypt, 182, 190, 247, 249–50

Pulcher, Clodius. *See* Clodius

Pulcher, Publius Claudius, brother of above, 114–17

Puteoli (Pozzuoli), 41–42

quartan fever, 5

Ravenna, Italy, 172–77
Rebilus, Gaius Caninius, 223
records bill, attempt at passing, 135–36
Republic of Rome
    Caesar assassination, 249–53
    choosing legions, 56
    and death of Strabo, 3–9
    divorce in, 33–34
    labeling, 19–20
    pirate campaign, 84–91
    territorial expansion of, 98
    traffic regulations in, 139
Rhodes, 52
Rhône River, 150
Roman Catholic Church, 41
Romulus, legend concerning his death, 86
Romulus and Remus, 207
Roscius, Lucius, 187
Rufus, Lucius Vibullius, 175
Rufus, Marcus Caelius, 233
Rufus, Servius Sulpicius, 149–50

Sabinus, Quintus Titurius, 150, 203
Salvius, centurion with Gabinians, 190, 249
Saône River, 151, 222
Satyricon, 185
Scaevola, Quintus Mucius, 30, 46
Scaurus, Marcus Aemilius, 92–93
Scheldt River, 165
Schwarzkopf, Norman, 1
2nd Legion, 23, 58, 148, 231
Second Punic War, 137
Second Triumvirate. See Board of Three
Seleucia, 207–9
Sempronia, 108, 111, 149
Seneca, 55
Sequani, tribe, 154

Sertorius, Quintus,

Sertorian War,

Sertorius, Quintus, 5

downfall of, 73–75

    versus Pompey, 65–68

    war against Sullan Rome, 77–78, 83, 94, 150

Servian Wall, 3, 5, 119

7th Legion, 123, 147, 167, 180, 196–97, 201–2, 231, 262

Shakespeare, William, 7, 127

16th Legion, 204, 231

6th Legion, 123, 221–22, 228, 231, 240–41, 245

Slave War, 78

Social War, 7

Spartacus, 71-73, 75–76, 78

Strabo, Gnaeus Pompeius, father of Pompey, 3–9, 16

Suetonius, 78, 103, 105, 108, 150

Sulla, Faustus, 100, 250

Sulla, Lucius Cornelius, 4, 19

    death of, 49–51

    as Dictator of Rome, 39–47

    Pompey as general of, 21–27

    Triumph to Pompey, 42–47

Sulla, Publius, 103, 245

Sulla's Student. *See* Pompey the Great

Syria, 98–101, 158, 172, 174, 182–83, 187, 189, 193–94, 197–98, 205–11, 226, 244–45

tabes, 227

tax farmers, 138

Temple of Capitoline Jupiter, 112, 127

Temple of Concord, 108

Temple of Cybele, 206

Temple of Julius, 253

Temple of Jupiter, 44

Temple of Solomon, 100–102

Temple of Venus, 128, 194, 207

Temple of Vesta, 30, 40

Tencteri, tribe, 190–93

10th Legion, 123, 147, 150–51, 155, 157, 166–67, 201, 214–15, 246

    in Britain, 195–97

    in German quarrel, 154–58

    in Helvetii quarrel, 250–54

Terentius, Lucius, 11–12

Tertia, Mucia, 46

Thames River, 202

Theater of Pompey, 101, 127-29, 194-95, 198, 220, 252, 255,
theaters, 127–28

Thermus, Marcus Minucius, 40–42

3rd Legion, 23, 58, 148, 245

Third Mithradatic War, 93–98, 101–2

13th Legion, 159, 167, 187, 201, 214, 221

Tigranes the Great of Armenia, 71, 74, 84, 90, 109, 120, 126, 208

Tigranes, prince, son of above, 96, 145,181

Tigris River, 207

Tongres, 203

tortoise formation (Testudo), 202

traffic regulations at Rome, 139

Transalpine Gaul, 58, 170–72, 174, 203, 218, 222, 232, 241

Treasury, Rome, 6, 13, 30, 63, 81, 88, 120, 125, 129, 142, 177, 224, 239

Trebonius, Gaius, 187–88, 202, 222

Treveri (Treverans), 167, 178, 223, 232

Tribune of the Plebs, 56–57, 77, 133, 137, 141–42, 144–45, 160–61, 173, 198, 219,
    224–26, 236

Triumph, celebration
    Caesar's, 216–17, 227
    Lucullus's, 94
    Pompey's, 42–47

Triumphal Gate (Porta Triumphalis), 46, 126

Tullianum, 111, 127

12th Legion, 148, 167, 170–72, 195, 201, 232

28th Legion, 242

24th Legion, 242

Ubii, tribe, 190–93

Usipetes, tribe, 190–93

Uxellodunum, 223

Varro, Marcus Terentius, 134–35, 137, 221, 226, 241

Vatia, Publius Servilius. See Isauricus

Vatinius, Publius, 173

Veneti, tribe, 177–80

Vento. See Perpenna

Vercingetorix, Gallic Revolt leader, 213–17

Vesontio (Besançon), 154, 158
Vestal Virgins, 40, 62, 106, 114, 139
Vetus, Gaius Antistius, 82-83
Viromandui, tribe, 166

Walmer Castle, 196

Zenodotia, 206
Zeugma, battle at, 206–11

ABOUT THE AUTHOR

S tephen Dando-Collins is the multi-award-winning author of forty-seven books, including biographies and nonfiction works on ancient Rome, Greece, and Persia, as well as American, British, French, and Australian history including World War I and World War II. These works focus on military history, with Stephen considered an authority on the legions of imperial Rome. He has also written several successful novels and children's novels. His books are widely published in the US, UK, Canada, Australia, and New Zealand, and they appear in translation in Spain, Italy, Poland, the Netherlands, Albania, Russia, Korea, and Latin America.